Taste *of* Home.
ONE-DISH
meals

TASTE OF HOME BOOKS • RDA ENTHUSIAST BRANDS, LLC • MILWAUKEE, WI

Visit us at **tasteofhome.com** for other
Taste of Home books and products.

International Standard Book Number:
979-8-88977-110-4

Chief Content Officer: Jason Buhrmester
Content Director: Mark Hagen
Creative Director: Raeann Thompson
Associate Creative Director:
Jami Geittmann
Senior Editor: Christine Rukavena
Senior Art Director: Courtney Lovetere
Assistant Art Director: Carrie Peterson
Manager, Production Design:
Satyandra Raghav
Senior Print Publication Designer:
Bipin Balakrishnan
Print Production Artist: Nandini Mittal
Deputy Editor, Copy Desk: Ann M. Walter
Senior Copy Editor: Elizabeth Bruch
Copy Editor: Rayan Naqash
Contributing Copy Editor: Pam Grandy

Cover Photography:
Photographer: Dan Roberts
Set Stylist: Stacey Genaw
Food Stylist: Josh Rink, Ellen Crowley

Pictured on front cover:
Beef & Biscuit Stew, p. 123; Stuffed Pasta
Shells, p.156; Sheet-Pan Honey Mustard
Chicken, p. 91

Pictured on back cover:
Turkey Club Pizza, p. 95; My Juicy Lucy,
p. 259; Copycat Cheesy Gordita Crunch,
p. 41; Slow-Cooked Balsamic Lentil Soup,
p. 226; Pennsylvania Pot Roast, p. 209;
Grilled Summer Sausage Salad, p. 291

Printed in China
1 3 5 7 9 10 8 6 4 2

CONTENTS

33

135

225

241

TORTELLINI WITH SAUSAGE & MASCARPONE, 55

21

41

74

STOVETOP SUPPERS

LIME CHICKEN TACOS

Our fun, simple recipe is perfect for taco Tuesdays or a relaxing dinner with friends. If we have any leftover filling, I toss it into a garden-fresh taco salad.

—Tracy Gunter, Boise, ID

PREP: 10 min. • **COOK:** 5½ hours • **MAKES:** 6 servings

1½ lbs. boneless skinless chicken breast halves
3 Tbsp. lime juice
1 Tbsp. chili powder
1 cup fresh or frozen corn, thawed
1 cup chunky salsa
12 fat-free flour tortillas (6 in.), warmed
Optional: Sour cream, pickled onions, shredded lettuce, sliced avocado, shredded cheddar or Cotija cheese, and lime wedges

1. Place chicken in a 3-qt. slow cooker. Pour lime juice over chicken; sprinkle with chili powder. Cook, covered, on low until chicken is tender, 5-6 hours.
2. Remove chicken. When cool enough to handle, shred meat with 2 forks; return to slow cooker. Stir in corn and salsa. Cook, covered, on low until heated through, about 30 minutes. Place filling on tortillas; if desired, serve with sour cream, pickled onions, lettuce, avocado slices, cheese and lime wedges.

2 TACOS 291 cal., 3g fat (1g sat. fat), 63mg chol., 674mg sod., 37g carb. (2g sugars, 2g fiber), 28g pro. **DIABETIC EXCHANGES** 3 lean meat, 2½ starch.

KEEPING CHICKEN MOIST

Chicken breasts are lean, so they will dry out if overcooked. But even perfectly cooked shredded chicken can dry out when exposed to air. After shredding the chicken, toss it with the cooking juices in the slow cooker to keep it moist. Or use boneless skinless chicken thighs, which have a higher fat content and are thus less dry-tasting.

RUSTIC ITALIAN TORTELLINI SOUP

This is my favorite soup recipe. It's quick to fix on a busy night and full of bright, tasty ingredients. It originally called for spicy sausage links, but I've found that turkey sausage, or even ground turkey breast, is just as good.

—Tracy Fasnacht, Irwin, PA

PREP: 20 min. • **COOK:** 20 min. • **MAKES:** 6 servings (2 qt.)

- ¾ lb. Italian turkey sausage links, casings removed
- 1 medium onion, chopped
- 6 garlic cloves, minced
- 2 cans (14½ oz. each) reduced-sodium chicken broth
- 1¾ cups water
- 1 can (14½ oz.) diced tomatoes, undrained
- 1 pkg. (9 oz.) refrigerated cheese tortellini
- 1 pkg. (6 oz.) fresh baby spinach, coarsely chopped
- 2¼ tsp. minced fresh basil or ¾ tsp. dried basil
- ¼ tsp. pepper
  Dash crushed red pepper flakes
  Shredded Parmesan cheese, optional

1. Crumble sausage into a Dutch oven; add onion. Cook and stir over medium heat until meat is no longer pink. Add garlic; cook 1 minute longer. Stir in broth, water and tomatoes. Bring to a boil.

2. Add tortellini; return to a boil. Cook for 5-8 minutes or until almost tender, stirring occasionally. Reduce heat; add spinach, basil, pepper and pepper flakes. Cook 2-3 minutes longer or until spinach is wilted and tortellini are tender. Serve with cheese if desired.

FREEZE OPTION Place individual portions of cooled soup in freezer containers and freeze. To use, partially thaw in refrigerator overnight. Heat through in a saucepan, stirring occasionally; add broth if necessary.

1⅓ CUPS 203 cal., 8g fat (2g sat. fat), 40mg chol., 878mg sod., 18g carb. (5g sugars, 3g fiber), 16g pro.

TORTELLINI SOUP TIPS

What type of tortellini is best for tortellini soup?
Refrigerated cheese tortellini is ideal for this soup—it cooks quickly and has a fresh taste. If you prefer tortellini filled with meat, vegetables or herbs, those work well too.

How do you thicken tortellini soup?
This soup has a brothy consistency, but you can thicken it by adding a few tablespoons of flour after cooking the sausage and onion. Or thicken it at the end with a cornstarch slurry: Mix equal parts cornstarch and cold water. Whisk the slurry into the soup, and simmer until it starts to thicken.

What do you serve with tortellini soup?
You can't go wrong with crusty bread and a green salad.

FIG-GLAZED CHICKEN WITH WHITE BEANS

Sauteed shallots, fig jam, rosemary, lemon and sherry vinegar make a delightful sauce for both the chicken and the beans. My husband couldn't believe how well the white beans absorbed the flavor, making this a grand slam. Matchstick carrots can be added to the bean mixture for extra color, flavor and crunch.

—Arlene Erlbach, Morton Grove, IL

PREP: 15 min. • **COOK:** 30 min. • **MAKES:** 6 servings

¾ cup fig preserves
⅓ cup water
2 Tbsp. lemon juice
2 Tbsp. sherry vinegar
4 tsp. minced fresh rosemary or 1 tsp. dried rosemary, crushed
1 Tbsp. Worcestershire sauce
¼ tsp. salt
¼ tsp. pepper
6 bone-in chicken thighs (about 2¼ lbs.)
4 shallots, coarsely chopped
1 can (15 oz.) cannellini beans, rinsed and drained

1. Mix first 8 ingredients. In a Dutch oven over medium-high heat, brown chicken in batches, starting skin side down. Remove from pan, reserving drippings.
2. In drippings, saute shallots until golden brown, 2-3 minutes. Stir in preserves mixture; bring to a boil, stirring to loosen browned bits from pan. Add chicken. Reduce heat; simmer, covered, 5 minutes.

3. Add beans; return to a boil. Cook, uncovered, until a thermometer inserted in chicken reads 170°-175°, 12-15 minutes.
1 SERVING 405 cal., 15g fat (4g sat. fat), 81mg chol., 287mg sod., 42g carb. (25g sugars, 3g fiber), 26g pro.

FIG-GLAZED CHICKEN TIPS

• Shallots add a mild yet distinctive flavor to sauces. When buying, choose shallots that are firm and heavy, with dry, papery skins. Avoid any that have shoots or feel soft. Store them as you would onions, in a cool, dry place with good air circulation.

• The flavorful sauce coats the chicken but will pool slightly, so serve it in a shallow bowl.

BALSAMIC CHICKEN PASTA SALAD

I love all the colors and flavors of this quick and easy dish and serve it often in summer, to the delight of guests! You can't beat the combination of Gorgonzola and bacon. Leftover grilled shrimp makes a tasty substitute for chicken.

—Terri McCarty, Oro Grande, CA

TAKES: 25 min. • **MAKES:** 8 servings

- 3 cups uncooked bow tie pasta
- 4 cups cubed cooked chicken breast
- 2 cups chopped tomatoes
- ½ cup chopped red onion
- 4 bacon strips, cooked and crumbled
- ¼ cup crumbled Gorgonzola cheese
- ½ cup olive oil
- ¼ cup minced fresh basil
- ¼ cup balsamic vinegar
- 2 Tbsp. brown sugar
- 1 tsp. minced garlic
- ¼ tsp. salt
- ¼ tsp. pepper
- ½ cup grated Parmesan cheese

1. Cook pasta according to package directions. Drain and rinse in cold water; transfer to a large bowl. Add the chicken, tomatoes, onion, bacon and Gorgonzola cheese.

2. In a small bowl, whisk the oil, basil, vinegar, brown sugar, garlic, salt and pepper. Drizzle over salad and toss to coat; sprinkle with Parmesan cheese.

1⅓ CUP 408 cal., 20g fat (5g sat. fat), 65mg chol., 323mg sod., 28g carb. (7g sugars, 2g fiber), 28g pro.

"Delightful! I swapped and doubled feta for the Gorgonzola, and I threw in some sugar snap peas from the garden, which was a perfect addition. This recipe's a keeper."

—BLUE_EYES998, TASTEOFHOME.COM

BLACK BEAN CHICKEN WITH RICE

This spicy family favorite calls for just a few basic ingredients, so it's quick and easy to stir up in your skillet on a weeknight.

—Molly Andersen, Portland, OR

TAKES: 25 min.
MAKES: 4 servings

- 3 tsp. chili powder
- 1 tsp. ground cumin
- 1 tsp. pepper
- ¼ tsp. salt
- 4 boneless skinless chicken breast halves (4 oz. each)
- 2 tsp. canola oil
- 1 can (15 oz.) black beans, rinsed and drained
- 1 cup frozen corn
- 1 cup salsa
- 2 cups hot cooked brown rice
  Minced fresh cilantro, optional

1. In a small bowl, mix seasonings; sprinkle over both sides of chicken. In a large nonstick skillet, heat oil over medium heat. Brown chicken on both sides.

2. Add beans, corn and salsa to skillet; cook, covered, 10-15 minutes or until a thermometer inserted in chicken reads 165°. Serve with rice and, if desired, cilantro.

1 CHICKEN BREAST HALF WITH ¾ CUP BEAN MIXTURE AND ½ CUP COOKED RICE 400 cal., 7g fat (1g sat. fat), 63mg chol., 670mg sod., 52g carb. (4g sugars, 8g fiber), 32g pro.

CREAMY CHICKEN RICE SOUP

I came up with this flavorful soup while making some adjustments to a favorite stovetop chicken casserole. We like this dish for lunch with crisp rolls and fresh fruit.

—Janice Mitchell, Aurora, CO

TAKES: 30 min. • **MAKES:** 4 servings

- 1 Tbsp. canola oil
- 1 medium carrot, chopped
- 1 celery rib, chopped
- ½ cup chopped onion
- ½ tsp. minced garlic
- ⅓ cup uncooked long grain rice
- ¾ tsp. dried basil
- ¼ tsp. pepper
- 2 cans (14½ oz. each) reduced-sodium chicken broth
- 3 Tbsp. all-purpose flour
- 1 can (5 oz.) evaporated milk
- 2 cups cubed cooked chicken breast

1. In a large saucepan, heat oil over medium-high heat; saute carrot, celery and onion until tender. Add garlic; cook and stir 1 minute. Stir in rice, seasonings and broth; bring to a boil. Reduce heat; simmer, covered, until rice is tender, about 15 minutes.
2. Mix flour and milk until smooth; stir into soup. Bring to a boil; cook and stir until thickened, about 2 minutes. Stir in chicken; heat through.

1¼ CUPS 312 cal., 9g fat (3g sat. fat), 71mg chol., 699mg sod., 26g carb. (6g sugars, 1g fiber), 29g pro. **DIABETIC EXCHANGES** 3 lean meat, 2 starch, 1 fat.

SZECHUAN CHICKEN

My whole family loves this Szechuan chicken. My husband prefers it without peppers, but he is happy to let others have his! I use the ginger paste that comes in a tube and pre-shredded carrots to save time.

—Christine Snyder, Boulder, CO

PREP: 20 min. • **COOK:** 15 min. • **MAKES:** 6 servings

¼ cup cold water
¼ cup soy sauce
3 Tbsp. sherry
1 Tbsp. cornstarch
2 tsp. sugar
¾ tsp. crushed red pepper flakes
1 small sweet red pepper
1 small green pepper
2 medium carrots
1 cup coarsely chopped cashews
2 Tbsp. canola oil, divided
1½ lbs. boneless skinless chicken breasts, cut into 1-in. cubes
6 green onions, thinly sliced
1 tsp. minced fresh gingerroot
4½ cups hot cooked rice

1. Mix first 6 ingredients until smooth. Cut peppers and carrots into matchsticks.
2. In a large skillet, cook cashews over low heat until lightly browned, stirring occasionally, 1-2 minutes. Remove from the pan.
3. In same skillet, heat 1 Tbsp. oil over medium-high heat; stir-fry chicken until no longer pink, 5-7 minutes. Remove from pan.
4. In same skillet, heat remaining 1 Tbsp. oil over medium-high heat; stir-fry peppers and carrots 4 minutes. Add green onions and ginger; cook and stir 1 minute.
5. Return chicken to skillet. Stir cornstarch mixture; add to the pan. Bring to a boil; cook and stir until thickened, 1-2 minutes. Stir in cashews. Serve with rice.

1 CUP CHICKEN MIXTURE WITH ¾ CUP RICE 489 cal., 18g fat (3g sat. fat), 63mg chol., 845mg sod., 48g carb. (5g sugars, 3g fiber), 32g pro.

"This is the type of meal that my husband just loves! Only cooking for the two of us now, but I still make full recipe because we like having leftovers— even though he could easily devour this whole pan! Quick, easy, economical."

—KOOKIEB, TASTEOFHOME.COM

CREAMY SPINACH CHICKEN DINNER

Cleanup is a breeze with this all-in-one supper. To make things even easier, tear the spinach with your hands instead of cutting it.

—*Taste of Home* Test Kitchen

TAKES: 30 min. • **MAKES:** 4 servings

1½ cups uncooked penne pasta
1 lb. boneless skinless chicken breasts, cut into 1-in. cubes
½ cup chopped onion
2 tsp. olive oil
1 can (10¾ oz.) condensed cream of mushroom soup, undiluted
1 cup heavy whipping cream
10 cups coarsely chopped fresh spinach
2 cups shredded part-skim mozzarella cheese
⅛ tsp. pepper
Optional: Crushed red pepper flakes and Parmesan cheese

1. Cook pasta according to package directions. Meanwhile, in a Dutch oven over medium heat, cook and stir chicken and onion in oil for 5 minutes or until chicken is no longer pink.

2. Stir in soup and cream. Bring to a boil over medium heat. Reduce heat; simmer, uncovered, for 2 minutes. Stir in the spinach, cheese and pepper; cook for 1-2 minutes or until spinach is wilted and cheese is melted.

3. Drain pasta; add to chicken mixture and toss to coat. If desired, sprinkle with red pepper flakes and Parmesan.

1¾ CUPS 698 cal., 42g fat (22g sat. fat), 170mg chol., 1061mg sod., 35g carb. (5g sugars, 4g fiber), 45g pro.

SPINACH CHICKEN DINNER TIPS

How can you make this creamy spinach chicken your own?
Customize the dish by adding ingredients like sun-dried tomatoes, sliced mushrooms or rinsed canned artichokes.

Can you use frozen spinach instead of fresh?
Yes, frozen spinach works well. Use a 10- to 12-oz. package.

How do you store lefotvers of this dish?
Allow the dish to cool completely before storing it in an airtight container. It will last up to 4 days in the fridge.

GENERAL TSO'S CHICKEN

An all-time favorite takeout dish, General Tso's is easy to make at home. The key is in the crisp chicken and the rich, flavorful sauce.

—*Taste of Home* Test Kitchen

TAKES: 30 min. • **MAKES:** 3 servings

1 Tbsp. cornstarch plus ¼ cup cornstarch, divided
¾ cup reduced-sodium chicken broth
2 Tbsp. reduced-sodium soy sauce
1 Tbsp. rice vinegar
1 Tbsp. hoisin sauce
2 tsp. sugar
2 tsp. sesame oil
  Oil for deep-fat frying
1 lb. boneless skinless chicken thighs, cut into 1-in. pieces
1 Tbsp. canola oil
1 Tbsp. minced fresh gingerroot
2 garlic cloves, minced
¼ tsp. crushed red pepper flakes
2 green onions, sliced
1 tsp. sesame seeds

1. In a small bowl, combine 1 Tbsp. cornstarch and broth until smooth. Stir in soy sauce, vinegar, hoisin sauce, sugar and sesame oil; set aside.

2. In an electric skillet or deep fryer, heat oil to 375°. Place remaining ¼ cup cornstarch in a shallow bowl. Add chicken, a few pieces at a time, and toss to coat; shake off excess. Fry chicken pieces, a few at a time, until golden brown, 2-3 minutes on each side. Drain on paper towels. Keep warm.

3. In a large skillet, heat canola oil over medium-high heat. Add ginger, garlic and pepper flakes; stir-fry until fragrant, about 30 seconds. Stir broth mixture and add to pan. Bring to a boil; cook and stir until thickened, about 2 minutes. Add chicken to pan; toss to coat. Sprinkle with green onions and sesame seeds.

1 CUP 524 cal., 35g fat (5g sat. fat), 101mg chol., 779mg sod., 22g carb. (6g sugars, 1g fiber), 30g pro.

SERVING SUGGESTION

General Tso's chicken goes well with a scoop of white rice to soak up some of the flavorful sauce. We also like it with a side of steamed or stir-fried veggies. Broccoli is a classic, but you could also serve carrots or bell peppers. For added interest, stir in rinsed canned baby corn or water chestnuts.

ONE-DISH TURKEY DINNER

This quick one-dish dinner helped keep my husband and me on track throughout the week while we were still learning to balance our busy schedules.

—Shannon Barden, Alpharetta, GA

TAKES: 30 min. • **MAKES:** 4 servings

1 lb. ground turkey
1 medium onion, chopped
1 shallot, finely chopped
3 garlic cloves, minced
¼ cup tomato paste
1 medium sweet potato, peeled and cubed
1 cup chicken broth
2 tsp. smoked paprika
½ tsp. salt
¼ tsp. pepper
3 cups chopped fresh kale
   Dash crushed red pepper flakes
1 medium ripe avocado, peeled and sliced
   Minced fresh mint, optional

1. In a large skillet, cook turkey, onion, shallot and garlic over medium heat until turkey is no longer pink and vegetables are tender, 8-10 minutes, breaking up turkey into crumbles; drain. Add tomato paste; cook and stir 1 minute longer.
2. Add sweet potato, broth, smoked paprika, salt and pepper. Bring to a boil; reduce heat. Simmer, covered, until sweet potato is tender, about 10 minutes, stirring occasionally. Add kale and red pepper flakes; cook and stir until kale is wilted, about 2 minutes longer. Serve with avocado and, if desired, mint.

FREEZE OPTION Once cool, freeze in freezer containers. To use, partially thaw in refrigerator overnight. Heat through in a saucepan, stirring occasionally; add broth or water if necessary. Serve with avocado and, if desired, mint.
1⅓ CUPS 318 cal., 14g fat (3g sat. fat), 76mg chol., 628mg sod., 24g carb. (8g sugars, 5g fiber), 26g pro. **DIABETIC EXCHANGES** 3 lean meat, 2 fat, 1½ starch.

ONE-DISH TURKEY DINNER TIPS

What sides can I serve with this dish?
Brown rice makes a hearty side. A simple green salad adds freshness, while roasted vegetables complement the rich flavors.

How can I adjust the spice level in this recipe?
For more heat, add extra crushed red pepper flakes or a pinch of cayenne. To make it milder, omit the red pepper flakes.

Can I add other vegetables to the turkey dinner?
Yes. Vegetables like zucchini, bell peppers or carrots work nicely. Add peppers and carrots along with the onion and shallot in the first step. Add softer veggies, such as zucchini, along with the sweet potato.

CRISPY CHICKEN
CAESAR SALAD

CRISPY CHICKEN CAESAR SALAD

This crispy chicken Caesar salad is loaded with herbs and happiness! The crouton crust on the chicken really boosts the flavor. You could also add tomato, onion or any topping you'd put on a salad.

—Susan Mason, Puyallup, WA

TAKES: 25 min. • **MAKES:** 4 servings

2 cups Caesar salad croutons, divided
1 lb. ground chicken
½ tsp. salt
½ tsp. pepper
2 Tbsp. olive oil
2 romaine hearts, coarsely chopped
½ cup Caesar salad dressing
½ cup shredded Parmesan cheese, divided

1. Finely crush 1 cup croutons and place in a shallow bowl. In a large bowl, gently combine chicken, salt and pepper. With wet hands, shape chicken mixture into four 5-in. patties. Coat both sides with crouton crumbs.

2. In a large skillet, heat oil over medium heat. Cook patties until lightly browned and a thermometer reads 165°, 4-5 minutes on each side. Remove to paper towel to drain. Cut each patty into 4-5 strips.

3. In a large bowl, toss romaine with dressing and ¼ cup cheese. Arrange on 4 individual serving plates. Top with chicken patty slices and remaining 1 cup whole croutons and ¼ cup cheese. Serve with additional salad dressing.

1 SERVING 515 cal., 39g fat (9g sat. fat), 95mg chol., 1054mg sod., 16g carb. (2g sugars, 3g fiber), 26g pro.

SIMPLE SAUSAGE PASTA TOSS

For a flash of tasty inspiration, grab a skillet and stir up turkey sausage with tomatoes, garlic and olives. Toss everything with spaghetti, and sprinkle with bread crumbs.

—*Taste of Home* Test Kitchen

TAKES: 25 min. • **MAKES:** 5 servings

8 oz. uncooked multigrain spaghetti
¼ cup seasoned bread crumbs
1 tsp. olive oil
¾ lb. Italian turkey sausage links, cut into ½-in. slices
1 garlic clove, minced
2 cans (14½ oz. each) no-salt-added diced tomatoes, undrained
1 can (2¼ oz.) sliced ripe olives, drained

1. Cook spaghetti according to package directions; drain. Meanwhile, in a large skillet, toss bread crumbs with oil; cook and stir over medium heat until toasted. Remove from pan.

2. Add sausage to same pan; cook and stir over medium heat until no longer pink. Add garlic; cook 30-60 seconds longer. Stir in tomatoes and olives; heat through. Add spaghetti and toss to combine. Sprinkle with toasted bread crumbs before serving.

1⅔ CUPS 340 cal., 10g fat (2g sat. fat), 41mg chol., 689mg sod., 44g carb. (6g sugars, 6g fiber), 21g pro. **DIABETIC EXCHANGES** 3 lean meat, 2 starch, 1 vegetable, ½ fat.

HONEY CHICKEN STIR-FRY

I am a new mom, so I like meals that can be ready in little time. This all-in-one chicken stir-fry recipe with a hint of sweetness from honey is a big timesaver.

—Caroline Sperry, Allentown, MI

TAKES: 30 min. • **MAKES:** 4 servings

- 2 tsp. cornstarch
- 1 Tbsp. cold water
- 3 tsp. olive oil, divided
- 1 lb. boneless skinless chicken breasts, cut into 1-in. pieces
- 1 garlic clove, minced
- 3 Tbsp. honey
- 2 Tbsp. reduced-sodium soy sauce
- ⅛ tsp. salt
- ⅛ tsp. pepper
- 1 pkg. (16 oz.) frozen broccoli stir-fry vegetable blend
  Hot cooked rice, optional

1. Mix cornstarch and water until smooth. In a large nonstick skillet, heat 2 tsp. oil over medium-high heat; stir-fry chicken and garlic 1 minute. Add honey, soy sauce, salt and pepper; cook and stir until chicken is no longer pink, 2-3 minutes. Remove from pan.
2. In same pan, stir-fry vegetable blend in remaining oil just until tender, 4-5 minutes. Return chicken to pan. Stir cornstarch mixture and add to pan; bring to a boil. Cook and stir until thickened, about 1 minute. Serve with rice if desired.
1 CUP STIR-FRY 249 cal., 6g fat (1g sat. fat), 63mg chol., 455mg sod., 21g carb. (15g sugars, 3g fiber), 25g pro. **DIABETIC EXCHANGES** 3 lean meat, 2 vegetable, ½ starch.

BARBARA'S ITALIAN WEDDING SOUP

My husband and I had an amazing soup with orzo in a little Italian restaurant. I tweaked it at home to make it healthier but kept the warm, comforting flavor.

—Barbara Spitzer, Lodi, CA

TAKES: 30 min. • **MAKES:** 6 servings

- 1 pkg. (19½ oz.) Italian turkey sausage links, casings removed
- 2 shallots, finely chopped
- 3 garlic cloves, minced
- 1 carton (32 oz.) reduced-sodium chicken broth
- ¾ cup uncooked whole wheat orzo pasta
- ¼ tsp. pepper
- 10 cups coarsely chopped escarole or spinach
- ½ cup coarsely chopped fresh Italian parsley

1. In a 6-qt. stockpot, cook sausage, shallots and garlic over medium heat until sausage is no longer pink, 6-8 minutes, breaking up sausage into crumbles. Drain.

2. Add broth to sausage mixture; bring to a boil. Stir in orzo, pepper and escarole; return to a boil. Reduce heat; simmer, uncovered, until orzo is tender, 10-12 minutes. Stir in parsley before serving.

1 CUP 197 cal., 6g fat (1g sat. fat), 34mg chol., 780mg sod., 20g carb. (1g sugars, 6g fiber), 16g pro.

TURKEY STEW WITH DUMPLINGS

My husband and I love dumplings, and this mild-tasting, homey dish has flavorful ones floating on a tasty turkey and vegetable stew. It really hits the spot on chilly fall and winter days.

—Rita Taylor, St. Cloud, MN

PREP: 30 min. • **COOK:** 45 min. • **MAKES:** 12 servings

8 medium carrots, cut into 1-in. chunks
4 celery ribs, cut into 1-in. chunks
1 cup chopped onion
½ cup butter, cubed
2 cans (10½ oz. each) condensed beef consomme, undiluted
4⅔ cups water, divided
2 tsp. salt
¼ tsp. pepper
3 cups cubed cooked turkey
2 cups frozen cut green beans
½ cup all-purpose flour
2 tsp. Worcestershire sauce

DUMPLINGS

1½ cups all-purpose flour
2 tsp. baking powder
1 tsp. salt
2 Tbsp. minced parsley
⅛ tsp. poultry seasoning
¾ cup 2% milk
1 large egg

1. In a Dutch oven, saute the carrots, celery and onion in butter for 10 minutes. Add the consomme, 4 cups water, salt and pepper. Bring to a boil. Reduce heat; cover and cook over low heat for 15 minutes or until vegetables are tender.
2. Add turkey and beans; cook 5 minutes. Combine the flour, Worcestershire sauce and remaining water until smooth; stir into turkey mixture. Bring to a boil. Reduce heat; cover and simmer for 5 minutes or until thickened.

3. For dumplings, combine the flour, baking powder and salt in a large bowl. Stir in parsley and poultry seasoning. Combine milk and egg; stir into flour mixture just until moistened. Drop by tablespoonfuls onto simmering stew. Cover and simmer for 20 minutes or until a toothpick inserted in a dumpling comes out clean (do not lift the cover while simmering).

1 SERVING 255 cal., 11g fat (6g sat. fat), 68mg chol., 995mg sod., 24g carb. (6g sugars, 3g fiber), 15g pro.

"This is a good recipe to use up leftover turkey. We use chicken also."

—OZZYB_NH, TASTEOFHOME.COM

MANGO CHICKEN THIGHS WITH BASIL-COCONUT SAUCE

This recipe brings the restaurant to my home kitchen. And it's easy too! The meal comes together quickly and fills my kitchen with wonderful aromas. Plus, if there are any leftovers, a reheat the next day is just as good!

—Kathi Jones-DelMonte, Rochester, NY

PREP: 20 min. • **COOK:** 30 min. • **MAKES:** 4 servings

4 boneless skinless chicken thighs (about 1 lb.)
½ tsp. salt
¼ tsp. pepper
1 Tbsp. olive oil
3 garlic cloves, minced
1 Tbsp. minced fresh gingerroot
1 can (13.66 oz.) coconut milk
1 medium mango, peeled and chopped
4 green onions, sliced
½ cup thinly sliced fresh basil, divided
¼ cup miso paste
2 tsp. Sriracha chili sauce
2 cups cooked jasmine rice
2 medium limes, quartered

1. Sprinkle chicken with salt and pepper. In a large skillet, heat oil over medium heat. Brown chicken on both sides. Add garlic and ginger; cook 1 minute longer.

2. Stir in coconut milk, mango, green onions, ¼ cup basil, miso paste and chili sauce. Cook and stir until sauce is slightly reduced and a thermometer inserted in chicken reads 170°, about 20 minutes. Sprinkle with remaining ¼ cup basil. Serve with rice and limes.

1 SERVING 552 cal., 28g fat (18g sat. fat), 76mg chol., 1209mg sod., 46g carb. (17g sugars, 4g fiber), 28g pro.

HOW TO CUBE A MANGO

To cut a mango, start by placing it on a cutting board with the 2 rounded sides facing left and right. Using a sharp chef's knife, slice as close to the seed as possible, removing both "cheeks." If your knife hits the pit, adjust slightly and continue cutting. For the remaining sections, carefully slice around the seed, then discard it.

Next, make "hedgehog" cuts. Score the mango cheeks lengthwise and widthwise, being careful not to pierce the skin, creating a grid pattern. Push the skin outward to expose the mango cubes, then gently slice them off.

SWEET CHILI & ORANGE CHICKEN

My husband loves this simple chicken dish so much he often requests it when he comes home from deployment. The sweet chili sauce adds just the right amount of heat to the bright, citrusy sauce.

—Jessica Eastman, Bremerton, WA

TAKES: 20 min. • **MAKES:** 4 servings

- 1 lb. boneless skinless chicken breasts, cut into 1-in. pieces
- ¼ tsp. salt
- ¼ tsp. pepper
- 2 Tbsp. butter
- ¾ cup sweet chili sauce
- ⅓ cup thawed orange juice concentrate
  Hot cooked jasmine or other rice
  Chopped fresh basil, optional

1. Toss chicken with salt and pepper. In a large skillet, heat butter over medium-high heat; stir-fry chicken until no longer pink, 5-7 minutes. Remove from pan; keep warm.

2. Add chili sauce and juice concentrate to skillet; cook and stir until heated through. Stir in chicken. Serve with rice. If desired, sprinkle with basil.

½ CUP CHICKEN MIXTURE 309 cal., 9g fat (4g sat. fat), 78mg chol., 1014mg sod., 33g carb. (31g sugars, 1g fiber), 24g pro.

"Great recipe! So easy and tasty! Will add in some broccoli or snow peas next time!"
—CROMYAK, TASTEOFHOME.COM

OKLAHOMA
ONION BURGERS

OKLAHOMA ONION BURGERS

Oklahoma onion burgers are a type of smash burger that came about during the Great Depression. Smothered in golden brown onions and topped with American cheese, they're fast, easy and delicious.

—Lauren Habermehl, Pewaukee, WI

TAKES: 25 min. • **MAKES:** 4 servings

1 large white onion
1 lb. ground beef
4 hamburger buns, split
1 Tbsp. butter
  Salt and pepper
4 slices American cheese, optional
  Yellow mustard
  Dill pickle slices
  Optional toppings: Lettuce leaves and sliced tomato

1. Using a mandolin, slice onion into paper-thin slices. Divide beef into 4 portions; gently shape each into a ball.
2. In a large cast-iron skillet or electric griddle over medium-high heat, melt butter. Place ground beef balls in the skillet. Season with salt and pepper. Top with a generous mound of onions. Using a cast-iron grill press or large metal spatula, flatten to about ¼-in. thickness, pressing the onion into the beef. Cook until lightly browned and edges are crisp, 4-6 minutes.

3. Carefully turn patties so onion is on the bottom. Cook until onions are golden brown, 4-6 minutes. If desired, top each patty with cheese and cook until melted, 1-2 minutes longer. Remove from the heat. Serve on buns with mustard, pickles and, if desired, lettuce and tomato.
1 BURGER 369 cal., 18g fat (7g sat. fat), 78mg chol., 304mg sod., 26g carb. (5g sugars, 1g fiber), 25g pro.

🅕

ASIAN BEEF & NOODLES

This yummy, economical dish takes only five ingredients—all of which are easy to keep on hand. Serve with a dash of soy sauce and a side of fresh pineapple slices. You can also try it with ground turkey instead of beef!

—Laura Shull Stenberg, Wyoming, MN

TAKES: 20 min. • **MAKES:** 4 servings

1 lb. lean ground beef (90% lean)
2 pkg. (3 oz. each) Soy sauce ramen noodles, crumbled
2½ cups water
2 cups frozen broccoli stir-fry vegetable blend
¼ tsp. ground ginger
2 Tbsp. thinly sliced green onion

1. In a large skillet, cook beef over medium heat until no longer pink. Crumble beef; drain. Add the contents of 1 ramen noodle flavoring packet; stir until dissolved. Remove beef and set aside.
2. In the same skillet, combine the water, vegetables, ginger, noodles and contents of remaining flavoring packet. Bring to a boil. Reduce heat; cover and simmer

until noodles are tender, 3-4 minutes, stirring occasionally. Return beef to the pan and heat through. Stir in onion.
1½ CUPS 383 cal., 16g fat (7g sat. fat), 71mg chol., 546mg sod., 29g carb. (2g sugars, 2g fiber), 27g pro.

CHEESEBURGER PARADISE SOUP

I've never met a person who didn't enjoy this creamy soup, and it's hearty enough to serve as a main course with bread or rolls.

—Nadina Iadimarco, Burton, OH

PREP: 30 min. • **COOK:** 25 min. • **MAKES:** 14 servings (about 3½ qt.)

6   medium potatoes, peeled and cubed
1   small carrot, grated
1   small onion, chopped
½   cup chopped green pepper
2   Tbsp. chopped seeded jalapeno pepper
3   cups water
2   Tbsp. plus 2 tsp. beef bouillon granules
2   garlic cloves, minced
⅛   tsp. pepper
2   lbs. ground beef
½   lb. sliced fresh mushrooms
2   Tbsp. butter
5   cups 2% milk, divided
6   Tbsp. all-purpose flour
1   pkg. (16 oz.) Velveeta, cubed
     Crumbled cooked bacon

1. In a Dutch oven, bring the first 9 ingredients to a boil. Reduce heat; cover and simmer for 10-15 minutes or until potatoes are tender.

2. Meanwhile, in a large skillet, cook beef and mushrooms in butter over medium heat until meat is no longer pink; drain. Add to soup. Stir in 4 cups milk; heat through.

3. In a small bowl, combine flour and remaining milk until smooth; gradually stir into soup. Bring to a boil; cook and stir for 2 minutes or until thickened. Reduce heat; stir in cheese until melted. Garnish with bacon.

NOTE Wear disposable gloves when cutting hot peppers; the oils can burn skin. Avoid touching your face.

1 CUP 370 cal., 20g fat (10g sat. fat), 79mg chol., 947mg sod., 24g carb. (8g sugars, 1g fiber), 23g pro.

CHOOSE THE RIGHT SPUD

Waxy potatoes (such as reds) hold their shape better than starchy potatoes (like russets). However, starchy varieties will absorb more flavor and help to thicken the creamy liquid. All-purpose potatoes (like Yukon Golds) offer the best of both worlds. Their skins are thin, so you can leave them unpeeled for a rustic look and improved nutrition.

PATTY MELTS

My husband often orders patty melts at restaurants, so I started fixing them at home. I added horseradish to give them more zip, and now he loves them my way.

—Leah Zimmerman, Ephrata, PA

TAKES: 30 min. • **MAKES:** 2 servings

- 10 thin slices sweet onion
- 2 Tbsp. butter, softened, divided
- ½ lb. lean ground beef (90% lean)
- ¼ tsp. salt
- ¼ tsp. pepper
- 4 slices rye bread
- 2 Tbsp. Thousand Island salad dressing
- 2 tsp. prepared horseradish
- 2 slices American cheese or Swiss cheese

1. In a large nonstick skillet, saute onion in 1 Tbsp. butter until tender. Remove and keep warm.
2. Shape beef into 2 oval patties; sprinkle with salt and pepper. In the same skillet, cook the patties over medium heat for 3-4 minutes on each side or until a thermometer reads 160° and meat juices run clear; drain. Remove and keep warm.
3. Spread remaining butter over 1 side of each slice of bread. Place in skillet, buttered side down, and toast until lightly browned.
4. Combine salad dressing and horseradish. On each of 2 slices of toast, layer a slice of cheese, a beef patty, and half of the onion and the dressing mixture. Top with remaining toast.

1 SANDWICH 516 cal., 24g fat (11g sat. fat), 108mg chol., 1278mg sod., 43g carb. (13g sugars, 5g fiber), 32g pro.

"We love patty melts, and this was no exception. I did leave out the horseradish because I didn't have any on hand, and I doubled the cheese—one on each side. It held the second piece of bread on better. Loved them! This is the second time I've made them."

—ANGELA32, TASTEOFHOME.COM

MONGOLIAN BEEF SALAD

This light and loaded beef salad even satisfies my meat-loving husband.

—Marla Clark, Albuquerque, NM

TAKES: 30 min. • **MAKES:** 4 servings

- ¼ cup olive oil
- 2 Tbsp. rice vinegar
- 1 Tbsp. reduced-sodium soy sauce
- 1 Tbsp. sesame oil
- 2 tsp. minced fresh gingerroot
- 1 small garlic clove, minced
- 1 tsp. sugar

BEEF
- 1 Tbsp. reduced-sodium soy sauce
- 2 garlic cloves, minced
- 2 tsp. sugar
- 1 to 2 tsp. crushed red pepper flakes
- 1 tsp. sesame oil
- 1 beef top sirloin steak (1 lb.), cut into ¼-in. strips
- 1 Tbsp. olive oil

SALAD
- 8 cups torn mixed salad greens
- 1 cup shredded carrots
- ½ cup thinly sliced cucumber
- 4 radishes, thinly sliced

1. For dressing, whisk together the first 7 ingredients.

2. Mix first 5 beef ingredients; toss with beef strips. In a large cast-iron or other heavy skillet, heat olive oil over medium-high heat; stir-fry beef mixture until browned, 2-3 minutes. Remove from pan.

3. Combine salad ingredients; divide among 4 plates. Top with beef. Drizzle with dressing.

1 SERVING 396 cal., 26g fat (5g sat. fat), 46mg chol., 550mg sod., 15g carb. (7g sugars, 3g fiber), 27g pro.

HAMBURGER STEAKS WITH MUSHROOM GRAVY

Here's a meat-and-potatoes meal that no one will want to miss. It makes for a hearty dish the whole family will cozy up to in no time!

—Denise Wheeler, Newaygo, MI

TAKES: 25 min. • **MAKES:** 4 servings

- 1 large egg
- ½ cup dry bread crumbs
- 1 envelope onion soup mix, divided
  Dash pepper
- 1 lb. ground beef
- 3 Tbsp. all-purpose flour
- 1¾ cups cold water
- 1 tsp. Worcestershire sauce
- 1 jar (4½ oz.) whole mushrooms, drained
  Hot cooked mashed potatoes

1. In a large bowl, combine the egg, bread crumbs, 2 Tbsp. soup mix and pepper. Crumble beef over mixture and mix lightly but thoroughly. Shape into 4 patties.
2. In a large cast-iron or other heavy skillet, cook patties over medium heat until a thermometer reads 160°, and juices run clear, 4-5 minutes on each side. Set aside and keep warm.
3. Combine the flour, water, Worcestershire sauce and remaining soup mix until blended; stir into skillet. Add mushrooms. Bring to a boil; cook and stir until thickened, about 5 minutes. Serve sauce with patties and mashed potatoes.

1 PATTY WITH ½ CUP GRAVY 325 cal., 15g fat (6g sat. fat), 123mg chol., 920mg sod., 20g carb. (2g sugars, 2g fiber), 25g pro.

COPYCAT CHEESY GORDITA CRUNCH

We wrapped a cheesy flour tortilla around a taco shell for a double dose of goodness. Serve with your favorite taco toppings.

—*Taste of Home* Test Kitchen

TAKES: 25 min. • **MAKES:** 8 servings

1 lb. ground beef
1 envelope taco seasoning
⅔ cup water
2 cups shredded cheddar cheese
8 flour tortillas (6 in.)
8 taco shells, warmed
8 Tbsp. spicy ranch salad dressing
  Optional toppings: Shredded cheddar cheese, sour cream, shredded lettuce, diced tomatoes, chopped red onion and lime wedges

1. In a large skillet, cook beef over medium heat until no longer pink, 5-7 minutes, breaking into crumbles; drain. Stir in taco seasoning and water. Bring to a boil. Reduce heat; simmer, uncovered, until thickened, 2-3 minutes.
2. Meanwhile, sprinkle ¼ cup cheese over 1 side of each tortilla. Place on a microwave-safe plate; heat, uncovered, on high for 15-20 seconds or until cheese is melted. Immediately wrap each tortilla around a taco shell. Fill with beef mixture. Drizzle with spicy ranch dressing. Serve with toppings of your choice.

1 TACO 357 cal., 22g fat (9g sat. fat), 60mg chol., 929mg sod., 22g carb. (2g sugars, 1g fiber), 18g pro.

MAKE 'EM AHEAD

For easy, on-demand Cheesy Gordita Crunch tacos, prepare the seasoned beef and toppings ahead of time. Store the beef in an airtight container in the fridge for up to 4 days, and keep the toppings in separate containers. Make the cheesy taco shells and fill them just before serving.

ST. PADDY'S IRISH BEEF DINNER

A variation on shepherd's pie, this hearty dish brings together saucy beef with mashed potatoes, parsnips and other vegetables. It's always the star of our March 17 meal.

—Lorraine Caland, Shuniah, ON

PREP: 25 min. • **COOK:** 35 min. • **MAKES:** 4 servings

2   medium Yukon Gold potatoes
2   small parsnips
¾   lb. lean ground beef (90% lean)
1   medium onion, chopped
2   cups finely shredded cabbage
2   medium carrots, halved and sliced
1   tsp. dried thyme
1   tsp. Worcestershire sauce
1   Tbsp. all-purpose flour
¼   cup tomato paste
1   can (14½ oz.) reduced-sodium chicken or beef broth
½   cup frozen peas
¾   tsp. salt, divided
½   tsp. pepper, divided
¼   cup 2% milk
1   Tbsp. butter

1. Peel potatoes and parsnips and cut into large pieces; place in a large saucepan and cover with water. Bring to a boil. Reduce heat; cover and cook for 10-15 minutes or until tender. Drain.

2. Meanwhile, in a large skillet, cook beef and onion over medium heat until meat is no longer pink; drain. Stir in the cabbage, carrots, thyme and Worcestershire sauce.

3. In a small bowl, combine the flour, tomato paste and broth until smooth. Gradually stir into meat mixture. Bring to a boil. Reduce heat; cover and simmer for 15-20 minutes or until vegetables are tender. Stir in the peas, ¼ tsp. salt and ¼ tsp. pepper.

4. Drain potatoes and parsnips; mash with milk, butter and the remaining ½ tsp. salt and ¼ tsp. pepper. Serve with meat mixture.

1 SERVING 369 cal., 11g fat (5g sat. fat), 62mg chol., 849mg sod., 46g carb. (13g sugars, 8g fiber), 24g pro. **DIABETIC EXCHANGES** 3 lean meat, 2 starch, 2 vegetable.

IRISH DINNER TIPS

How do I store this St. Patrick's Irish beef dinner recipe?
Cool the mashed potato and beef mixtures completely before storing them separately in airtight containers. They will last 3 to 4 days in the fridge.

What are some variations of this Irish beef dinner recipe?
You can add vegetables like corn to the dish for variety, or prepare it with ground lamb instead of beef.

What other recipes can I make for St. Patrick's Day?
Complement this dish with classic Irish soda bread or Irish brown bread. Don't forget to pair your meal with an Irish beer!

BULGOGI SALAD BOWL

Since beef is so expensive these days, I found a great way to make a little go a long way. If salad isn't your thing, the recipe also works well served over rice.

—Stacy Schneidmiller, Beaumont, AB

PREP: 30 min. + marinating • **COOK:** 5 min. • **MAKES:** 4 servings

3 Tbsp. soy sauce
1 Tbsp. brown sugar
1 Tbsp. sesame oil
1 Tbsp. grated fresh gingerroot
2 garlic cloves, minced
1 beef top sirloin steak (1 lb.), cut into ¼-in.-thick strips
2 large carrots, thinly sliced
½ medium cucumber, thinly sliced
1 Tbsp. rice vinegar
6 cups chopped lettuce
3 Tbsp. chopped fresh cilantro
3 Tbsp. chopped fresh mint
2 green onions, thinly sliced
  Sesame seeds

DRESSING

2 Tbsp. rice vinegar
2 tsp. sesame oil
  Dash salt

1. In a shallow bowl, combine the first 5 ingredients. Add beef and turn to coat. Cover and refrigerate for 8 hours or overnight.
2. In a small bowl, toss carrots, cucumber and vinegar.
3. In a large skillet, saute beef over medium-high heat. Cook and stir until beef is no longer pink, 4-5 minutes.
4. In a large bowl, toss lettuce and herbs; divide among 4 individual salad bowls. Sprinkle with green onions and sesame seeds. In a small bowl, whisk vinegar, sesame oil and salt; drizzle over salads. Top with carrot mixture and beef.

1 BOWL 271 cal., 11g fat (3g sat. fat), 46mg chol., 997mg sod., 16g carb. (11g sugars, 3g fiber), 28g pro.

"This is a quick and easy recipe to make on a weeknight."
—KIMSPACC, TASTEOFHOME.COM

TRIPLE-CITRUS STEAKS WITH JICAMA & MANGO

This is a recipe I made up several years ago. It seems to be one of our family favorites. It is colorful to bring to the table and it's easy.

—Sheryl Little, Cabot, AR

PREP: 30 min. + marinating • **COOK:** 15 min. • **MAKES:** 4 servings

1 medium orange
1 medium lemon
1 medium lime
4 Tbsp. honey
1¼ tsp. salt, divided
4 beef flat iron steaks or top sirloin steaks (6 oz. each and ¾ in. thick)
½ cup water
1 cup julienned peeled jicama
1 medium mango, peeled and cubed

1. Cut orange, lemon and lime crosswise in half; squeeze juice from fruits. Stir in honey and 1 tsp. salt. Pour ⅓ cup marinade into a bowl or shallow dish. Add steaks and turn to coat. Refrigerate at least 3 hours, turning once. Cover and refrigerate remaining marinade.
2. Drain steaks, discarding marinade. Heat a large skillet over medium heat. Cook the steaks until meat reaches desired doneness (for medium-rare, a thermometer should read 135°; medium, 140°; medium-well, 145°), 6-8 minutes on each side. Remove and keep warm.
3. Add water and reserved marinade. Bring to a boil; cook until liquid is reduced to 3 Tbsp., 10-12 minutes. Add jicama, mango and remaining ¼ tsp. salt; heat through. Serve with steaks. If desired, garnish with orange, lemon or lime slices.

1 SERVING 412 cal., 18g fat (7g sat. fat), 109mg chol., 609mg sod., 29g carb. (24g sugars, 3g fiber), 34g pro.

REUBEN SANDWICHES

My mouth waters just thinking of these sandwiches. I adapted the recipe from one my mother found several years ago.

—Kathy Jo Scott, Hemingford, NE

TAKES: 15 min. • **MAKES:** 4 servings

12 oz. thinly sliced corned beef
8 slices light or dark rye bread
1 can (8 oz.) sauerkraut, rinsed and well drained
½ cup Thousand Island dressing
4 slices Swiss cheese
4 Tbsp. butter, softened

1. Arrange corned beef on 4 slices of bread. Layer each with a quarter of the sauerkraut, 2 Tbsp. of dressing and a slice of cheese. Top with remaining bread slices. Butter outsides of sandwiches.
2. In a small skillet over medium heat, toast sandwiches until bread is lightly browned on both sides and cheese is melted.

1 SANDWICH 547 cal., 31g fat (13g sat. fat), 106mg chol., 2346mg sod., 39g carb. (10g sugars, 5g fiber), 28g pro.

TRIPLE-CITRUS STEAKS WITH JICAMA & MANGO

PUMPKIN CHILI

This unique chili freezes well ... but it still doesn't last around our farmhouse very long, especially when my five children and 13 grandchildren are around!

—Betty Butler, Greencastle, IN

PREP: 10 min. • **COOK:** 70 min.
MAKES: 11 servings (2¾ qt.)

- 3 lbs. ground beef
- 1 medium onion, chopped
- 2 cans (16 oz. each) hot chili beans, undrained
- 2 bottles (12 oz. each) chili sauce
- 2 cans (10¾ oz. each) condensed tomato soup, undiluted
- 1 cup canned pumpkin
- 2 tsp. pumpkin pie spice
- 1 tsp. salt
- 1 tsp. sugar
- 1 tsp. pepper
- 1 tsp. chili powder
  Optional toppings: Corn chips and shredded white cheddar cheese

In a Dutch oven, cook beef and onion over medium heat until no longer pink; drain. Stir in remaining ingredients except toppings. Add water if desired to reduce thickness. Bring chili to a boil. Reduce heat; cover and simmer for 1 hour. If desired, top with corn chips and cheese.

1 CUP 293 cal., 12g fat (5g sat. fat), 61mg chol., 1034mg sod., 21g carb. (10g sugars, 4g fiber), 25g pro.

EASY GROUND BEEF TACO SALAD

Every time I have to bring a dish to a party, friends ask for my taco salad. Even players on my son's football team ask for it.

—Lori Buntrock, Wisconsin Rapids, WI

TAKES: 30 min. • **MAKES:** 6 servings

- 1 lb. ground beef
- 1 envelope reduced-sodium taco seasoning
- ¾ cup water
- 1 medium head iceberg lettuce, torn (about 8 cups)
- 2 cups shredded cheddar cheese
- 2 cups broken nacho-flavored tortilla chips
- ¼ cup Catalina salad dressing
  Optional toppings: Diced tomatoes, black beans, cubed avocado, salsa or pico de gallo

1. In a large skillet, cook beef over medium heat 6-8 minutes or until no longer pink, breaking into crumbles; drain. Stir in taco seasoning and water; bring to a boil. Reduce heat; simmer, uncovered, 4-6 minutes or until thickened, stirring occasionally. Cool slightly.
2. In a large bowl, toss lettuce with cheese. Top with beef mixture and chips; drizzle with dressing and toss to combine. Serve immediately with toppings as desired.

1⅔ CUPS 416 cal., 27g fat (12g sat. fat), 86mg chol., 830mg sod., 19g carb. (7g sugars, 2g fiber), 25g pro.

FAMILY-FAVORITE CHEESEBURGER PASTA

I created this recipe to satisfy a cheeseburger craving. The result was a delicious new classic!

—Raquel Haggard, Edmond, OK

TAKES: 30 min. • **MAKES:** 4 servings

1½ cups uncooked whole wheat penne pasta
¾ lb. lean ground beef (90% lean)
2 Tbsp. finely chopped onion
1 can (14½ oz.) no-salt-added diced tomatoes
2 Tbsp. dill pickle relish
2 Tbsp. prepared mustard
2 Tbsp. ketchup
1 tsp. steak seasoning
¼ tsp. seasoned salt
¾ cup shredded reduced-fat cheddar cheese
   Chopped green onions, optional

1. Cook pasta according to package directions. Meanwhile, in a large skillet, cook beef and onion over medium heat until meat is no longer pink; drain. Drain pasta; add to meat mixture.
2. Stir in the tomatoes, relish, mustard, ketchup, steak seasoning and seasoned salt. Bring to a boil. Reduce heat; simmer, uncovered, for 5 minutes.

3. Sprinkle with cheese. Remove from the heat; cover and let stand until cheese is melted. Garnish with green onions if desired.
1½ CUPS 391 cal., 12g fat (6g sat. fat), 57mg chol., 759mg sod., 43g carb. (10g sugars, 4g fiber), 28g pro. **DIABETIC EXCHANGES** 3 lean meat, 2 starch, 1 vegetable, ½ fat.

MAKE IT A ONE-POT MEAL

If you want t to save yourself some dishes, begin by browning the beef and onion in a Dutch oven, then add the uncooked pasta and 2 cups beef broth. Bring to a boil, then simmer until al dente, 8-10 minutes. Proceed with steps 2 and 3.

HEARTY PENNE BEEF

This is comfort food at its finest! The best of everything is found here—it's tasty, easy and a smart way to sneak in some spinach for extra nutrition.

—*Taste of Home* Test Kitchen

TAKES: 30 min. • **MAKES:** 4 servings

1¾ cups uncooked penne pasta
1 lb. ground beef
1 tsp. minced garlic
1 can (15 oz.) tomato puree
1 can (14½ oz.) beef broth
1½ tsp. Italian seasoning
1 tsp. Worcestershire sauce
¼ tsp. salt
¼ tsp. pepper
2 cups chopped fresh spinach
2 cups shredded part-skim mozzarella cheese

1. Cook pasta according to package directions. Meanwhile, in a Dutch oven, cook beef over medium heat until no longer pink, 6-8 minutes, breaking into crumbles. Add garlic; cook 1 minute longer. Drain. Stir in tomato puree, broth, Italian seasoning, Worcestershire sauce, salt and pepper.
2. Bring to a boil. Reduce heat; simmer, uncovered, until slightly thickened, 10-15 minutes. Add spinach; cook until wilted, 1-2 minutes.

3. Drain pasta; stir into beef mixture. Sprinkle with cheese; cover and cook until cheese is melted, 3-4 minutes.
FREEZE OPTION Freeze cooled pasta mixture in freezer containers. To use, partially thaw in refrigerator overnight. Heat through in a saucepan, stirring occasionally; add broth or water if necessary.
1½ CUPS 482 cal., 20g fat (10g sat. fat), 88mg chol., 1001mg sod., 33g carb. (5g sugars, 2g fiber), 41g pro.

KOREAN BEEF & RICE

A friend raved about Korean bulgogi, which is beef cooked in soy sauce and ginger, so I tried it. It's delicious! You'll dazzle the table with this tasty version of beef and rice.

—Elizabeth King, Duluth, MN

TAKES: 15 min. • **MAKES:** 4 servings

1 lb. lean ground beef (90% lean)
3 garlic cloves, minced
¼ cup packed brown sugar
¼ cup reduced-sodium soy sauce
2 tsp. sesame oil
¼ tsp. ground ginger
¼ tsp. crushed red pepper flakes
¼ tsp. pepper
2⅔ cups hot cooked brown rice
3 green onions, thinly sliced

1. In a large skillet, cook beef and garlic over medium heat 6-8 minutes or until beef is no longer pink, breaking beef into crumbles. Meanwhile, in a small bowl, mix brown sugar, soy sauce, oil and seasonings.
2. Stir sauce into beef; heat through. Serve with rice. Sprinkle with green onions.
½ CUP BEEF MIXTURE WITH ⅔ CUP RICE 413 cal., 13g fat (4g sat. fat), 71mg chol., 647mg sod., 46g carb. (14g sugars, 3g fiber), 27g pro. **DIABETIC EXCHANGES** 3 starch, 3 lean meat, ½ fat.

TORTELLINI WITH SAUSAGE & MASCARPONE

TORTELLINI WITH SAUSAGE & MASCARPONE

When I crave Italian comfort food on a busy night and don't have a lot of time to cook, this dish is fast and yummy. You can have it on the table in less time than a takeout order.

—Gerry Vance, Millbrae, CA

TAKES: 20 min. • **MAKES:** 6 servings

1 pkg. (20 oz.) refrigerated cheese tortellini
8 oz. bulk Italian sausage
1 jar (24 oz.) pasta sauce with mushrooms
½ cup shredded Parmesan cheese
1 carton (8 oz.) mascarpone cheese
   Crushed red pepper flakes, optional

1. Prepare tortellini according to package directions. Meanwhile, in a large cast-iron or other heavy skillet, cook sausage over medium heat until no longer pink, 6-8 minutes, breaking into crumbles; drain. Stir in pasta sauce; heat through.
2. Drain tortellini, reserving 1 cup cooking water. Add tortellini to sauce with enough reserved cooking water to reach desired consistency; toss to coat. Stir in Parmesan cheese; dollop with mascarpone cheese. If desired, sprinkle with red pepper flakes.

1 CUP 637 cal., 37g fat (17g sat. fat), 113mg chol., 1040mg sod., 57g carb. (11g sugars, 4g fiber), 24g pro.

"This is amazing and quick to make! My husband loved it! I had some leftover mushrooms and garlic that I added. This will be added to my dinner rotation."

—LOR207, TASTEOFHOME.COM

BACON & TOMATO SPAGHETTI

Our summer-perfect pasta features baby spinach, cherry tomatoes and crisp bacon tossed with a tangy balsamic vinaigrette.

—*Taste of Home* Test Kitchen

TAKES: 25 min. • **MAKES:** 4 servings

8 oz. uncooked spaghetti
½ lb. thick-sliced bacon strips, chopped
2 cups cherry tomatoes, halved
3 cups fresh baby spinach
¼ cup balsamic vinaigrette
½ tsp. salt
¼ tsp. pepper
   Grated Parmesan cheese

1. Cook spaghetti according to package directions.
2. Meanwhile, in a large skillet, cook bacon over medium heat until crisp. Remove to paper towels with a slotted spoon; drain, reserving 2 Tbsp. drippings. Saute tomatoes in drippings until tender. Drain spaghetti; stir into skillet.

Add the spinach, bacon, vinaigrette, salt and pepper; heat through. Sprinkle with cheese.

1¼ CUPS 407 cal., 17g fat (5g sat. fat), 21mg chol., 880mg sod., 49g carb. (6g sugars, 3g fiber), 15g pro.

PORK TENDERLOIN STEW

This thick, creamy stew is one my family requests often. It does an especially good job of warming us up on cold winter days.

—Janet Allen, Belleville, IL

PREP: 20 min. • **COOK:** 40 min. • **MAKES:** 8 servings

- 2 lbs. pork tenderloin, cut into 1-in. cubes
- 1 Tbsp. olive oil
- 1 medium onion, chopped
- 1 garlic clove, minced
- 4 cups reduced-sodium chicken broth
- 2 lbs. red potatoes, peeled and cubed
- 1 cup sliced fresh carrots
- 1 cup sliced celery
- ½ lb. sliced fresh mushrooms
- 2 Tbsp. cider vinegar
- 2 tsp. sugar
- 1½ tsp. dried tarragon
- 1 tsp. salt
- 2 Tbsp. all-purpose flour
- ½ cup fat-free milk
- ½ cup sour cream
  Optional: Chopped fresh parsley and cracked pepper

1. In a medium Dutch oven over medium heat, cook pork in batches in oil until no longer pink; remove and keep warm.
2. In the same pan, saute onion until crisp-tender. Add garlic; cook 1 minute longer. Add the broth, vegetables, vinegar, sugar, tarragon and salt; bring to a boil. Reduce heat; cover and simmer for 25-30 minutes or until vegetables are tender.
3. Combine flour and milk until smooth; gradually stir into vegetable mixture. Bring to a boil; cook and stir for 2 minutes or until thickened. Add pork and heat through. Reduce heat; stir in sour cream just before serving (do not boil). If desired, top with parsley and cracked pepper.

1¼ CUPS 305 cal., 9g fat (3g sat. fat), 74mg chol., 665mg sod., 27g carb. (5g sugars, 3g fiber), 29g pro. **DIABETIC EXCHANGES** 3 lean meat, 1 starch, 1 vegetable, ½ fat.

"So good! The second time I wanted to make it, the store didn't have pork tenderloin. So I made this with pork chops instead. Still really yummy!"

—JACKLYN0810, TASTEOFHOME.COM

SPICY PLUM PORK MEATBALLS WITH BOK CHOY

I am a huge fan of sweet, salty and spicy, and with the new year in full swing, I'm trying to make healthier choices. This recipe is so satisfying and delicious, you won't miss any pasta or rice. If you don't want spiralized zucchini, any thin noodles will work too.

—Susan Mason, Puyallup, WA

PREP: 30 min. • **COOK:** 30 min. • **MAKES:** 4 servings

1   jar (7 oz.) plum sauce
½   cup hoisin sauce
3   Tbsp. reduced-sodium soy sauce
2   Tbsp. rice vinegar
1   Tbsp. Sriracha chili sauce
1   large egg, lightly beaten
1½ cups panko bread crumbs, divided
1   lb. ground pork
4   Tbsp. olive oil, divided
2   medium zucchini, spiralized
1   lb. bok choy, trimmed and cut into
    1-in. pieces
    Sesame seeds, optional

1. Whisk together first 5 ingredients. Reserve 1¼ cups for sauce. Pour remaining mixture into a large bowl; add egg and ½ cup bread crumbs. Add pork; mix lightly but thoroughly. Shape into 16 balls. Place remaining 1 cup bread crumbs in a shallow bowl. Roll meatballs in bread crumbs to coat.

2. In a large skillet, heat 3 Tbsp. oil over medium heat. In batches, cook meatballs until cooked through, turning occasionally. Remove and keep warm. Heat remaining 1 Tbsp. oil in the same skillet. Add zucchini and bok choy; cook and stir over medium-high heat until crisp-tender, 6-8 minutes. Add meatballs and reserved sauce; heat through. If desired, sprinkle with sesame seeds.

1 SERVING 647 cal., 34g fat (9g sat. fat), 123mg chol., 1656mg sod., 55g carb. (16g sugars, 4g fiber), 29g pro.

"I don't have a spiralizer, so I julienned the zucchini on a mandolin, and that worked out just fine."

—NEON3CMR, TASTEOFHOME.COM

CINNAMON-APPLE PORK CHOPS

When I found this recipe online years ago, it quickly became a favorite.
The ingredients are easy to keep on hand, and the one-pan cleanup is a bonus.

—Christina Price, Colorado Springs, CO

TAKES: 25 min. • **MAKES:** 4 servings

- 2 Tbsp. butter, divided
- 4 boneless pork loin chops (4 oz. each)
- 3 Tbsp. brown sugar
- 1 tsp. ground cinnamon
- ½ tsp. ground nutmeg
- ¼ tsp. salt
- 4 medium tart apples, thinly sliced
- 2 Tbsp. chopped pecans

1. In a large skillet, heat 1 Tbsp. butter over medium heat. Add pork chops; cook 4-5 minutes on each side or until a thermometer reads 145°. Meanwhile, in a small bowl, mix brown sugar, cinnamon, nutmeg and salt.
2. Remove chops; keep warm. Add apples, pecans, brown sugar mixture and remaining 1 Tbsp. butter to pan; cook and stir until apples are tender. Serve with chops.

1 PORK CHOP WITH ⅔ CUP APPLE MIXTURE 345 cal., 15g fat (6g sat. fat), 70mg chol., 229mg sod., 32g carb. (26g sugars, 4g fiber), 23g pro.

APPLE PICKING
Granny Smith or Braeburn apples work best for this dish. Their juicy flavor pairs well with buttery pecans and savory pork.

5i

HAM & BROCCOLI PASTA

It's hard to beat a meal that is created in one pan, takes 30 minutes and your kids will actually thank you for making. Sounds like a keeper in my book!

—Jana Cathey, Ada, MI

TAKES: 30 min. • **MAKES:** 6 servings

- 4½ cups uncooked bow tie pasta (12 oz.)
- 1 pkg. (16 oz.) frozen broccoli florets
- 3 cups cubed fully cooked ham
- 1 carton (8 oz.) spreadable chive and onion cream cheese
- ⅓ cup milk
- ¼ tsp. salt
- ½ tsp. pepper

1. In a Dutch oven, cook pasta according to package directions, adding broccoli during the last 5 minutes of cooking; drain and set aside.
2. In same pan, combine remaining ingredients; cook and stir over medium heat until heated through and cream cheese is melted. Return pasta mixture to pan and toss to combine.

1¾ CUPS 452 cal., 17g fat (10g sat. fat), 79mg chol., 1135mg sod., 48g carb. (6g sugars, 4g fiber), 26g pro.

KIMCHI CAULIFLOWER FRIED RICE

This is one of my favorite recipes because it's so customizable. If there's a vegetarian in the family, leave out the bacon. You can also add your favorite veggies.

—Stefanie Schaldenbrand,
Los Angeles, CA

TAKES: 30 min. • **MAKES:** 2 servings

- 2   bacon strips, chopped
- 1   green onion, chopped
- 2   garlic cloves, minced
- 1   cup kimchi, chopped
- 3   cups frozen riced cauliflower
- 2   large eggs
- 1   to 3 Tbsp. kimchi juice
     Optional: Sesame oil and sesame seeds

1. In a skillet, cook bacon over medium heat until partially cooked but not crisp, stirring occasionally. Add green onion and garlic; cook 1 minute longer. Add kimchi; heat through. Stir in cauliflower; cook until tender, 8-10 minutes.

2. Meanwhile, heat a large nonstick skillet over medium-high heat. Break eggs, 1 at a time, into pan; reduce heat to low. Cook until whites are set and yolks begin to thicken, turning once if desired. Stir enough kimchi juice into cauliflower mixture to moisten. Divide between 2 serving bowls. Top with fried eggs, additional green onions and, if desired, sesame oil and sesame seeds.

1 SERVING 254 cal., 17g fat (5g sat. fat), 204mg chol., 715mg sod., 13g carb. (6g sugars, 6g fiber), 15g pro. **DIABETIC EXCHANGES** 2 vegetable, 2 high-fat meat.

SAUSAGE & ASPARAGUS PASTA WITH CAJUN CREAM SAUCE

I needed to use up some ingredients in my refrigerator, so I threw together this dish. It's delicious and everyone loves it. I only use Tony Chachere's Creole seasoning mix.

—Angela Lively, Conroe, TX

TAKES: 25 min. • **MAKES:** 8 servings

1 pkg. (16 oz.) spiral pasta
1 lb. fresh asparagus, trimmed and cut into 2-in. pieces
1 pkg. (14 oz.) smoked sausage, sliced
2 garlic cloves, minced
1 cup heavy whipping cream
½ cup shredded Parmesan cheese
1 Tbsp. Creole seasoning
¼ tsp. pepper

1. In a Dutch oven, cook pasta according to package directions, adding asparagus during the last 4 minutes of cooking. Meanwhile, in a large nonstick skillet, cook sausage over medium heat until browned. Add garlic; cook 1 minute longer. Stir in cream, Parmesan cheese, Creole seasoning and pepper; cook and stir until slightly thickened, about 3 minutes.

2. Drain pasta mixture, reserving ½ cup cooking water; add to sausage mixture. Toss to coat, gradually adding enough reserved cooking water to reach desired consistency.
1¼ CUPS 496 cal., 26g fat (14g sat. fat), 71mg chol., 909mg sod., 46g carb. (4g sugars, 2g fiber), 18g pro.

BLT SKILLET

This weeknight meal is fast and reminiscent of a BLT, with its chunks of bacon and tomato. The whole wheat linguine gives the skillet dish extra flavor and texture.

—Edrie O'Brien, Denver, CO

TAKES: 25 min. • **MAKES:** 2 servings

4 oz. uncooked whole wheat linguine
4 bacon strips, cut into 1½-in. pieces
1 plum tomato, cut into 1-in. pieces
1 garlic clove, minced
1½ tsp. lemon juice
¼ tsp. salt
¼ tsp. pepper
2 Tbsp. grated Parmesan cheese
1 Tbsp. minced fresh parsley

1. Cook linguine according to package directions. Meanwhile, in a large skillet, cook bacon over medium heat until crisp. Remove to paper towels; drain, reserving 1 tsp. drippings.
2. In the drippings, saute tomato and garlic for 1-2 minutes or until heated through. Stir in the bacon, lemon juice, salt and pepper.
3. Drain linguine; add to the skillet. Sprinkle with cheese and parsley; toss to coat.
1½ CUPS 314 cal., 11g fat (4g sat. fat), 23mg chol., 682mg sod., 46g carb. (2g sugars, 7g fiber), 14g pro.

OPEN-FACED BRATWURST SANDWICHES WITH BEER GRAVY

A nod to my Volga German heritage, this classic diner fare comes together in a snap and can be made all in one skillet! I serve it with a green vegetable and french fries or mashed potatoes on the side. Cook the sausages in lager or stout beer for a deeper flavor profile.

—Allison Ochoa, Hays, KS

TAKES: 30 min. • **MAKES:** 5 servings

¼ cup butter, divided
1 pkg. uncooked bratwurst links (20 oz.)
1 medium onion, thinly sliced
1 bottle (12 oz.) beer or nonalcoholic beer
2 Tbsp. all-purpose flour
⅛ tsp. dill weed
⅛ tsp. pepper
5 thick slices bread

1. In a Dutch oven, heat 2 Tbsp. butter over medium-high heat. Add bratwurst and onion; cook and stir until bratwurst starts to brown and onion softens. Stir in beer. Bring to a boil. Reduce heat; simmer, covered, turning occasionally, until a thermometer inserted in bratwurst reads 165° and brats are no longer pink, 12-14 minutes.

2. Remove brats and onions; keep warm. Add remaining butter to pan; whisk in flour, dill weed and pepper. Bring to a boil, stirring constantly until thickened, 3-5 minutes. To serve, place 1 brat on each slice of bread; top evenly with onions and gravy.

1 BRATWURST SANDWICH WITH ¼ CUP GRAVY 567 cal., 43g fat (17g sat. fat), 108mg chol., 1176mg sod., 23g carb. (3g sugars, 1g fiber), 19g pro.

SERVING SUGGESTIONS

You can serve the sausage, onions and gravy over mashed potatoes, noodles or spaetzel. Using a dark beer will give the gravy a more deep, rich flavor but watch out for intense dark beers; you don't want to make the gravy bitter.

CHINESE PORK FRIED RICE

Here's an all-time classic scaled down for two. The peas and carrots add color and crunch to this savory dinner.

—Peggy Vaught, Glasgow, WV

TAKES: 25 min. • **MAKES:** 2 servings

- 1 boneless pork loin chop (6 oz.), cut into ½-in. pieces
- ¼ cup finely chopped carrot
- ¼ cup chopped fresh broccoli
- ¼ cup frozen peas
- 1 green onion, chopped
- 1 Tbsp. butter
- 1 large egg, lightly beaten
- 1 cup cold cooked long grain rice
- 4½ tsp. reduced-sodium soy sauce
- ⅛ tsp. garlic powder
- ⅛ tsp. ground ginger

1. In a large skillet, saute the pork, carrot, broccoli, peas and onion in butter until pork is no longer pink, 3-5 minutes. Remove from skillet and set aside.
2. In same skillet, cook and stir egg over medium heat until completely set. Stir in the rice, soy sauce, garlic powder, ginger and pork mixture; heat through. If desired, garnish with additional green onions.

1 CUP 338 cal., 13g fat (6g sat. fat), 163mg chol., 597mg sod., 29g carb. (3g sugars, 2g fiber), 24g pro. **DIABETIC EXCHANGES** 3 lean meat, 2 starch.

5i

TORTELLINI CARBONARA

Bacon, cream and Parmesan cheese make a classic pasta sauce that's absolutely heavenly. It's a delightful option for company!

—Cathy Croyle, Davidsville, PA

TAKES: 20 min. • **MAKES:** 4 servings

1   pkg. (9 oz.) refrigerated cheese tortellini
8   bacon strips, chopped
1   cup heavy whipping cream
½   cup grated Parmesan cheese
½   cup chopped fresh parsley

1. Cook tortellini according to package directions; drain.
2. Meanwhile, in a large skillet, cook bacon over medium heat until crisp, stirring occasionally. Remove with a slotted spoon; drain on paper towels. Pour off drippings.
3. In same pan, combine cream, cheese, parsley and bacon; heat through over medium heat. Stir in tortellini. Serve immediately.

1 CUP 527 cal., 36g fat (20g sat. fat), 121mg chol., 728mg sod., 33g carb. (3g sugars, 2g fiber), 19g pro.

SODA POP CHOPS WITH SMASHED POTATOES

Root beer gives this family-friendly recipe a tangy taste kids will love. Served alongside the smashed potatoes, this makes a scrumptious stick-to-the-ribs meal any weeknight.

—*Taste of Home* Test Kitchen

PREP: 25 min. • **COOK:** 15 min. • **MAKES:** 4 servings

1½ lbs. small red potatoes, halved
1 cup root beer
1 cup ketchup
1 Tbsp. brown sugar
2 tsp. chili powder
2 tsp. Worcestershire sauce
½ tsp. garlic powder, divided
2 Tbsp. all-purpose flour
¾ tsp. pepper, divided
½ tsp. salt, divided
4 bone-in pork loin chops (7 oz. each)
2 Tbsp. olive oil
2 Tbsp. butter

1. Place potatoes in a large saucepan and cover with water. Bring to a boil over high heat. Reduce heat to medium; cover and cook until tender, 15-20 minutes.

2. Meanwhile, in a small bowl, combine the root beer, ketchup, brown sugar, chili powder, Worcestershire sauce and ¼ tsp. garlic powder; set aside. In a shallow dish, combine the flour, ½ tsp. pepper and ¼ tsp. salt. Add pork chops, 1 at a time, and shake to coat.

3. In a large cast-iron or other ovenproof skillet, cook chops in oil over medium heat until chops are lightly browned, 2-3 minutes on each side. Drain. Add root beer mixture; bring to a boil. Reduce heat; cover and simmer until a thermometer reads 145°, 6-8 minutes. Remove pork and keep warm. Let stand for 5 minutes before serving.

4. Bring sauce to a boil; cook until liquid is reduced by half. Meanwhile, drain potatoes; mash with butter, remaining garlic powder and the remaining salt and pepper. Serve with pork chops and sauce.

1 PORK CHOP WITH ½ CUP POTATOES AND ⅓ CUP SAUCE 637 cal., 29g fat (11g sat. fat), 112mg chol., 1222mg sod., 59g carb. (29g sugars, 4g fiber), 36g pro.

"My family liked the root beer sauce so much that I have used it for chicken and even on grilled burgers. Definite keeper."

—LADIEPHOENIX, TASTEOFHOME.COM

VEGAN TORTILLA SOUP

Quinoa may be unconventional in tortilla soup, but it lends enough protein to make this soup a hearty main dish.

—Taste of Home Test Kitchen

TAKES: 30 min. • **MAKES:** 8 servings (3 qt.)

1 Tbsp. olive oil
1 medium onion, chopped
4 garlic cloves, minced
1 jalapeno pepper, seeded and chopped
8 cups vegetable broth
1 cup quinoa, rinsed
2 tsp. chili powder
½ tsp. ground cumin
½ tsp. salt
¼ tsp. pepper
1 can (15 oz.) black beans, rinsed and drained
3 medium tomatoes, chopped
1 cup fresh or frozen corn
⅓ cup minced fresh cilantro
Optional ingredients: Cubed avocado, lime wedges and additional chopped cilantro

Heat oil in a Dutch oven over medium-high heat. Add the onion, garlic and jalapeno pepper; cook and stir until tender, 3-5 minutes. Add broth, quinoa, and seasonings. Bring to a boil; reduce heat. Simmer, uncovered, until quinoa is tender, about 10 minutes. Add the beans, tomatoes, corn and cilantro; heat through. Serve with optional ingredients as desired.

NOTE Wear disposable gloves when cutting hot peppers; the oils can burn skin. Avoid touching your face.
1½ CUPS 182 cal., 4g fat (1g sat. fat), 0 chol., 792mg sod., 31g carb. (5g sugars, 5g fiber), 7g pro. **DIABETIC EXCHANGES** 2 starch, ½ fat.

TORTILLA SOUP TIPS

What can you serve with tortilla soup?
Pair this Vegan Tortilla Soup with a fresh green salad topped with a vegan vinaigrette, homemade tortilla chips, or guacamole and raw veggies. For a heartier meal, serve it alongside seasoned rice and beans or a vegan quesadilla with plant-based cheese and vegetables.

What can you use as a substitute for quinoa?
You can use rice for a similar texture, or try barley for a chewier texture and nutty flavor. Bulgur wheat and farro are also good options. For gluten-free substitutes, use millet or buckwheat groats.

Can you make this soup in a pressure cooker?
Yes. Simply saute the onion, garlic and jalapeno in a pressure cooker. Add vegetable broth, quinoa, spices, black beans, tomatoes and corn. Lock lid; close pressure-release valve. Adjust to pressure-cook on high for 5 minutes. Allow pressure to release naturally for 10 minutes, then quick-release any remaining pressure.

GRANDMA'S SWEDISH MEATBALLS

My mother made these hearty meatballs when we were growing up, and now my kids love them too. My daughter likes to help toss the meatballs in flour.

—Karin Ness, Big Lake, MN

TAKES: 30 min. • **MAKES:** 4 servings

1 large egg, lightly beaten
½ cup crushed saltines (about 10 crackers)
¼ tsp. seasoned salt
¼ tsp. pepper
¼ tsp. ground nutmeg, optional
½ lb. ground beef
½ lb. bulk pork sausage
¼ cup plus 2 Tbsp. all-purpose flour, divided
2½ cups reduced-sodium beef broth, divided
Hot mashed potatoes
Minced fresh parsley, optional

1. Mix first 4 ingredients and nutmeg if desired. Add beef and sausage; mix lightly but thoroughly. Shape into 1-in. balls; toss with ¼ cup flour, coating lightly.

2. In a large skillet, brown meatballs over medium-high heat. Add 2 cups broth; bring to a boil. Reduce heat; simmer, covered, until meatballs are cooked through, 5-6 minutes.

3. Remove meatballs with a slotted spoon. Mix the remaining 2 Tbsp. flour and ½ cup broth until smooth; add to pan. Bring to a boil; cook and stir until thickened, 1-2 minutes. Return meatballs to pan; heat through. Serve with mashed potatoes. If desired, sprinkle with parsley.

1 SERVING 348 cal., 21g fat (7g sat. fat), 115mg chol., 846mg sod., 17g carb. (1g sugars, 1g fiber), 21g pro.

HOW TO MAKE GREAT MEATBALLS

For tender meatballs, mix the ingredients gently—overmixing can make them tough. Use a light hand when combining the egg, crackers and seasonings with the meat, mixing just until the ingredients come together.

To save time and ensure uniform meatballs, use a cookie scoop to shape them. Add them to a hot pan and avoid overcrowding. This helps the meatballs brown nicely while keeping their shape.

SINGAPORE NOODLE SOUP

This hearty noodle soup is a beloved favorite in southeast Asia, especially Singapore, where it is called *laska*. It is perfect for busy dinners because it has protein, starch and vegetables cooked together in one pot. Every household has its own recipe. You can serve it with lime juice or chili garlic paste.

—Loanne Chiu, Fort Worth, TX

PREP: 15 min. • **COOK:** 25 min.
MAKES: 6 servings (2¼ qt.)

- 1 carton (32 oz.) seafood stock
- 1 can (13.66 oz.) coconut milk
- 2 Tbsp. grated fresh gingerroot
- 2 Tbsp. massaman curry paste or red curry paste
- 1 Tbsp. fish sauce or soy sauce
- 3 tsp. grated lime zest
- 2 tsp. brown sugar
- 2 cups frozen stir-fry vegetable blend
- 1 small sweet red pepper, chopped
- 1½ lbs. uncooked shrimp (26-30 per lb.), peeled and deveined
- 8 oz. refrigerated angel hair pasta
- 2 Tbsp. lime juice
- 2 Tbsp. chopped fresh basil

1. In a large saucepan, combine first 7 ingredients. Bring to a boil. Reduce heat; simmer, uncovered, 15 minutes.
2. Stir in frozen vegetables and chopped red pepper. Return to a boil. Add shrimp and pasta. Cook until shrimp turn pink and pasta is tender, 4-5 minutes. Stir in lime juice and basil. If desired, garnish with additional basil.

1½ CUPS 359 cal., 13g fat (11g sat. fat), 157mg chol., 952mg sod., 33g carb. (6g sugars, 2g fiber), 27g pro.

LENTIL BURRITOS

I incorporate healthy but tasty meals into our menus. Everyone loves these mildly spiced burritos that combine filling lentils with zucchini. They're healthy, satisfying, fast and tasty!

—Pam Masters, Wickenburg, AZ

TAKES: 30 min. • **MAKES:** 8 burritos

- 2 cups water
- 1 cup dried brown lentils
- 2 Tbsp. dried minced onion
- ½ tsp. dried minced garlic
- ½ tsp. ground cumin
- ⅛ tsp. hot pepper sauce
- 1 small zucchini, chopped
- 1 cup taco sauce
- 1 cup shredded part-skim mozzarella cheese
- 8 flour tortillas (8 in.), warmed

1. Place the first 6 ingredients in a large saucepan; bring to a boil. Reduce heat; simmer, covered, until lentils are tender, 15-20 minutes. Drain if necessary.
2. Stir zucchini, taco sauce and cheese into lentils. To serve, place about ½ cup lentil mixture on each tortilla and roll up.
1 BURRITO 313 cal., 7g fat (3g sat. fat), 9mg chol., 452mg sod., 47g carb. (4g sugars, 5g fiber), 14g pro. **DIABETIC EXCHANGES** 3 starch, 2 lean meat, 1 fat.

"Great idea for a healthy lunch. I didn't have taco sauce so I used salsa and topped the burrito with cheddar, hot sauce and more salsa. Plain yogurt might also taste good on top."
—CANDEYACID, TASTEOFHOME.COM

TRADITIONAL LAMB STEW

This is a delicious, nourishing and economical dish. The flavor improves if you make the stew the day before you serve it.

—Margery Richmond, Fort Collins, CO

PREP: 20 min. • **COOK:** 1 hour • **MAKES:** 6 servings

1½ lbs. lamb stew meat
2 Tbsp. olive oil, divided
3 large onions, quartered
3 medium carrots, cut into 1-in. pieces
4 small potatoes, peeled and cubed
1 can (14½ oz.) beef broth
¾ tsp. salt
¼ tsp. pepper
1 Tbsp. butter
1 Tbsp. all-purpose flour
1½ tsp. minced fresh parsley
1½ tsp. minced chives
½ tsp. minced fresh thyme

1. In a Dutch oven, brown meat in 1 Tbsp. oil over medium heat until meat is no longer pink. Remove with a slotted spoon; set aside. Add onions, carrots and remaining oil to pan. Cook for 5 minutes or until onions are tender, stirring occasionally. Add potatoes, broth, salt, pepper and lamb; bring to a boil.
2. Remove from the heat. Cover and bake at 350° for 50-60 minutes or until meat and vegetables are tender.
3. With a slotted spoon, remove meat and vegetables to a large bowl; set aside and keep warm. Pour pan juices into another bowl; set aside.

4. In the Dutch oven, melt butter over medium heat. Stir in flour until smooth. Gradually whisk in pan juices. Bring to a boil; cook and stir for 2 minutes or until thickened. Stir in the parsley, chives, thyme, and meat and vegetables; heat through.
1¼ CUPS 360 cal., 13g fat (4g sat. fat), 79mg chol., 721mg sod., 34g carb. (6g sugars, 4g fiber), 27g pro. **DIABETIC EXCHANGES** 3 lean meat, 2 starch, 2 fat.

LAMB STEW TIPS

What cut of meat is best for lamb stew?
Lamb shoulder is the ideal cut for lamb stew. It comes from a part of the animal with more connective tissue, which breaks down during slow cooking, making the meat tender and flavorful. While precut stew meat is convenient, it often includes mixed cuts, leading to uneven textures. Using lamb shoulder ensures consistent, melt-in-your-mouth results after braising.

Can you overcook lamb stew?
Yes, overcooking lamb stew can cause the meat to lose moisture and become tough, even though it's been slow-cooked. The goal is to cook the stew just until the meat is fork-tender and still holds its shape. Prolonged cooking breaks down the fibers too much, causing the meat to dry out. Keep an eye on it to maintain the perfect texture.

Why is lamb stew meat tough?
Lamb stew meat is typically cut from well-worked muscles, such as the shoulder or leg, which contain a lot of connective tissue. These tougher cuts need low and slow cooking methods to break down the collagen and become tender. Boiling or cooking over high heat can result in tough, chewy meat. Braising or simmering over a longer period allows the collagen to melt, creating a tender, flavorful dish.

SHRIMP LETTUCE WRAPS WITH PEANUT SAUCE

Tender shrimp meets crisp Bibb lettuce for this light and tasteful lettuce wrap. Shrimp, carrots and cucumbers are layered on a leaf of lettuce and then topped with a flavorful sauce made of peanut butter, soy sauce and brown sugar. Try it for a simple and easy lunch!

—*Taste of Home* Test Kitchen

TAKES: 20 min. • **MAKES:** 6 servings

⅓ cup water
1 Tbsp. reduced-sodium soy sauce
1 Tbsp. creamy peanut butter
1 Tbsp. packed brown sugar
1 Tbsp. canola oil
1½ lbs. uncooked shrimp (31-40 per lb.), peeled and deveined
1 Tbsp. minced fresh gingerroot
2 garlic cloves, minced
4 green onions, chopped
12 Bibb or butter lettuce leaves
1 cup julienned carrot
1 small cucumber, cut into strips
1 Additional chopped green onions, optional

1. Whisk together first 4 ingredients until smooth. In a large skillet, heat oil over medium-high heat. Add shrimp; cook and stir until shrimp turn pink, 2-3 minutes. Add ginger and garlic; cook and stir 1 minute. Stir in sauce mixture and green onions; heat through.

2. Serve in lettuce leaves; top with carrots and cucumber. If desired, garnish with additional chopped green onions. **2 WRAPS** 163 cal., 5g fat (1g sat. fat), 138mg chol., 260mg sod., 8g carb. (4g sugars, 1g fiber), 20g pro. **DIABETIC EXCHANGES** 3 lean meat, ½ starch.

SHRIMP LETTUCE WRAP VARIATIONS

- **Try different sauces:** These shrimp lettuce wraps are versatile enough to be enjoyed with a variety of Asian sauces. Instead of this peanut sauce, try it with sweet and sour sauce, sriracha sauce or wasabi mayo.

- **Change up the protein:** We love these wraps with shrimp, but they also work made with tofu, ground pork or chicken.

- **Add some herbs:** Adding fresh herbs like cilantro, mint and basil is a delicious way to use up any leftover clamshells you have in your crisper drawer.

TUNA PASTA SALAD

Mustard and dill add wonderful flair to the flavor of this simple salad. It's really very inexpensive to serve. This is one of my favorite take-to-work salads. I sometimes substitute peas for the shredded carrot and add some Italian dressing.

—Pat Kordas, Nutley, NJ

PREP: 15 min. + chilling • **MAKES:** 4 servings

2½ cups small pasta shells, cooked and drained
1 can (5 oz.) light tuna in water, drained and flaked
1 large carrot, shredded
¼ cup chopped onion
¾ cup mayonnaise
¼ cup 2% milk
1 Tbsp. lemon juice
2 tsp. prepared mustard
1 tsp. dill weed
½ tsp. salt
⅛ tsp. pepper
Snipped fresh dill, optional

In a large bowl, combine pasta, tuna, carrot and onion. Combine the next 7 ingredients; whisk until smooth. Pour over pasta mixture; toss to coat. Cover and refrigerate for 1-2 hours. If desired, garnish with fresh dill.

¾ CUP 538 cal., 32g fat (5g sat. fat), 29mg chol., 644mg sod., 47g carb. (4g sugars, 3g fiber), 15g pro.

5i
ASIAN SALMON TACOS

This Asian/Mexican fusion dish is ready in minutes—perfect for an on-the-run meal! If the salmon begins to stick, add 2 to 3 tablespoons of water and continue cooking.

—Marisa Raponi, Vaughan, ON

TAKES: 20 min. • **MAKES:** 4 servings

1 lb. salmon fillet, skin removed, cut into 1-in. cubes
2 Tbsp. hoisin sauce
1 Tbsp. olive oil
Shredded lettuce
8 corn tortillas (6 in.), warmed
1½ tsp. black sesame seeds
Mango salsa, optional

1. Toss salmon with hoisin sauce. In a large nonstick skillet, heat oil over medium-high heat. Cook salmon for 3-5 minutes or until it begins to flake easily with a fork, turning gently to brown all sides.

2. Serve salmon and lettuce in tortillas; sprinkle with sesame seeds. If desired, top with mango salsa.

2 TACOS 335 cal., 16g fat (3g sat. fat), 57mg chol., 208mg sod., 25g carb. (3g sugars, 3g fiber), 22g pro. **DIABETIC EXCHANGES** 3 lean meat, 2 starch, 1 fat.

ITALIAN WEDDING SOUP SUPPER

Classic Italian wedding soup is a marriage of meatballs, pasta and veggies in a flavorful broth. My family loves it, so I created a stick-to-your-ribs skillet version you can eat with a fork.

—Patricia Harmon, Baden, PA

PREP: 25 min. • **COOK:** 15 min. • **MAKES:** 6 servings

2 cups small pasta shells
½ lb. boneless skinless chicken breasts, cut into ¾-in. cubes
2 Tbsp. olive oil, divided
1 medium onion, chopped
1 medium carrot, finely chopped
1 celery rib, chopped
1 pkg. (12 oz.) frozen fully cooked Italian meatballs, thawed
1 can (10¾ oz.) reduced-fat reduced-sodium condensed cream of chicken soup, undiluted
1 pkg. (10 oz.) frozen chopped spinach, thawed and squeezed dry
1 cup reduced-sodium chicken broth
2 tsp. minced fresh thyme or ½ tsp. dried thyme
½ tsp. salt
⅛ tsp. pepper
¾ cup shredded Asiago cheese

1. Cook pasta according to package directions. Meanwhile, in a large skillet, saute chicken in 1 Tbsp. oil until no longer pink; remove and keep warm.

2. In the same skillet, saute the onion, carrot and celery in remaining 1 Tbsp. oil until tender. Add the meatballs, soup, spinach, broth, thyme, salt, pepper and sauteed chicken; cover and cook until heated through, 4-6 minutes.

3. Drain pasta; stir into skillet. Sprinkle with cheese.

1⅓ CUPS 473 cal., 24g fat (10g sat. fat), 63mg chol., 1006mg sod., 38g carb. (7g sugars, 4g fiber), 28g pro.

ITALIAN HERB-LENTIL PATTIES WITH MOZZARELLA

My family has requested this meatless recipe over and over again. It is simple to prepare and even meat lovers like it.

—Geraldine Lucas, Oldsmar, FL

PREP: 50 min. • **COOK:** 10 min./batch
MAKES: 10 servings

- 3 cups dried lentils, rinsed
- 3 large eggs, lightly beaten
- 1 Tbsp. dried minced onion
- 1 Tbsp. dried parsley flakes
- 1 tsp. dried basil
- 1 tsp. salt
- ½ tsp. dried thyme
- ¼ tsp. pepper
- 2 cups uncooked instant oatmeal
- 2 Tbsp. canola oil
- 10 slices part-skim mozzarella cheese or provolone cheese
     Marinara sauce, warmed, optional

1. Cook lentils according to package directions; drain and cool slightly.
2. In a large bowl, combine eggs and seasonings; stir in lentils and oatmeal. Shape into ten ¾-in.-thick patties.
3. In a large nonstick skillet, heat 1 Tbsp. oil over medium heat. Cook patties in batches, 4-6 minutes on each side or until golden brown and a thermometer reads 160°, adding additional oil as needed. Top with cheese; cook 1-2 minutes longer or until cheese is melted. If desired, serve with marinara sauce.

1 PATTY 416 cal., 12g fat (4g sat. fat), 74mg chol., 517mg sod., 54g carb. (2g sugars, 9g fiber), 26g pro.

FAVORITE BAKED SPAGHETTI, 127

95

139

153

OVEN ENTREES

GREEK ROASTED CHICKEN & POTATOES

You'll find this meal is a nice one to prepare for company or to serve your family for Sunday dinner. All you need with it is tossed salad and some crusty French bread.

—Pella Visnick, Dallas, TX

PREP: 10 min. • **BAKE:** 2 hours + standing • **MAKES:** 8 servings

1 roasting chicken (6 to 7 lbs.)
  Salt and pepper to taste
2 to 3 tsp. dried oregano, divided
4 baking potatoes, peeled and quartered
¼ cup butter, melted
3 Tbsp. lemon juice
¾ cup chicken broth

1. Preheat oven to 350°. Place chicken breast side up on a rack in a roasting pan. Sprinkle with salt and pepper and half of the oregano. Arrange potatoes around chicken; sprinkle with salt, pepper and remaining oregano. Pour butter and lemon juice over chicken and potatoes. Add chicken broth to pan.

2. Bake, uncovered, 2-2½ hours or until a thermometer inserted in thigh reads 170°, basting frequently with pan drippings.

3. Remove chicken from oven; tent with foil. Let stand 15 minutes before carving. If desired, skim fat and thicken pan drippings for gravy. Serve with chicken.

6 OZ. COOKED CHICKEN WITH 2 PIECES POTATO 530 cal., 30g fat (10g sat. fat), 150mg chol., 262mg sod., 19g carb. (1g sugars, 2g fiber), 45g pro.

ROSEMARY-LEMON ROAST CHICKEN
Brush chicken with 1 Tbsp. olive oil. Combine 2 Tbsp. each grated lemon zest and minced fresh rosemary with 2 tsp. each salt and coarsely ground pepper; sprinkle over chicken and potatoes. Add broth to pan and bake as directed.

TASTES LIKE THANKSGIVING CASSEROLE

This hearty, rich-tasting dish is sure to be a hit with your family. It's a delicious way to use up Thanksgiving turkey, and you can substitute 5½ cups leftover mashed potatoes for the six potatoes.

—Mary Lou Timpson, Colorado City, AZ

PREP: 30 min. • **BAKE:** 30 min. • **MAKES:** 10 servings

- 6 medium potatoes, peeled and cut into chunks
- 1¼ cups chopped celery
- ¾ cup chopped onion
- ½ cup butter, cubed
- 6 cups unseasoned stuffing cubes
- 1 tsp. poultry seasoning
- ¼ tsp. rubbed sage
- 1 cup chicken broth
- 4 cups cubed cooked turkey
- 2 cans (10¾ oz. each) condensed cream of chicken soup, undiluted
- 1 tsp. garlic powder
- ¾ cup sour cream, divided
- 4 oz. cream cheese, softened
- ½ tsp. pepper
- ¼ tsp. salt
- 1½ cups shredded cheddar cheese

1. Place potatoes in a Dutch oven and cover with water. Bring to a boil. Reduce heat; cover and cook 10-15 minutes or until tender.

2. Meanwhile, in a large skillet, saute celery and onion in butter until tender, about 5 minutes. Remove from the heat. Preheat oven to 350°.

3. In a large bowl, combine the stuffing cubes, poultry seasoning and sage. Stir in broth and celery mixture. Transfer to a greased 13x9-in. baking dish.

4. In another large bowl, combine the turkey, soup, garlic powder and ¼ cup sour cream; spoon over stuffing mixture. Drain potatoes; mash in a large bowl. Beat in the cream cheese, pepper, salt and remaining sour cream; spread over turkey mixture. Sprinkle with cheese.

5. Bake, uncovered, until heated through, 30-35 minutes.

1¼ CUPS 572 cal., 30g fat (15g sat. fat), 119mg chol., 1142mg sod., 49g carb. (5g sugars, 4g fiber), 29g pro.

THANKSGIVING CASSEROLE TIPS

How do you store Thanksgiving casserole?

Store Thanksgiving casserole tightly covered in the refrigerator for up to 4 days. To make it even easier, package it in individual portions for quick meals. If any ingredients were already a couple of days old when making the casserole, consider that extra time when storing.

Can you make Thanksgiving casserole ahead of time?

Yes, you can assemble Thanksgiving casserole the night before. Let it sit at room temperature for about 15 minutes before baking. If it's still chilled, plan to add 10 extra minutes to the baking time to heat it through evenly.

SHEET-PAN HONEY MUSTARD CHICKEN

This sheet-pan chicken is an easy gluten-free, low-carb meal ideal for busy weekdays. The chicken is tender, juicy and so delicious! It's now on the list of our favorite meals. You can substitute any low-carb vegetable for green beans.

—Denise Browning, San Antonio, TX

PREP: 20 min. • **BAKE:** 40 min. • **MAKES:** 6 servings

6 bone-in chicken thighs (about 2¼ lbs.)
¾ tsp. salt, divided
½ tsp. pepper, divided
2 medium lemons
⅓ cup olive oil
⅓ cup honey
3 Tbsp. Dijon mustard
4 garlic cloves, minced
1 tsp. paprika
½ cup water
½ pound fresh green beans, trimmed
6 miniature sweet peppers, sliced into rings
¼ cup pomegranate seeds, optional

1. Preheat oven to 425°. Place chicken in a greased 15x10x1-in. baking pan. Sprinkle with ½ tsp. salt and ¼ tsp. pepper. Thinly slice 1 lemon; place over chicken. Cut remaining lemon crosswise in half; squeeze juice into a small bowl. Whisk in the oil, honey, mustard, garlic and paprika. Pour half the sauce over chicken; reserve remaining sauce for beans. Pour water into pan. Bake 25 minutes.

2. Meanwhile, combine beans, sweet peppers and the remaining sauce, ¼ tsp. salt and ¼ tsp. pepper; toss to coat. Arrange vegetables around the chicken in pan. Bake until a thermometer inserted into chicken reads 170°-175° and beans are tender, 15-20 minutes. If desired, sprinkle with pomegranate seeds before serving.

1 SERVING 419 cal., 26g fat (6g sat. fat), 81mg chol., 548mg sod., 22g carb. (17g sugars, 2g fiber), 24g pro.

"A great way to get a hearty meal with very little effort! It was easy to assemble, the chicken cooked perfectly, and the honey mustard sauce (plus lemon) made for a flavorful dish. We decided to omit the pomegranate seeds and just ate them separately."

—NH-RESCUE, TASTEOFHOME.COM

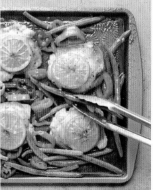

CONTEST-WINNING BROCCOLI CHICKEN CASSEROLE

This delicious twist on chicken divan came from an old boss who gave the recipe to me when I got married. It's quick, satisfying comfort food.

—Jennifer Schlachter, Big Rock, IL

PREP: 15 min. • **BAKE:** 30 min. • **MAKES:** 6 servings

- 1 pkg. (6 oz.) chicken stuffing mix
- 2 cups cubed cooked chicken
- 1 cup frozen broccoli florets, thawed
- 1 can (10¾ oz.) condensed broccoli cheese soup, undiluted
- 1 cup shredded cheddar cheese

1. Preheat oven to 350°. Prepare stuffing mix according to package directions, using only 1½ cups water.

2. In large bowl, combine the chicken, broccoli and soup; transfer to a greased 11x7-in. baking dish. Top with stuffing; sprinkle with cheese. Bake, covered, 20 minutes. Uncover; bake until heated through, 10-15 minutes longer.

FREEZE OPTION Transfer individual portions of cooled casserole to freezer containers; freeze. To use, partially thaw in refrigerator overnight. Place in a microwave-safe dish and microwave, covered, on high until a thermometer inserted in center reads 165°, stirring occasionally; add a little broth if necessary.

1⅓ CUPS 317 cal., 13g fat (5g sat. fat), 62mg chol., 899mg sod., 19g carb. (4g sugars, 1g fiber), 21g pro.

"It was a hit, even with the teenagers. I doubled everything but used 3 cups of rotisserie chicken and used a 9x13-in. baking dish. I think next time I will add more broccoli."

—LISA2805, TASTEOFHOME.COM

TURKEY CLUB PIZZA

TURKEY CLUB PIZZA

This easy pizza will be a hit with your family. And it'll keep you out of the kitchen! It's perfect for busy school nights, hectic weekends or any time you just don't want to wait on dinner.

—Pippa Milburn, Dover, OH

TAKES: 20 min. • **MAKES:** 8 servings

1 prebaked 12-in. pizza crust
½ cup mayonnaise
1½ cups shredded Monterey Jack cheese, divided
1 cup chopped cooked turkey
8 bacon strips, cooked and crumbled
2 plum tomatoes, sliced
Shredded lettuce, optional

Preheat oven to 450°. Place pizza crust on a baking sheet; spread with mayonnaise. Top with 1 cup cheese, turkey, bacon and tomatoes. Sprinkle with remaining ½ cup cheese. Bake until cheese is melted, 10-12 minutes. If desired, top with lettuce.

1 PIECE 367 cal., 22g fat (6g sat. fat), 42mg chol., 688mg sod., 23g carb. (1g sugars, 0 fiber), 18g pro.

BRUSCHETTA CHICKEN

We enjoy serving this tasty chicken to both family and guests. It just might become your new favorite way to use up summer tomatoes and basil.

—Carolin Cattoi-Demkiw, Lethbridge, AB

PREP: 10 min. • **BAKE:** 30 min. • **MAKES:** 4 servings

½ cup all-purpose flour
½ cup egg substitute or 2 large eggs, beaten
4 boneless skinless chicken breast halves (4 oz. each)
¼ cup grated Parmesan cheese
¼ cup dry bread crumbs
1 Tbsp. butter, melted
2 large tomatoes, seeded and chopped
3 Tbsp. minced fresh basil
1 Tbsp. olive oil
2 garlic cloves, minced
½ tsp. salt
¼ tsp. pepper

1. Preheat oven to 375°. Place flour and egg substitute in separate shallow bowls. Dip chicken in flour, then in egg substitute; place in a greased 13x9-in. baking dish. In a small bowl, mix cheese, bread crumbs and butter; sprinkle over chicken.
2. Loosely cover the baking dish with foil. Bake 20 minutes. Uncover; bake for 5-10 minutes longer or until a thermometer reads 165°.
3. Meanwhile, in a small bowl, toss tomatoes with the remaining ingredients. Spoon over chicken; bake 3-5 minutes or until tomato mixture is heated through.

1 SERVING 316 cal., 11g fat (4g sat. fat), 75mg chol., 563mg sod., 22g carb. (4g sugars, 2g fiber), 31g pro. **DIABETIC EXCHANGES** 3 lean meat, 1½ fat, 1 starch, 1 vegetable.

"Great dish! I added a little balsamic vinegar to the tomato mixture to make it a true bruschetta."

—CBYBEE, TASTEOFHOME.COM

CRANBERRY TURKEY BURGERS WITH ARUGULA SALAD

These healthy burgers taste just like the holidays, all in one bite. They are a little sweet and a little savory, and they're delicious over a bed of peppery arugula.

—Nicole Stevens, Charleston, SC

TAKES: 25 min. • **MAKES:** 4 servings

¾ lb. ground turkey
⅓ cup dried cranberries
⅓ cup soft bread crumbs
3 green onions, finely chopped
2 to 3 Tbsp. crumbled goat cheese
2 Tbsp. pepper jelly
3 garlic cloves, minced
1 large egg yolk
¼ tsp. salt
¼ tsp. pepper
4 cups fresh arugula
1 Tbsp. grapeseed oil or olive oil
1 Tbsp. honey

1. Preheat oven to 375°. Combine the first 10 ingredients, mixing lightly but thoroughly. Shape into four ½-in.-thick patties; transfer to a greased baking sheet. Bake for 12 minutes. Heat broiler; broil until a thermometer inserted in burgers reads 165°, about 5 minutes.

2. Meanwhile, toss arugula with oil. Drizzle with honey; toss to combine. Top salad with turkey burgers.

1 BURGER WITH 1 CUP SALAD 281 cal., 12g fat (3g sat. fat), 107mg chol., 240mg sod., 26g carb. (21g sugars, 2g fiber), 19g pro.

CHICKEN TATER BAKE

You'll please everyone in the family with this inviting dish. It tastes like chicken potpie with a crispy Tater Tot crust.

—Fran Allen, St. Louis, MO

PREP: 20 min. • **BAKE:** 35 min.
MAKES: 2 casseroles (6 servings each)

- 2 cans (10¾ oz. each) condensed cream of chicken soup, undiluted
- ½ cup 2% milk
- ¼ cup butter, cubed
- 3 cups cubed cooked chicken
- 1 pkg. (16 oz.) frozen peas and carrots, thawed
- 1½ cups shredded cheddar cheese, divided
- 1 pkg. (32 oz.) frozen Tater Tots

1. In a large saucepan, combine the soup, milk and butter. Cook and stir over medium heat until heated through. Remove from heat; stir in the chicken, peas and carrots, and 1 cup cheese.
2. Transfer to 2 greased 8-in. square baking dishes. Top with Tater Tots.
3. Cover and freeze 1 casserole for up to 3 months. Bake the remaining casserole at 400° until bubbling, 25-30 minutes. Sprinkle with ¼ cup cheese; bake until cheese is melted, about 5 minutes longer.
4. To use frozen casserole: Remove from the freezer 30 minutes before baking (do not thaw). Sprinkle with ¼ cup cheese. Cover and bake at 350° until heated through, 1½-1¾ hours.
1 SERVING 374 cal., 22g fat (8g sat. fat), 60mg chol., 925mg sod., 27g carb. (2g sugars, 4g fiber), 18g pro.

PAN-ROASTED CHICKEN & VEGETABLES

This one-dish meal tastes as if it took hours of hands-on time, but the simple ingredients can be prepped in minutes. The rosemary gives it a rich flavor, and the meat juices cook the veggies to perfection. So easy!

—Sherri Melotik, Oak Creek, WI

PREP: 15 min. • **BAKE:** 45 min. • **MAKES:** 6 servings

2 lbs. red potatoes (about 6 medium), cut into ¾-in. pieces
1 large onion, coarsely chopped
2 Tbsp. olive oil
3 garlic cloves, minced
1 Tbsp. minced fresh rosemary or 1 tsp. dried rosemary, crushed
1¼ tsp. salt, divided
¾ tsp. pepper, divided
½ tsp. paprika
6 bone-in chicken thighs (about 2¼ lbs.), skin removed
6 cups fresh baby spinach (about 6 oz.)
Lemon wedges, optional

1. Preheat oven to 425°. In a large bowl, combine potatoes, onion, oil, garlic, fresh or dried rosemary, ¾ tsp. salt and ½ tsp. pepper; toss to coat. Transfer to a 15x10x1-in. baking pan coated with cooking spray.

2. In a small bowl, mix paprika and the remaining salt and pepper. Sprinkle chicken with paprika mixture; arrange over the vegetables. Roast until a thermometer inserted in chicken reads 170°-175° and vegetables are just tender, 35-40 minutes.

3. Remove chicken to a serving platter; keep warm. Top vegetables with spinach. Roast until vegetables are tender and spinach is wilted, 8-10 minutes longer. Stir vegetables to combine; serve with chicken. If desired, serve with additional fresh rosemary and lemon wedges.

1 CHICKEN THIGH WITH 1 CUP VEGETABLES 357 cal., 14g fat (3g sat. fat), 87mg chol., 597mg sod., 28g carb. (3g sugars, 4g fiber), 28g pro. **DIABETIC EXCHANGES** 4 lean meat, 1½ starch, 1 vegetable, 1 fat.

VEGGIE MIX-UP

Many other vegetables would pair well with this chicken dish. Consider root vegetables, like carrots or parsnips, or use sweet potatoes instead of reds. Baby kale or other greens make a fine substitute for spinach.

CREAMY TURKEY ENCHILADAS

This is a fantastic way to use leftover turkey. It's always in the rotation during the week after a holiday feast. The recipe works with chicken as well.

—Brenda Baskerville, Fair Oaks, CA

PREP: 20 min. • **BAKE:** 20 min. • **MAKES:** 4 servings

¼ cup chopped onion
3 Tbsp. butter, divided
1 garlic clove, minced
2 cups cubed cooked turkey
1 can (4 oz.) chopped green chiles
½ tsp. dried oregano
3 Tbsp. all-purpose flour
2 cups chicken broth
½ cup sour cream
8 corn tortillas (6 in.)
1½ cups shredded Colby-Monterey Jack cheese
1 can (3.8 oz.) sliced ripe olives, drained

1. Preheat oven to 375°. In a large skillet, saute onion in 1 Tbsp. butter until tender. Add garlic; cook 1 minute longer. Add the turkey, chiles and oregano; heat through.
2. In a small saucepan, melt remaining butter. Stir in the flour until blended; gradually add broth. Bring to a boil; cook and stir until thickened, about 2 minutes. Remove from heat; stir in sour cream. Stir ½ cup sauce into the turkey mixture and set aside.
3. Spread ¼ cup sauce mixture into a greased 13x9-in. baking dish. Dip both sides of each tortilla in sauce mixture.

Place ⅓ cup turkey mixture down the center of each tortilla and sprinkle with 2 Tbsp. cheese. Roll up and place seam side down in prepared dish.
4. Pour remaining sauce mixture over top; sprinkle with olives and remaining cheese. Bake, uncovered, until heated through and the cheese is melted, 20-25 minutes.
2 ENCHILADAS 636 cal., 37g fat (21g sat. fat), 145mg chol., 1,340mg sod., 36g carb., 4g fiber, 38g pro.

5i

QUICK CHICKEN & WAFFLES

My first experience with chicken and waffles sent my taste buds into orbit. I first made the dish as appetizers, but we all love it as a main course too.

—Lisa Renshaw, Kansas City, MO

TAKES: 25 min. • **MAKES:** 4 servings

12 frozen crispy chicken strips (about 18 oz.)
½ cup honey
2 tsp. hot pepper sauce
8 frozen waffles, toasted

1. Bake chicken strips according to package directions. Meanwhile, in a small bowl, mix honey and pepper sauce.
2. Cut chicken into bite-sized pieces; serve on waffles. Drizzle with honey mixture.
1 SERVING 643 cal., 22g fat (3g sat. fat), 32mg chol., 958mg sod., 93g carb. (39g sugars, 6g fiber), 21g pro.

FAST CHICKEN DIVAN

Frozen broccoli and leftover chicken get an easy—but elegant—treatment in this dish. I use a saucy blend of cream soup and mayonnaise, then cover it all with a golden, cheesy crumb topping.

—Bertille Cooper, California, MD

PREP: 15 min. • **BAKE:** 30 min. + standing
MAKES: 6 servings

- 8 cups frozen broccoli florets or chopped broccoli
- 2 cans (10¾ oz. each) condensed cream of chicken soup, undiluted
- 1 cup mayonnaise
- 1 tsp. lemon juice
- 3 cups cubed cooked chicken
- 1 cup shredded sharp cheddar cheese
- ¾ cup dry bread crumbs
- 3 Tbsp. butter, melted
- 1 Tbsp. sliced pimientos, optional

1. Preheat the oven to 325°. In a large saucepan, cook broccoli in boiling water for 1 minute; drain. Set aside.
2. In a large bowl, combine soup, mayonnaise and lemon juice; add broccoli and chicken. Gently stir to combine; transfer to a greased 11x7-in. baking dish. Sprinkle with cheese. Combine bread crumbs and butter; sprinkle over the top.
3. Bake, uncovered, until bubbly and golden brown, about 30 minutes. Let stand for 10 minutes before serving. If desired, garnish with pimientos.
1 SERVING 629 cal., 49g fat (14g sat. fat), 115mg chol., 944mg sod., 16g carb. (1g sugars, 2g fiber), 28g pro.

ROASTED TUSCAN CHICKEN DINNER

When an Italian friend shared many years ago that she often added Italian sausages to her pan of baked chicken, I had to give it a try! The sausages give the chicken an amazing flavor. Over the years, I have turned it into a one-dish meal by adding potatoes, onions and peppers. It has now become a family favorite that I often use for holidays, spur-of-the-moment company and Sunday dinners.

—Teri Lindquist, Gurnee, IL

PREP: 20 min. • **BAKE:** 40 min. • **MAKES:** 6 servings

6   medium red potatoes, cut into thin wedges
3   Tbsp. olive oil, divided
6   bone-in chicken thighs (about 2 lbs.)
3   sweet Italian sausage links (4 oz. each), cut in half lengthwise
1   large onion, cut into wedges
1   large green pepper, cut into 1-in. pieces
1   large sweet red pepper, cut into 1-in. pieces
1   tsp. garlic salt
1   tsp. dried oregano
1   tsp. dried thyme
1   tsp. dried rosemary, crushed
1   tsp. paprika
1   tsp. pepper

1. Preheat oven to 425°. Place potatoes in a shallow roasting pan; drizzle with 1 Tbsp. oil and toss to coat. Rub chicken and sausage with 1 Tbsp. oil; arrange over potatoes.

2. In a large bowl, toss onion and peppers with remaining 1 Tbsp. oil; spoon over chicken and sausage. Sprinkle with seasonings.

3. Bake, uncovered, until a meat thermometer inserted into chicken reads 170°-175° and potatoes are tender, 40-45 minutes.

1 SERVING 673 cal., 44g fat (13g sat. fat), 149mg chol., 1181mg sod., 26g carb. (5g sugars, 4g fiber), 43g pro.

CHICKEN CORDON BLEU BAKE

A friend shared this awesome hot dish recipe with me. I freeze several pans to share with neighbors or for days when I'm scrambling at mealtime.

—Rea Newell, Decatur, IL

PREP: 20 min. • **BAKE:** 40 min. • **MAKES:** 2 casseroles (6 servings each)

2 pkg. (6 oz. each) reduced-sodium stuffing mix
1 can (10¾ oz.) condensed cream of chicken soup, undiluted
1 cup 2% milk
8 cups cubed cooked chicken
½ tsp. pepper
¾ lb. sliced deli ham, cut into 1-in. strips
1 cup shredded Swiss cheese
3 cups shredded cheddar cheese

1. Preheat oven to 350°. Prepare stuffing mixes according to package directions. Meanwhile, whisk together the soup and milk.

2. Toss chicken with pepper; divide between 2 greased 13x9-in. baking dishes. Layer with ham, Swiss cheese, 1 cup cheddar cheese, soup mixture and stuffing. Sprinkle with remaining cheddar cheese.

3. Bake, covered, 30 minutes. Uncover; bake 10-15 minutes or until cheese is melted.

FREEZE OPTION Cover and freeze unbaked casseroles. To use, partially thaw in refrigerator overnight. Remove from refrigerator 30 minutes before baking. Preheat oven to 350°. Bake, covered, until heated through and a thermometer inserted in center reads 165°, about 45 minutes. Uncover; bake until cheese is melted, 10-15 minutes.

1 CUP 555 cal., 29g fat (15g sat. fat), 158mg chol., 1055mg sod., 26g carb. (5g sugars, 1g fiber), 46g pro.

SHARP CHEDDAR

Sharp cheddar cheese has been aged longer than regular cheddar. As cheese ages, its flavor becomes more pronounced. Using aged cheese in a recipe can add complexity and rich flavor, even to humble casseroles.

KABOBLESS CHICKEN & VEGETABLES

As the primary caregiver for my grandma, I am trying to cook healthier for her. I am fascinated with Mediterranean cuisine. It is much easier to have chicken and vegetables off the kabob, which inspired this sheet-pan dinner.

—Chelsea Madren, Anaheim, CA

PREP: 10 min. + marinating • **BAKE:** 45 min. • **MAKES:** 6 servings

½ cup olive oil
½ cup balsamic vinegar
2 tsp. lemon-pepper seasoning
2 tsp. Italian seasoning
2 lbs. boneless skinless chicken breasts, cut into 1-in. pieces
2 medium yellow summer squash, sliced
2 medium zucchini, sliced
1 medium carrot, sliced
1 cup grape tomatoes

1. In a large bowl, combine oil, vinegar, lemon pepper and Italian seasoning. Pour half the marinade into a separate bowl or shallow dish. Add chicken; turn to coat. Cover and refrigerate overnight. Cover and refrigerate the remaining marinade.

2. Preheat oven to 350°. Line a 15x10x1-in. baking pan with foil. Drain the chicken, discarding that marinade. Place squash, zucchini, carrot and tomatoes in pan in a single layer. Place chicken on top of the vegetables; pour reserved marinade over top. Cook 45-60 minutes or until chicken is no longer pink and vegetables are tender. Let stand 5 minutes before serving.

1 SERVING 305 cal., 15g fat (3g sat. fat), 84mg chol., 158mg sod., 9g carb. (7g sugars, 2g fiber), 32g pro. **DIABETIC EXCHANGES** 4 lean meat, 2 fat, 1 vegetable.

CHICKEN CROUTON HOT DISH

This recipe has practically made my mom famous. When she takes it to potluck, it's loved by all who taste it. Whenever she serves it to family, the dish is empty at the end of the meal.

—Beth Gramling, Warren, PA

PREP: 10 min. • **BAKE:** 20 min. • **MAKES:** 8 servings

1 can (14½ oz.) chicken broth
1 can (10¾ oz.) condensed cream of chicken soup, undiluted
1 cup sour cream
½ cup butter, melted
1 pkg. (12 oz.) seasoned stuffing cubes
4 cups shredded cooked chicken
Minced fresh parsley, optional

1. Preheat oven to 375°. In a large bowl, combine the broth, soup, sour cream and butter. Stir in croutons and chicken.
2. Transfer to a greased 13x9-in. baking dish. Bake, uncovered, until heated through, 20-25 minutes. If desired, sprinkle with parsley.
1 CUP 515 cal., 26g fat (12g sat. fat), 115mg chol., 1393mg sod., 41g carb. (4g sugars, 3g fiber), 28g pro.

TURKEY WITH SAUSAGE STUFFING

Here's a super way to savor roast turkey and stuffing without having to cook the big holiday bird. The stuffing is hearty, and the meat always comes out juicy.

—Aura Lee Johnson, Vermilion, OH

PREP: 25 min. • **BAKE:** 2 hours + standing • **MAKES:** 12 servings

1 bone-in turkey breast (5 to 7 lbs.)
¼ cup butter, melted
1½ lbs. bulk pork sausage
2 cups sliced celery
2 medium onions, chopped
4 cups dry bread cubes
2 cups pecan halves
1 cup raisins
⅔ cup chicken broth
2 large eggs, beaten
1 tsp. salt
½ tsp. rubbed sage
¼ tsp. pepper

1. Place turkey breast side up in a shallow roasting pan. Brush with butter. Bake, uncovered, at 325° for 2-2½ hours or until a thermometer reads 170° (cover loosely with foil to prevent overbrowning if necessary).
2. Meanwhile, in a large skillet over medium heat, cook the sausage, celery and onions until meat is no longer pink; drain. Transfer to a bowl; stir in the bread cubes, pecans, raisins, broth, eggs, salt, sage and pepper.

3. Spoon into a greased 3-qt. baking dish. Cover and bake at 325° for 1 hour.
4. Let turkey stand for 10 minutes before slicing. Serve with stuffing.
1 SERVING 452 cal., 25g fat (7g sat. fat), 118mg chol., 663mg sod., 18g carb. (8g sugars, 3g fiber), 39g pro.

GREEK CHICKEN SHEET-PAN DINNER

I love roasted vegetables and keeping things simple. One bowl and one sheet pan, that's it. You could use boneless chicken and add other veggies. Serve it with cucumber salad.

—Sara Martin, Whitefish, MT

PREP: 10 min. • **BAKE:** 30 min. • **MAKES:** 4 servings

4 bone-in chicken thighs, skin removed
½ cup Greek vinaigrette
8 small red potatoes, quartered
1 medium sweet red pepper, cut into ½-in. strips
1 can (14 oz.) water-packed artichoke hearts, drained and halved
¾ cup pitted ripe olives, drained
1 small red onion, cut into 8 wedges
¼ tsp. pepper
⅓ cup crumbled feta cheese

1. Preheat the oven to 375°. Spray a 15x10x1-in. baking pan with cooking spray; set aside.
2. In a large bowl, combine the first 7 ingredients; toss to coat. Place the chicken and vegetables in a single layer on baking pan; sprinkle with pepper. Bake until a thermometer inserted into chicken reads 170°- 175° and vegetables are tender, 30-35 minutes.

3. If desired, preheat the broiler. Broil chicken and vegetables 3-4 in. from the heat until lightly browned, 2-3 minutes. Remove from oven; cool slightly. Sprinkle with feta cheese.

1 SERVING 481 cal., 24g fat (5g sat. fat), 92mg chol., 924mg sod., 31g carb. (3g sugars, 4g fiber), 31g pro.

TEXAN RANCH CHICKEN CASSEROLE

Every time I serve this creamy chicken ranch casserole, it gets rave reviews. The recipe was passed down to me and is so good! It is really easy to make, freezes well and has just a touch of heat.

—Kendra Doss, Colorado Springs, CO

PREP: 25 min. • **BAKE:** 30 min. • **MAKES:** 8 servings

---

1 large onion, finely chopped
2 celery ribs, finely chopped
1 medium green pepper, finely chopped
1 medium sweet red pepper, finely chopped
1 Tbsp. canola oil
1 garlic clove, minced
3 cups cubed cooked chicken breast
1 can (10¾ oz.) reduced-fat reduced-sodium condensed cream of celery soup, undiluted
1 can (10¾ oz.) reduced-fat reduced-sodium condensed cream of chicken soup, undiluted
1 can (10 oz.) diced tomatoes and green chiles, undrained
1 Tbsp. chili powder
12 corn tortillas (6 in.), cut into 1-in. strips
2 cups shredded reduced-fat cheddar cheese, divided

1. In a large skillet coated with cooking spray, cook and stir onion, celery and peppers in oil until crisp-tender. Add garlic; cook 1 minute longer. Stir in the chicken, soups, tomatoes and chili powder.

2. Line the bottom of a 3-qt. baking dish with half of the tortilla strips; top with half of the chicken mixture and 1 cup cheese. Repeat layers. Bake, uncovered, at 350° for 30-35 minutes or until bubbly.

1 CUP 329 cal., 12g fat (5g sat. fat), 65mg chol., 719mg sod., 31g carb. (4g sugars, 3g fiber), 26g pro. **DIABETIC EXCHANGES** 3 lean meat, 1½ starch, 1 vegetable, 1 fat.

"Amazing meal. Husband, boys and I loved it. At first I wondered about the peppers for the younger kids, but my 9-year-old went up for seconds. Definitely going to make it again."

—HEATHER375, TASTEOFHOME.COM

TRADITIONAL SHEPHERD'S PIE

Instead of a pastry crust, this recipe creates a savory crust with mashed potatoes. The bacon adds a fabulous flavor to the filling! Just add a tossed salad or green vegetable and dessert, and you'll have a complete meal that's sure to please your family.

—Chris Eschweiler, Dallas, TX

PREP: 30 min. • **BAKE:** 30 min. • **MAKES:** 8 servings

1   lb. ground beef
3   bacon strips, diced
1   small onion, chopped
2   garlic cloves, minced
¼   tsp. dried oregano
½   cup tomato sauce
1   can (4¼ oz.) chopped ripe olives, drained
5½ cups hot mashed potatoes (prepared without milk and butter)
2   large eggs, lightly beaten
2   Tbsp. butter, softened
1   Tbsp. minced fresh cilantro
¼   tsp. salt
    Additional butter, melted

1. Preheat oven to 375°. In a large skillet, cook beef over medium heat until no longer pink; drain and set aside. In the same skillet, cook bacon, onion, garlic and oregano until bacon is crisp; drain. Stir in the tomato sauce, olives and beef. Simmer, uncovered, until heated through, about 10 minutes.

2. Meanwhile, combine mashed potatoes, eggs, butter, cilantro and salt. Spread half the potato mixture onto bottom and up side of a greased 9-in. deep-dish pie plate. Layer with the beef mixture and remaining potato mixture.

3. Bake 20 minutes. Brush pie with melted butter. Bake until top is golden brown, about 10 minutes longer. If desired, garnish with additional cilantro.
1 PIECE 288 cal., 13g fat (5g sat. fat), 100mg chol., 354mg sod., 23g carb. (1g sugars, 5g fiber), 16g pro.

SHEPHERD'S PIE TIPS

Can you use leftover mashed potatoes to make shepherd's pie?
Yes, leftover mashed potatoes work perfectly for shepherd's pie. If your mashed potatoes already contain butter and salt, there's no need to add extra. Just spread them evenly on top of the meat and vegetable mixture before baking.

What else can you add to shepherd's pie?
Shepherd's pie is highly customizable. It's traditionally made with ground lamb, but you can switch to beef or even mix in additional vegetables. Frozen peas, carrots, green beans, or corn are fantastic additions to stir in with the tomato sauce for extra flavor and nutrition.

What can you serve with shepherd's pie?
Pair this rich, savory dish with lighter sides like a fresh green salad or roasted vegetables. A simple vinaigrette salad or a medley of root vegetables roasted with herbs would complement the flavors nicely.

LASAGNA CASSEROLE

While growing up, I always wanted this meal on my birthday. Mother made the sauce from scratch, but now I use store-bought spaghetti sauce to save time. Replace the ground beef with Italian sausage if you want more spice.

—Deb Morrison, Skiatook, OK

PREP: 15 min. • **BAKE:** 1 hour + standing • **MAKES:** 8 servings

- 1 lb. ground beef
- ¼ cup chopped onion
- ½ tsp. salt
- ½ tsp. pepper, divided
- 1 lb. medium pasta shells, cooked and drained
- 4 cups shredded part-skim mozzarella cheese, divided
- 3 cups 4% cottage cheese
- 2 large eggs, lightly beaten
- ⅓ cup grated Parmesan cheese
- 2 Tbsp. dried parsley flakes
- 1 jar (24 oz.) pasta sauce

1. In a large skillet, cook the beef and onion over medium heat until meat is no longer pink, breaking meat into crumbles; drain. Sprinkle with salt and ¼ tsp. pepper; set aside.

2. In a large bowl, combine pasta, 3 cups mozzarella cheese, cottage cheese, eggs, Parmesan cheese, parsley and the remaining pepper. Transfer to a greased shallow 3-qt. or 13x9-in. baking dish. Top with beef mixture and spaghetti sauce (dish will be full).

3. Cover and bake at 350° for 45 minutes. Sprinkle with remaining mozzarella cheese. Bake, uncovered, until bubbly and cheese is melted, about 15 minutes longer. Let stand for 10 minutes before serving.

FREEZE OPTION Sprinkle casserole with remaining mozzarella cheese. Cover and freeze unbaked casserole. To use, partially thaw in refrigerator overnight. Remove from refrigerator 30 minutes before baking. Preheat oven to 350°. Bake casserole as directed, increasing time as necessary until heated through and a thermometer inserted in center reads 165°.

1 SERVING 667 cal., 30g fat (14g sat. fat), 157mg chol., 1209mg sod., 56g carb. (12g sugars, 4g fiber), 44g pro.

BEYOND SHELLS

While pasta shells work great for this Lasagna Casserole, you can use any small pasta shape. Options such as elbow macaroni, penne, ziti, rigatoni or spirals all hold the sauce and cheese well, creating a deliciously hearty dish.

GARLIC BEEF ENCHILADAS

Enchiladas are typically prepared with corn tortillas, but we prefer flour tortillas in this saucy casserole with a subtle kick.

—Jennifer Standridge, Dallas, GA

PREP: 30 min. • **BAKE:** 40 min. • **MAKES:** 5 servings

1 lb. ground beef
1 medium onion, chopped
2 Tbsp. all-purpose flour
1 Tbsp. chili powder
1 tsp. salt
1 tsp. garlic powder
½ tsp. ground cumin
¼ tsp. rubbed sage
1 can (14½ oz.) stewed tomatoes, cut up

SAUCE
⅓ cup butter
4 to 6 garlic cloves, minced
½ cup all-purpose flour
1 can (14½ oz.) beef broth
1 can (15 oz.) tomato sauce
1 to 2 Tbsp. chili powder
1 to 2 tsp. ground cumin
1 to 2 tsp. rubbed sage
½ tsp. salt
10 flour tortillas (6 in.), warmed
2 cups shredded Colby-Monterey Jack cheese, divided
Optional toppings: Halved grape tomatoes, minced fresh cilantro, sliced jalapeno peppers, chopped red onion and cubed avocado

1. Preheat oven to 350°. In a large skillet, cook beef and onion over medium heat until beef is no longer pink, 6-8 minutes, breaking meat into crumbles; drain. Stir in flour and seasonings. Add tomatoes; bring to a boil. Reduce heat; simmer, covered, 15 minutes.

2. In a saucepan, heat the butter over medium-high heat. Add garlic; cook and stir 1 minute or until tender. Stir in flour until blended; gradually whisk in broth. Bring to a boil; cook and stir until thickened, about 2 minutes. Stir in tomato sauce and seasonings; heat through.

3. Pour 1½ cups sauce into an ungreased 13x9-in. baking dish. Place about ¼ cup beef mixture off-center on each tortilla; top with 1-2 Tbsp. cheese. Roll up and place over sauce, seam side down. Top with remaining sauce.

4. Bake, covered, until heated through, 30-35 minutes. Sprinkle with remaining cheese. Bake, uncovered, until cheese is melted, 10-15 minutes longer. Serve with toppings as desired.

2 ENCHILADAS 766 cal., 42g fat (24g sat. fat), 129mg chol., 2643mg sod., 61g carb. (9g sugars, 6g fiber), 37g pro.

ENCHILADA TIPS

How do you keep beef enchiladas from getting soggy?
To prevent soggy enchiladas, avoid rolling sauce inside the tortillas. Instead, spread a thin layer of enchilada sauce on the bottom of the casserole dish, and pour just enough over the top to coat the tortillas. This helps control moisture and keeps the enchiladas from becoming too soft.

What do you serve with beef enchiladas?
Load up your enchiladas with lots of fresh toppings like cherry tomatoes, red onions, jalapenos or avocado. Serve them alongside Mexican-inspired sides such as street corn, refried beans, or a light tomato and avocado salad.

Can you substitute corn tortillas in this recipe?
Yes, corn tortillas can be used instead of flour. To prevent them from becoming soggy, fry the corn tortillas in hot oil for about 10 seconds on each side before filling. This adds a little firmness to the tortillas and prevents them from soaking up too much sauce.

FRITO PIE

Frito pie is legendary in the Southwest for being spicy, salty, cheesy … and fabulous! Here's my easy take on this crunchy classic.

—Jan Moon, Alamogordo, NM

TAKES: 30 min. • **MAKES:** 6 servings

- 1 lb. ground beef
- 1 medium onion, chopped
- 2 cans (15 oz. each) Ranch Style beans (pinto beans in seasoned tomato sauce)
- 1 pkg. (9¼ oz.) Frito corn chips
- 2 cans (10 oz. each) enchilada sauce
- 2 cups shredded cheddar cheese
  Thinly sliced green onions, optional

1. Preheat oven to 350°. In a large skillet, cook beef and onion over medium heat 6-8 minutes or until beef is no longer pink and onion is tender, crumbling meat; drain. Stir in beans; heat through.
2. Reserve 1 cup corn chips for topping. Place remaining corn chips in a greased 13x9-in. baking dish. Layer with meat mixture, enchilada sauce and cheese; top with reserved chips.
3. Bake, uncovered, 15-20 minutes or until cheese is melted. If desired, sprinkle with green onion.
1 SERVING 718 cal., 40g fat (14g sat. fat), 84mg chol., 1719mg sod., 53g carb. (6g sugars, 8g fiber), 33g pro.

"I loved how quick and easy this dish was to put together. Very tasty as well. The whole family really enjoyed it."

—ANGEL182009, TASTEOFHOME.COM

FRENCH ONION POTPIE

I came up with this dish knowing that my husband loves French onion soup—which I turned into the perfect base for the hearty, beefy potpie.

—Sara Hutchens, Du Quoin, IL

TAKES: 30 min. • **MAKES:** 4 servings

- 1 lb. ground beef
- 1 small onion, chopped
- 1 can (10½ oz.) condensed French onion soup, undiluted
- 1½ cups shredded part-skim mozzarella cheese
- 1 tube (12 oz.) refrigerated buttermilk biscuits

1. Preheat oven to 350°. In a large skillet, cook the beef and onion over medium heat 6-8 minutes or until beef is no longer pink, breaking the meat into crumbles; drain. Stir in soup; bring to a boil.

2. Transfer mixture to an ungreased 9-in. deep-dish pie plate; sprinkle with mozzarella cheese. Bake for 5 minutes or until cheese is melted. Top with the biscuits. Bake 15-20 minutes longer or until the biscuits are golden brown.

1 SERVING 553 cal., 23g fat (10g sat. fat), 98mg chol., 1550mg sod., 47g carb. (4g sugars, 1g fiber), 38g pro.

ZUCCHINI PIZZA CASSEROLE

My husband has a hearty appetite, our two kids never tire of pizza, and I grow lots of zucchini. So this tasty, tomatoey casserole is absolutely tops with us throughout the entire year. Once you've tried the recipe, you may even decide to grow more zucchini in your own garden next summer!

—Lynn Bernstetter, White Bear Lake, MN

PREP: 20 min. • **BAKE:** 40 min. • **MAKES:** 8 servings

- 4 cups shredded unpeeled zucchini
- ½ tsp. salt
- 2 large eggs
- ½ cup grated Parmesan cheese
- 2 cups shredded part-skim mozzarella cheese, divided
- 1 cup shredded cheddar cheese, divided
- 1 lb. ground beef
- ½ cup chopped onion
- 1 can (15 oz.) Italian tomato sauce
- 1 medium green or sweet red pepper, chopped

1. Preheat oven to 400°. Place zucchini in colander; sprinkle with salt. Let stand 10 minutes, then squeeze out moisture.

2. In a bowl, combine zucchini with eggs, Parmesan and half the mozzarella and cheddar cheeses. Press into a greased 13x9-in. or 3-qt. baking dish. Bake for 20 minutes.

3. Meanwhile, in a large saucepan, cook beef and onion over medium heat until meat is no longer pink, breaking meat into crumbles; drain. Add the tomato sauce; spoon over zucchini mixture. Sprinkle with remaining cheeses; add green pepper. Bake until heated through, about 20 minutes longer.

FREEZE OPTION Cool baked casserole; cover and freeze. To use, partially thaw in refrigerator overnight. Remove from refrigerator 30 minutes before baking. Preheat oven to 350°. Unwrap casserole; reheat on a lower oven rack until heated through and a thermometer inserted in center reads 165°.

1 CUP 315 cal., 20g fat (10g sat. fat), 119mg chol., 855mg sod., 10g carb. (4g sugars, 2g fiber), 25g pro.

BEEF & BISCUIT STEW

This easy-to-prepare dish is a meal in itself. That made it a real favorite of my mother's—she had to cook for nine children! Better yet, my brothers, sisters and I loved it.

—Sylvia Sonneborn, York, PA

PREP: 2¾ hours • **BAKE:** 20 min. • **MAKES:** 10 servings

2 lbs. beef stew meat (1-in. cubes)
   All-purpose flour
2 Tbsp. canola oil
2 beef bouillon cubes
2 cups boiling water
   Salt and pepper to taste
6 to 8 small potatoes, peeled and quartered
3 small onions, quartered
4 carrots, sliced
1 package (9 oz.) frozen cut green beans, thawed
2 Tbsp. cornstarch
¼ cup water

BISCUIT DOUGH
2 cups all-purpose flour
4 tsp. baking powder
½ tsp. salt
2 Tbsp. canola oil
¾ to 1 cup 2% milk
   Melted butter

1. Coat beef cubes with flour. Heat oil in an oven-safe Dutch oven; add beef in batches and brown on all sides. Dissolve bouillon in boiling water; add to Dutch oven, stirring to loosen browned bits. Season with salt and pepper.
2. Simmer, covered, for 1½-2 hours or until meat is tender. Add the potatoes, onions, carrots and beans; cook until vegetables are tender, 30-45 minutes. Mix the cornstarch and cold water; stir into stew and cook until thickened and bubbly.

3. For biscuits, combine flour, baking powder and salt in a large bowl. Stir in oil and enough milk to form a light, soft dough, mixing just until combined. Drop by tablespoonfuls on top of stew. Brush tops of biscuits with melted butter. Bake, uncovered, at 350° for 20-30 minutes or until biscuits are done.
1 CUP 382 cal., 13g fat (4g sat. fat), 59mg chol., 542mg sod., 43g carb. (6g sugars, 4g fiber), 23g pro.

HOW TO BRAISE

To brown stew meat for braising, first pat it dry to prevent steaming, or coat it with flour, as in this recipe. Heat a heavy pan with oil until shimmering, then add the meat in small batches to avoid overcrowding. This ensures a good sear.

Let the meat brown without moving it until a golden crust forms. Turn and repeat on all sides. Remove the browned meat, then deglaze the pan to capture the flavorful browned bits for the braising liquid. To do this, add a small amount of liquid and scrape the bottom of the pan with a wooden spoon. Then add remaining liquid.

MEXICAN LASAGNA

I enjoy collecting cookbooks and recipes. My husband loves this dish!

—Rose Ann Buhle, Minooka, IL

PREP: 20 min. • **BAKE:** 65 min. + standing
MAKES: 12 servings

2	lbs. ground beef
1	can (16 oz.) refried beans
1	can (4 oz.) chopped green chiles
1	envelope taco seasoning
2	Tbsp. hot salsa
12	oz. uncooked lasagna noodles
4	cups shredded Colby-Monterey Jack cheese, divided
1	jar (16 oz.) mild salsa
2	cups water
2	cups sour cream
1	can (2¼ oz.) sliced ripe olives, drained
3	green onions, chopped
1	medium tomato, chopped, optional

1. Preheat oven to 350°. In a large skillet, cook beef over medium heat until no longer pink; drain. Stir in beans, chiles, taco seasoning and hot salsa.

2. In a greased 13x9-in. baking dish, layer a third of the noodles and meat mixture. Sprinkle with 1 cup cheese. Repeat the layers twice.

3. Combine mild salsa and water; pour over top. Cover and bake 1 hour or until heated through.

4. Top with remaining cheese. Bake, uncovered, until cheese is browned, 5-7 minutes longer. Let stand 10-15 minutes. Garnish with sour cream, olives, green onions and, if desired, tomato.

1 SERVING 520 cal., 29g fat (16g sat. fat), 108mg chol., 929mg sod., 35g carb. (4g sugars, 3g fiber), 29g pro.

SHEET-PAN STEAK DINNER

Asparagus and steak form a classic combination for a delicious dinner. Cooking them together makes for easy prep and cleanup. In our house, any meal that can be put in the oven while we get a few more things done for the day is a win!

—Pamela Forrest, Springfield, OR

PREP: 15 min. • **BAKE:** 25 min.
MAKES: 4 servings

- 1 tsp. minced fresh rosemary
- ½ tsp. each salt, pepper, paprika and garlic powder
- 1½ lbs. beef flank steak
- 1 lb. fresh asparagus, trimmed
- 2 Tbsp. avocado oil
- 2 Tbsp. butter, melted
- 1 garlic clove, minced

1. Preheat oven to 400°. Combine rosemary and seasonings; set aside.
2. Place steak on 1 side of a 15x10x1-in. baking pan; place asparagus on the other side in a single layer. Brush steak with oil and sprinkle with seasoning mix. Combine butter and garlic; pour over asparagus.
3. Cover with foil; bake until meat reaches desired doneness (for medium-rare, a thermometer should read 135°; medium, 140°; medium-well, 145°), 25-30 minutes. Let the steak stand for 5-10 minutes before slicing. Serve with asparagus.

5 OZ. COOKED BEEF WITH 8 ASPARAGUS SPEARS 380 cal., 25g fat (10g sat. fat), 96mg chol., 448mg sod., 3g carb. (1g sugars, 1g fiber), 34g pro.

FAVORITE BAKED SPAGHETTI

This is my grandchildren's most-loved dish. It feels like a special dinner and is so cozy for cooler months.

—Louise Miller, Westminster, MD

PREP: 25 min. • **BAKE:** 1 hour + standing • **MAKES:** 10 servings

- 1   pkg. (16 oz.) spaghetti
- 1   lb. ground beef
- 1   medium onion, chopped
- 1   jar (24 oz.) pasta sauce
- ½   tsp. seasoned salt
- 2   large eggs
- ⅓   cup grated Parmesan cheese
- 5   Tbsp. butter, melted
- 2   cups 4% cottage cheese
- 4   cups shredded part-skim mozzarella cheese
     Chopped fresh basil, optional

1. Preheat oven to 350°. Cook spaghetti according to package directions for al dente. Meanwhile, in a large skillet, cook beef and onion over medium heat for 6-8 minutes or until onion is tender and beef is no longer pink, breaking meat into crumbles; drain. Stir in pasta sauce and seasoned salt.

2. In a large bowl, whisk the eggs, Parmesan cheese and butter. Drain spaghetti; add to the egg mixture and toss to coat.

3. Place half the mixture in a greased 13x9-in. baking dish. Top with half the cottage cheese, meat sauce and mozzarella cheese. Repeat layers. Place baking dish on a rimmed baking sheet.

4. Cover and bake for 40 minutes. Uncover and bake for 20-25 minutes longer or until heated through. Let stand for 15 minutes before serving. If desired, sprinkle with basil.

1¼ CUPS 526 cal., 24g fat (13g sat. fat), 127mg chol., 881mg sod., 45g carb. (9g sugars, 3g fiber), 31g pro.

BAKED SPAGHETTI PUTTANESCA Add 1 Tbsp. minced garlic while cooking the ground beef mixture. After draining, stir in 3 Tbsp. rinsed and drained capers, 1 cup coarsely chopped black olives, 3 finely chopped anchovy fillets and ¾ tsp. red pepper flakes. Proceed as directed, topping with additional olives and capers before serving.

OVEN SWISS STEAK

I was really glad to find this recipe since it's a great way to use round steak and it picks up fabulous flavor from one of my favorite herbs—tarragon. I am a homemaker with three children and enjoy cooking tasty dinners like this one for my family.

—Lorna Dickau, Vanderhoof, BC

PREP: 30 min. • **BAKE:** 1¼ hours • **MAKES:** 4 servings

8 bacon strips
2 lbs. beef top round steak (¾ in. thick)
2 cups sliced fresh mushrooms
1 can (14½ oz.) diced tomatoes, undrained
½ cup chopped onion
1 to 2 tsp. dried tarragon
2 Tbsp. cornstarch
2 Tbsp. water
1 cup heavy whipping cream
  Minced fresh parsley, optional

1. In a large cast-iron or ovenproof skillet, cook bacon over medium heat until crisp. Remove to paper towels to drain, reserving ¼ cup drippings. Crumble bacon and set aside.
2. Trim beef; cut into serving-size pieces. Brown on both sides in drippings. Top meat with mushrooms, tomatoes and onion. Sprinkle with tarragon and bacon. Cover and bake at 325° until meat is tender, 1¼-1¾ hours, basting twice.

3. Remove meat from skillet; keep warm. Combine cornstarch and water until smooth; add to skillet. Bring to a boil; cook and stir until thickened, about 2 minutes. Reduce heat; stir in cream. Simmer, uncovered, until heated through, 3-4 minutes. Return meat to skillet and turn to coat with sauce. If desired, sprinkle with parsley.
1 SERVING 385 cal., 26g fat (12g sat. fat), 116mg chol., 308mg sod., 7g carb. (4g sugars, 1g fiber), 31g pro.

5i

CHEESEBURGER & FRIES CASSEROLE

Kids love this casserole because it combines two of their favorite fast foods. And I like the fact that I can whip it up with just a few ingredients and little prep time.

—Karen Owen, Rising Sun, IN

PREP: 10 min. • **BAKE:** 50 min. • **MAKES:** 8 servings

2 lbs. lean ground beef (90% lean)
1 can (10¾ oz.) condensed golden mushroom soup, undiluted
1 can (10¾ oz.) condensed cheddar cheese soup, undiluted
1 pkg. (20 oz.) frozen crinkle-cut french fries

1. Preheat oven to 350°. In a large skillet, cook and crumble beef over medium heat until no longer pink; drain. Stir in soups. Pour into a greased 13x9-in. baking dish.
2. Top with french fries. Bake, uncovered, until golden brown, 50-55 minutes.
1½ CUPS 352 cal., 17g fat (5g sat. fat), 62mg chol., 668mg sod., 25g carb. (1g sugars, 2g fiber), 25g pro.

ROAST PORK WITH APPLES & ONIONS

⑤ ROAST PORK WITH APPLES & ONIONS

The sweetness of the apples and onions nicely complements the roast pork. With its crisp exterior and melt-in-your-mouth flavor, this is my family's favorite dinner.

—Lily Julow, Lawrenceville, GA

PREP: 30 min. • **BAKE:** 45 min. + standing • **MAKES:** 8 servings

- 1 boneless pork loin roast (2 lbs.)
- ¼ tsp. salt
- ¼ tsp. pepper
- 1 Tbsp. olive oil
- 3 large Golden Delicious apples, cut into 1-in. wedges
- 2 large onions, cut into ¾-in. wedges
- 5 garlic cloves, peeled
- 1 Tbsp. minced fresh rosemary or 1 tsp. dried rosemary, crushed

1. Preheat oven to 350°. Sprinkle roast with salt and pepper. In a large nonstick skillet, heat oil over medium heat; brown roast on all sides. Transfer to a roasting pan coated with cooking spray. Place apples, onions and garlic around roast; sprinkle with rosemary.

2. Roast until a thermometer inserted in the pork reads 145°, 45-55 minutes, turning apples, onion and garlic once.

Remove from oven; tent with foil. Let stand 10 minutes before slicing roast. Serve with apple mixture.

1 SERVING 210 cal., 7g fat (2g sat. fat), 57mg chol., 109mg sod., 14g carb. (9g sugars, 2g fiber), 23g pro. **DIABETIC EXCHANGES** 3 lean meat, 1 starch, ½ fat.

PIZZA MACARONI & CHEESE

My grandma made this for us once during a visit and I never forgot just how good it was. Since my kids love anything with pepperoni and cheese, I bake it so they can enjoy it as much as I did.

—Juli Meyers, Hinesville, GA

PREP: 30 min. • **BAKE:** 25 min. • **MAKES:** 12 servings

- 2 pkg. (14 oz. each) deluxe macaroni and cheese dinner mix
- ½ cup sour cream
- 1 can (14½ oz.) petite diced tomatoes, drained
- 1 can (15 oz.) pizza sauce
- 1 small green pepper, chopped
- 1 small sweet red pepper, chopped
- 2 cups shredded Italian cheese blend
- 2 oz. sliced pepperoni

1. Preheat oven to 350°. Cook macaroni according to package directions for al dente. Drain; return to pan. Stir in contents of cheese packets and sour cream. Transfer to a greased 13x9-in. baking dish.

2. In a small bowl, combine tomatoes and pizza sauce; drop by spoonfuls over macaroni. Top with peppers, cheese and pepperoni. Bake, uncovered, until bubbly, 25-30 minutes.

1 CUP 340 cal., 14g fat (7g sat. fat), 37mg chol., 927mg sod., 37g carb. (5g sugars, 3g fiber), 14g pro.

"Loved how quick and easy this was to make. It was a big hit with the family too. I may try spicing things up next time with jalapenos."

—ANGEL182009, TASTEOFHOME.COM

MOTHER'S HAM CASSEROLE

This ham casserole recipe was one of my mother's favorite dishes and it always brings back fond memories of her when I prepare it. It's a terrific use of leftover ham from a holiday dinner.

—Linda Childers, Murfreesboro, TN

PREP: 35 min. • **BAKE:** 25 min. • **MAKES:** 6 servings

- 2 cups cubed peeled potatoes
- 1 large carrot, sliced
- 2 celery ribs, chopped
- 3 cups water
- 2 cups cubed fully cooked ham
- 2 Tbsp. chopped green pepper
- 2 tsp. finely chopped onion
- 7 Tbsp. butter, divided
- 3 Tbsp. all-purpose flour
- 1½ cups 2% milk
- ¾ tsp. salt
- ⅛ tsp. pepper
- 1 cup shredded cheddar cheese
- ½ cup soft bread crumbs

1. Preheat oven to 375°. In a saucepan, bring the potatoes, carrot, celery and water to a boil. Reduce heat; cover and cook until tender, about 15 minutes. Drain.

2. In a large skillet, saute ham, green pepper and onion in 3 Tbsp. butter until tender. Add the potato mixture. Transfer to a greased 1½-qt. baking dish.

3. In a large saucepan, melt remaining 4 Tbsp. butter; stir in flour until smooth. Gradually whisk in the milk, salt and pepper. Bring to a boil; cook and stir for 2 minutes or until thickened. Reduce heat; add cheddar cheese and stir until melted.

4. Pour over ham mixture. Sprinkle with soft bread crumbs. Bake until heated through, 25-30 minutes.

NOTE To make soft bread crumbs, tear bread into pieces and place in a food processor or blender. Cover and pulse until crumbs form. One slice of bread yields ½-¾ cup crumbs.

1 CUP 360 cal., 23g fat (14g sat. fat), 87mg chol., 1157mg sod., 21g carb. (5g sugars, 2g fiber), 18g pro.

"I made this according to the recipe, and it was delicious. My husband loved it and thought it would be good with eggs for breakfast. Will make again!"

—CANDI213, TASTEOFHOME.COM

SHEET-PAN PORK SUPPER

I created this recipe to suit our family's needs. It's a delicious meal in one, and so quick and easy to clean up since you use one pan for everything! Use any variety of small potatoes—fingerlings or other colored potatoes are a fun and delicious option.

—Debbie Johnson, Centertown, MO

PREP: 10 min. • **BAKE:** 35 min. • **MAKES:** 8 servings

¼ cup butter, softened
2 tsp. minced fresh chives or 1 tsp. dried minced chives
1 garlic clove, minced
1½ lbs. fresh green beans, trimmed
2 Tbsp. olive oil
¾ tsp. salt
½ tsp. pepper
1½ lbs. baby red potatoes, halved
2 pork tenderloins (about 1 lb. each)
½ cup teriyaki glaze or hoisin sauce
    Optional: Toasted sesame seeds and additional fresh minced chives

1. Preheat oven to 450°. In a small bowl, combine butter, chives and garlic. In a second bowl, combine green beans with 1 Tbsp. olive oil, ¼ tsp. salt and ¼ tsp. pepper. Arrange the green beans down 1 side of a 15x10x1-in. baking pan. In the same bowl, combine potatoes with remaining 1 Tbsp. olive oil, ½ tsp. salt and ¼ tsp. pepper. Arrange potatoes on other side of pan.
2. Pat pork dry with paper towels; brush with teriyaki glaze. Place on top of green beans.
3. Bake until a thermometer inserted in pork reads 145°, 25-30 minutes. Remove tenderloins to a cutting board and top with 2 Tbsp. seasoned butter. Tent pork with aluminum foil; let stand.

4. Stir green beans and potatoes; return to oven and cook about 10 minutes longer or until vegetables are tender and lightly browned. Stir remaining seasoned butter into vegetables.
5. Slice the pork; serve with roasted vegetables and pan drippings. If desired, top with sesame seeds and additional minced chives.
3 OZ. COOKED PORK WITH 1¼ CUPS VEGETABLES 354 cal., 14g fat (6g sat. fat), 79mg chol., 1186mg sod., 30g carb. (9g sugars, 5g fiber), 28g pro.

5i

PORK CHOPS WITH APPLES & STUFFING

The heartwarming taste of cinnamon and apples is the perfect accompaniment to these tender pork chops. The dish is always a winner with my family. Because it calls for only four ingredients, it's a main course that I can serve with little preparation.

—Joan Hamilton, Worcester, MA

PREP: 15 min. • **BAKE:** 45 min.
MAKES: 6 servings

- 6 boneless pork loin chops (6 oz. each)
- 1 Tbsp. canola oil
- 1 pkg. (6 oz.) crushed stuffing mix
- 1 can (21 oz.) apple pie filling with cinnamon
  Minced fresh parsley, optional

1. In a large skillet, brown pork chops in oil over medium-high heat. Meanwhile, prepare stuffing according to package directions. Spread pie filling into a greased 13x9-in. baking dish. Place the pork chops on top; spoon stuffing over chops.

2. Cover and bake at 350° for 35 minutes. Uncover; bake until a thermometer inserted in pork reads 145°, about 10 minutes longer. If desired, sprinkle with parsley.

1 SERVING 527 cal., 21g fat (9g sat. fat), 102mg chol., 550mg sod., 48g carb. (15g sugars, 3g fiber), 36g pro.

BLT PIZZA

Take a prebaked crust and layer bacon, tomatoes, cheese and other savory toppings on top. This is my family's favorite way to eat pizza.

—Marilyn Ruggles, Lee's Summit, MO

TAKES: 25 min. • **MAKES:** 6 servings

1   prebaked 12-in. pizza crust
½   cup Miracle Whip
2   tsp. dried basil
½   tsp. garlic powder
⅛   tsp. onion powder
12 bacon strips, cooked and crumbled
¾   cup shredded cheddar cheese
¾   cup shredded part-skim mozzarella cheese
1½ cups shredded lettuce
2   medium tomatoes, thinly sliced

1. Place the crust on an ungreased 12-in. pizza pan. In a small bowl, combine the Miracle Whip, basil, garlic powder and onion powder; spread over crust. Set aside ¼ cup bacon. Sprinkle cheeses and remaining bacon over crust.
2. Bake at 425° for 8-12 minutes or until the cheese is melted. Top with lettuce, tomatoes and reserved bacon. Cut into wedges.
1 PIECE 416 cal., 22g fat (8g sat. fat), 46mg chol., 961mg sod., 35g carb. (4g sugars, 2g fiber), 20g pro.

"I was a little unsure of heating the Miracle Whip but was surprised how this came out! We love BLTs and thought this was amazing!"

—KARENKEEFE, TASTEOFHOME.COM

CHRISTMAS PORK PIE

When my mother was growing up, her mom made mince pies that contained meat.
I created this recipe with my grandmother in mind.

—Candice Salazar, Los Alamos, NM

PREP: 35 min. • **BAKE:** 30 min. + cooling • **MAKES:** 6 servings

2 cups beef broth
¾ cup chopped onion
½ cup chopped dried apricots
½ cup raisins
½ cup whole-berry cranberry sauce
½ cup undrained crushed pineapple
½ tsp. curry powder
¼ tsp. ground cinnamon
1 Tbsp. cornstarch
1 Tbsp. water
3 cups cubed cooked pork
½ cup chopped pecans
½ tsp. salt
   Dough for double-crust pie
   Milk and sugar

1. Preheat oven to 400°. In a large saucepan, combine first 8 ingredients. Cook over medium heat for 20 minutes. Combine the cornstarch and water until smooth; stir into fruit mixture. Bring to a boil; cook and stir until thickened, about 2 minutes. Remove from the heat; stir in pork, pecans and salt.
2. On a lightly floured surface, roll half of the dough to a ⅛-in.-thick circle; transfer to a 9-in. pie plate. Trim even with rim. Fill with meat mixture. Roll remaining dough to a ⅛-in.-thick circle; make decorative cutouts in crust. Set cutouts aside. Place top crust over filling; trim, seal and flute edge.

3. Brush crust and cutouts with milk; place cutouts on top of pie. Sprinkle with sugar. Bake 30-35 minutes or until golden brown. Cool 10 minutes before serving. Refrigerate leftovers.

DOUGH FOR DOUBLE-CRUST PIE
Combine 2½ cups all-purpose flour and ½ tsp. salt; cut in 1 cup cold butter until crumbly. Gradually add ⅓-⅔ cup ice water, tossing with a fork until dough holds together when pressed. Divide dough in half. Shape each into a disk; wrap and refrigerate 1 hour.

1 PIECE 665 cal., 33g fat (11g sat. fat), 77mg chol., 795mg sod., 69g carb. (27g sugars, 3g fiber), 25g pro.

HOW TO MAKE A REVERSE CUTOUT CRUST

For a decorative reverse cutout crust, roll out the top crust and use small or medium cookie cutters to cut shapes in select areas, spacing them apart.

Place the crust over your filled pie and seal the edges. If desired, attach some cutouts on top of the pie, securing them with a bit of egg wash (1 egg whisked with 1 tsp. of water). Then lightly brush the entire crust with more egg wash before baking. This will give your pie a beautiful shine.

HOT DOG CASSEROLE

When our children were small and I was busy trying to get all those extra things done, I would make this quick hot dish. Kids love it!

—JoAnn Gunio, Franklin, NC

PREP: 20 min. • **BAKE:** 70 min. • **MAKES:** 8 servings

3 Tbsp. butter
2 Tbsp. all-purpose flour
1 to 1½ tsp. salt
¼ to ½ tsp. pepper
1½ cups 2% milk
5 medium red potatoes, thinly sliced
1 pkg. (1 lb.) hot dogs, halved lengthwise and cut into ½-in. slices
1 medium onion, chopped
⅓ cup shredded cheddar cheese
Chopped green onions, optional

1. Preheat oven to 350°. In a small saucepan, melt butter. Stir in the flour, salt and pepper until smooth. Gradually add the milk. Bring to a boil; cook and stir until thickened and bubbly, about 2 minutes.

2. In a greased 2½-qt. baking dish, layer with a third of the potatoes, half the hot dogs and half the onion. Repeat layers. Top with remaining potatoes. Pour white sauce over all.

3. Bake, covered, for 1 hour. Uncover; sprinkle with cheese. Bake until potatoes are tender, 10-15 minutes longer. If desired, garnish with green onions.

1 CUP 330 cal., 24g fat (11g sat. fat), 52mg chol., 967mg sod., 18g carb. (4g sugars, 2g fiber), 11g pro.

HARVEST SHEET-PAN DINNER

This foolproof weeknight dinner is naturally gluten free, and is on your table in no time! It's easily adaptable to use seasonal fruits or veggies.

—Melissa Erdelac, Valparaiso, IN

PREP: 15 min. • **BAKE:** 45 min. • **MAKES:** 5 servings

2 large sweet potatoes, peeled and cut into ½-in. cubes
1 large sweet onion, cut into wedges
2 Tbsp. olive oil
1 Tbsp. brown sugar
½ tsp. salt
½ tsp. ground allspice
¼ tsp. ground cinnamon
⅛ tsp. pepper
3 small pears, quartered
1 pkg. (19 oz.) Italian sausage links

1. Preheat oven to 425°. Place the sweet potatoes and onion in a 15x10x1-in. baking pan; drizzle with oil. Sprinkle with brown sugar and seasonings; toss to coat. Bake for 15 minutes.

2. Gently stir in pears; top with sausages. Bake 20 minutes longer, stirring once. Increase oven temperature to 450°. Bake for 8-10 minutes or until the sausages are golden brown and a thermometer inserted into sausage reads at least 160°, turning once.

1 SERVING 533 cal., 29g fat (8g sat. fat), 58mg chol., 912mg sod., 56g carb. (28g sugars, 8g fiber), 15g pro.

OKTOBERFEST CASSEROLE

In northeastern Ohio, we love German flavors. This delicious casserole is a trifecta mashup of my favorite dishes. It combines the flavors of cheesy hash brown casseroles with bratwursts and sauerkraut, plus pretzels and beer cheese. It takes less than 10 minutes to mix and uses only one bowl. It's sure to please everyone any time of the year.

—Sarah Markley, Ashland, OH

PREP: 15 min. • **BAKE:** 1½ hours + standing • **MAKES:** 12 servings

2 cans (10½ oz. each) condensed cheddar cheese soup, undiluted
1 cup beer or chicken broth
1 cup sour cream
1 pkg. (32 oz.) frozen cubed hash brown potatoes, thawed
1 can (14 oz.) sauerkraut, rinsed and well drained
2 cups shredded cheddar cheese
1 pkg. (14 oz.) fully cooked bratwurst links, chopped
2 cups pretzel pieces

1. Preheat oven to 350°. In a large bowl, whisk soup, beer and sour cream until combined. Stir in potatoes, sauerkraut, cheese and chopped bratwurst. Transfer to a greased 13x9-in. baking dish. Cover and bake for 45 minutes.

2. Uncover; bake 30 minutes. Top with pretzel pieces. Bake the casserole for 12-15 minutes longer or until bubbly and heated through. Let stand 10 minutes before serving.

FREEZE OPTION Freeze cooled potato mixture in freezer containers. To use, partially thaw in refrigerator overnight. Heat through in a saucepan, stirring occasionally; add broth or water if necessary.

1 SERVING 356 cal., 21g fat (10g sat. fat), 49mg chol., 884mg sod., 29g carb. (4g sugars, 3g fiber), 13g pro.

"Excellent casserole! Very tasty! My family likes sauerkraut, so this was a great way to use it."
—BEV, TASTEOFHOME.COM

CAST-IRON SAUSAGE PIZZA

This shortcut pizza starts with frozen dough in a cast-iron pan. Add your family's favorite toppings for variety.

—*Taste of Home* Test Kitchen

PREP: 30 min. • **BAKE:** 20 min. • **MAKES:** 6 servings

- 1 loaf (1 lb.) frozen bread dough, thawed
- 2 tsp. cornmeal
- 1½ cups pizza sauce
- ½ lb. bulk Italian sausage, cooked and drained
- 1½ cups shredded part-skim mozzarella cheese, divided
- 1 tsp. dried oregano
- 1 small green pepper, sliced into rings
  Crushed red pepper flakes, optional

1. Preheat oven to 425°. On a lightly floured surface, roll and stretch dough into a 10-in. circle. Cover; let rest for 10 minutes. Roll and stretch the dough into a 12-in. circle. Grease a 10-in. cast-iron or other ovenproof skillet; sprinkle with cornmeal. Press dough onto bottom and 1 in. up side of the prepared skillet.

2. Spread with pizza sauce; top with sausage, 1 cup cheese, oregano and green pepper. Sprinkle with remaining ½ cup cheese. Bake until the crust is golden brown, 20-25 minutes. If desired, sprinkle with red pepper flakes.

1 PIECE 424 cal., 18g fat (6g sat. fat), 39mg chol., 1092mg sod., 45g carb. (7g sugars, 4g fiber), 20g pro.

FRENCH ONION PORK CHOPS

These tasty pork chops, baked in a rich, beefy onion sauce, would be great served over rice or mashed potatoes, or with crusty bread to soak up the juices.

—*Taste of Home* Test Kitchen

PREP: 65 min. • **BAKE:** 10 min. • **MAKES:** 4 servings

- 2 Tbsp. butter
- 2 Tbsp. olive oil, divided
- 2 large onions, halved and thinly sliced
- 4 boneless pork loin chops (1 in. thick and 6 oz. each)
- 1 tsp. minced fresh thyme or ½ tsp. dried thyme
- ½ tsp. salt
- ½ tsp. garlic powder
- ¼ tsp. pepper
- 2 Tbsp. all-purpose flour
- 1¼ cups beef stock
- 1 cup shredded Gruyere or Swiss cheese

1. In a large cast-iron or other ovenproof skillet, heat butter and 1 Tbsp. oil over medium heat. Add the onions; cook and stir until softened, 8-10 minutes. Reduce heat to medium-low; cook until deep golden brown, 30-40 minutes, stirring occasionally. Remove and keep warm.

2. Preheat oven to 400°. Sprinkle chops with thyme, salt, garlic powder and pepper. In the same skillet, cook chops in remaining 1 Tbsp. oil until lightly browned, 2-3 minutes on each side. Remove from pan. Return onions to skillet. Stir in flour until blended; gradually whisk in stock. Bring to a boil, stirring constantly; cook and stir until thickened, 1-2 minutes.

3. Return pork chops to skillet. Bake, uncovered, until a thermometer inserted in pork reads 145°, 8-10 minutes. Top with cheese; bake until cheese is melted, 2-3 minutes longer. If desired, top with additional fresh thyme before serving.

1 SERVING 510 cal., 31g fat (14g sat. fat), 128mg chol., 750mg sod., 11g carb. (4g sugars, 1g fiber), 44g pro.

CAST-IRON
SAUSAGE PIZZA

SHEET-PAN NEW ENGLAND CLAMBAKE

This recipe transports you to hot summer nights on the beach enjoying fresh seafood, corn on the cob, spicy sausage and potatoes any time of the year! Bathed in garlicky, spicy butter, this one-pan wonder is beautiful, delicious and easy on cleanup! You could mix up the seafood and add pieces of salmon or haddock, use other quick-cooking veggies like cherry tomatoes or asparagus, or substitute kielbasa for the chorizo. It's so versatile!

—Pamela Gelsomini, Wrentham, MA

PREP: 25 min. • **BAKE:** 45 min. • **MAKES:** 6 servings

1 lb. assorted baby potatoes
2 Tbsp. olive oil
2 tsp. Italian seasoning
6 half-ears frozen corn on the cob, thawed
2 lbs. fresh mussels, scrubbed and beards removed
1½ dozen fresh littleneck clams, scrubbed
1 lb. uncooked shrimp (26-30 per lb.), peeled and deveined
½ lb. fully cooked Spanish chorizo links, cut into ½-in. pieces
¼ cup dry white wine or chicken broth
1 medium lemon, cut into wedges
½ cup butter, melted
4 garlic cloves, chopped
2 tsp. seafood seasoning
1¼ tsp. Cajun seasoning
¼ tsp. pepper
2 Tbsp. minced fresh parsley
French bread, optional

1. Preheat oven to 400°. Place potatoes in a 15x10x1-in. baking pan. Drizzle with oil and sprinkle with Italian seasoning; toss to coat. Bake 25-30 minutes or until tender. Using a potato masher, flatten potatoes to ½-in. thickness; remove and keep warm.
2. Add corn, mussels, clams, shrimp and chorizo to same pan; top with potatoes. Pour wine into pan. Squeeze the lemon wedges over top; add to pan.
3. Combine the butter, garlic, seafood seasoning and Cajun seasoning. Pour half the butter mixture over top. Bake until shrimp turn pink and mussels and clams open, 20-25 minutes. Discard any unopened mussels or clams.
4. Drizzle with remaining butter mixture. Sprinkle with pepper; top with parsley. If desired, serve with bread.

1 SERVING 639 cal., 35g fat (15g sat. fat), 214mg chol., 1302mg sod., 37g carb. (4g sugars, 3g fiber), 46g pro.

BUDGET SPICE BLEND

If you don't have Cajun seasoning on hand, you can make your own with the spices you have. There are many different blends, but a typical mix will include salt, cayenne pepper, garlic powder, paprika, thyme, pepper and onion powder.

VEGETABLE TOFU POTPIE

We raised our daughters as vegetarians. I wanted to give them more options than just pizza and pasta, so when they were around 11 years old, I went to work trying to expand their palates by experimenting with recipes. This one is still a hit.

—Mark Sirota, New York, NY

PREP: 25 min. • **COOK:** 45 min. + standing • **MAKES:** 6 servings

1½ cups frozen mixed vegetables (about 8 oz.)
1 large potato, peeled , chopped
2 cups chopped cauliflower
2 Tbsp. water
8 oz. extra-firm tofu
3 Tbsp. cornstarch
½ tsp. onion salt
2 Tbsp. canola oil
2 large eggs, lightly beaten
1 can (10½ oz.) condensed cream of potato soup, undiluted
½ cup 2% milk
½ tsp. dried thyme
¼ tsp. pepper
¼ tsp. salt
Dough for double-crust pie

1. Preheat the oven to 375°. In a large microwave-safe bowl, combine frozen mixed vegetables, potato, cauliflower and water. Cover and microwave on high 8-10 minutes or until potato is almost tender; drain.

2. Cut tofu into ½-in. cubes; pat dry with paper towels. In a large bowl, combine cornstarch and onion salt. Add tofu and toss to coat. In a large skillet, heat oil over medium-high heat. Add tofu; cook 5-7 minutes or until crisp and golden brown, stirring occasionally. Remove from pan; drain on paper towels.

3. In another large bowl, whisk eggs, soup, milk, thyme, pepper and salt until combined. Stir in vegetable mixture and tofu. On a lightly floured surface, roll half the dough to a ⅛-in.-thick circle; transfer to a 9-in. pie plate. Trim even with rim. Add filling. Roll remaining dough to a ⅛-in.-thick circle. Place over filling. Trim, seal and flute edge. Cut slits in top.

4. Bake on a lower oven rack until crust is golden brown and filling is bubbly, 45-50 minutes. Let stand 15 minutes before cutting.

DOUGH FOR DOUBLE-CRUST PIE
Combine 2½ cups all-purpose flour and ½ tsp. salt; cut in 1 cup cold butter until crumbly. Gradually add ⅓-⅔ cup ice water, tossing with a fork until dough holds together when pressed. Divide dough in half. Shape each into a disk; wrap and refrigerate 1 hour.

1 PIECE 679 cal., 40g fat (21g sat. fat), 146mg chol., 973mg sod., 65g carb. (5g sugars, 6g fiber), 15g pro.

EASY FALAFEL BURGERS

I love to get falafel at our local Middle Eastern restaurant. It's not always cheap or convenient to eat out, so I tried making an at-home version burger-style. This falafel burger is baked, making it a little more calorie-friendly.

—Kristyne McDougle Walter, Lorain, OH

PREP: 1 hour + soaking • **BAKE:** 20 min. • **MAKES:** 8 servings

2 cups dried garbanzo beans or chickpeas
½ Tbsp. baking soda
1 cup fresh parsley leaves
1 cup fresh cilantro leaves
⅓ cup all-purpose flour
1 jalapeno pepper, seeded
6 garlic cloves
2 Tbsp. lemon juice
2 tsp. grated lemon zest
2 tsp. ground cumin
¾ tsp. salt
½ tsp. pepper
1 tsp. baking powder

YOGURT SAUCE
¾ cup plain Greek yogurt
3 Tbsp. tahini
3 Tbsp. lemon juice
½ tsp. salt

BURGERS
8 hamburger buns, split and toasted or whole pita breads
Optional toppings: Lettuce leaves, pickled onion, feta cheese, red onion, tomato or cucumber

1. In a large bowl, cover garbanzo beans with water. Stir in baking soda. Cover; let stand overnight. Drain; rinse and pat dry.

2. In a food processor, combine garbanzo beans, parsley, cilantro, 6 Tbsp. flour, jalapeno, garlic, 2 Tbsp. lemon juice, lemon zest, cumin, salt, pepper and baking powder. Pulse until crumbly. Using hands, try to shape a small portion into a ball. If mixture is too dry, add water 1 Tbsp. at a time. If mixture is too wet, add more flour, 1 Tbsp. at a time. Transfer to a large bowl. Cover and refrigerate 30 minutes.

3. Shape garbanzo bean mixture into 8 ¾-in.-thick patties. Arrange patties on a parchment-lined baking sheet. Refrigerate 30 minutes. Preheat oven to 450°.

4. Bake 18-22 minutes or until lightly browned, turning once. Meanwhile, in a small bowl, combine yogurt, tahini, lemon juice and salt. Serve patties on buns with yogurt sauce and desired toppings.

NOTE Wear disposable gloves when cutting hot peppers; the oils can burn skin. Avoid touching your face.

1 BURGER 327 cal., 10g fat (2g sat. fat), 6mg chol., 692mg sod., 59g carb. (6g sugars, 16g fiber), 15g pro.

FALAFEL BURGER TIPS

Can you use canned garbanzo beans in this recipe?
Yes, canned garbanzo beans will work, but they're not ideal. They lack the starch of soaked dried beans, resulting in a stickier patty that may not hold together as well.

Is there an alternative to using all-purpose flour?
For a gluten-free option, use chickpea flour in place of all-purpose flour in the patties and replace a standard bun with a gluten-free bun or chickpea flatbread.

What can I serve with falafel burgers?
You might find that a side of fries is too heavy to go with these burgers, so try serving them with a fresh Mediterranean salad or sliced cucumbers.

SWISS & CRAB SUPPER PIE

Though some parts of Alaska are suitable for farming, we're on the Gulf, where commercial fishing is the main industry. Crab is plentiful here, and so is salmon, halibut, shrimp and sea herring. You don't need fresh crab for this tasty, easy-to-make supper pie. With canned crabmeat, it becomes a terrific off-the-shelf meal. Hope your family enjoys it as much as mine does!

—Kathy Crow, Cordova, AK

PREP: 15 min. • **BAKE:** 45 min. + standing • **MAKES:** 8 servings

1   sheet refrigerated pie crust
1   can (6 oz.) lump crabmeat, drained
1   cup shredded Swiss cheese
2   green onions, thinly sliced
3   large eggs, beaten
1   cup half-and-half cream
½   tsp. salt
½   tsp. grated lemon zest
¼   tsp. ground mustard
    Dash mace
¼   cup sliced almonds

1. Preheat oven to 450°. Line a 9-in. tart pan with unpricked crust; line with heavy-duty foil. Bake for 5 minutes. Remove foil; reduce oven temperature to 325°.

2. Arrange crab evenly in baked crust; top with the cheese and green onion. Combine remaining ingredients except almonds; pour into tart shell. Sprinkle top with almonds.

3. Bake until set, about 45 minutes. Let stand for 10 minutes before serving.

1 PIECE 276 cal., 18g fat (8g sat. fat), 123mg chol., 435mg sod., 15g carb. (2g sugars, 0 fiber), 13g pro.

SHEET-PAN SHRIMP FAJITAS

I love easy weeknight dinners like this. This meal comes together so quickly.

—Carla Hubl, Hastings, NE

PREP: 30 min. • **COOK:** 20 min.
MAKES: 6 servings

- 1½ lbs. uncooked shrimp (31-40 per lb.), peeled and deveined
- 1 each medium green, sweet red and yellow peppers, cut into ½-in. strips
- 1 sweet onion, cut into ½-in. strips
- 2 garlic cloves, minced
- 2 Tbsp. olive oil
- 2 tsp. chili powder
- 1 tsp. ground cumin
- ¾ tsp. salt
- 12 corn tortillas (6 in.), warmed
  Optional: Lime wedges, crema, fresh cilantro and sliced avocado

1. Preheat oven to 425°. In a large bowl, combine shrimp, peppers, onion and garlic. Drizzle with oil; sprinkle with chili powder, cumin and salt. Toss to coat. Spread evenly between 2 greased 15x10x1-in. baking pans.

2. Roast for 10 minutes, rotating pans halfway through cooking. Remove pans from oven; preheat broiler.

3. Broil shrimp mixture, 1 pan at a time, 3-4 in. from heat until vegetables are lightly browned and shrimp turn pink, 4-5 minutes. Serve in tortillas, with toppings as desired.

2 FAJITAS 280 cal., 8g fat (1g sat. fat), 138mg chol., 484mg sod., 31g carb. (5g sugars, 5g fiber), 22g pro. **DIABETIC EXCHANGES** 3 lean meat, 1½ starch, 1 vegetable, 1 fat.

EASY TAMALE PIE WITH PEPPERS

My family loves anything with southwestern flavor, so this recipe is a big hit. It's super quick and easy to prepare, and cleanup afterward is fast because everything cooks in one dish.

—Joan Hallford, North Richland Hills, TX

PREP: 20 min. + standing • **BAKE:** 30 min. • **MAKES:** 6 servings

- 2 poblano peppers
- 6 chicken or beef tamales
- 1 can (15 oz.) chili with beans
- 2 cups shredded sharp cheddar cheese
- 1 small onion, chopped
  Chopped fresh cilantro and thinly sliced green onions

1. Cut the peppers lengthwise in half; remove stems and seeds. Place peppers on a foil-lined baking sheet, skin side up. Broil 4 in. from heat until skins blister, about 5 minutes. Immediately place peppers in a large bowl; let stand, covered, 20 minutes. Reduce oven setting to 350°.
2. Peel off and discard charred skins. Place peppers in a greased 11x7-in. baking dish. Remove husks from tamales.

Cut tamales into quarters; place over peppers. Top with chili, cheese and chopped onion. Bake until hot and bubbly, 30-35 minutes. Serve with cilantro and green onions.

NOTE Wear disposable gloves when cutting hot peppers; the oils can burn skin. Avoid touching your face.

1 SERVING 439 cal., 25g fat (9g sat. fat), 59mg chol., 1152mg sod., 34g carb. (3g sugars, 5g fiber), 23g pro.

KATHY'S SMOKED SALMON PIZZA

This is wonderful for a light supper. It's easy, too, so put away that frozen pizza!

—Kathy Petty, Portland, OR

TAKES: 25 min. • **MAKES:** 8 servings

- 1 prebaked 12-in. thin pizza crust
- ½ cup ranch salad dressing
- 4 slices provolone cheese, cut in half
- 6 slices tomato
- 1 pkg. (3 oz.) smoked salmon or lox
- ½ cup crumbled feta cheese
  Chopped chives, optional

1. Preheat oven to 425°. Place crust on an ungreased 14-in. pizza pan. Spread with ranch dressing; top with provolone cheese. Arrange tomato and salmon over provolone; sprinkle with feta cheese.
2. Bake until cheese is melted and golden, 15-20 minutes. If desired, top with chopped chives.

1 PIECE 231 cal., 12g fat (4g sat. fat), 19mg chol., 584mg sod., 20g carb. (2g sugars, 1g fiber), 10g pro.

STUFFED PASTA SHELLS

These savory shells never fail to make a big impression, even though the recipe is very easy. One or two of these shells makes a great individual serving at a potluck, so a single batch goes a long way.

—Jena Coffey, St. Louis, Missouri

PREP: 15 min. • **BAKE:** 30 min. • **MAKES:** 12 servings

4 cups shredded mozzarella cheese
1 carton (15 oz.) ricotta cheese
1 package (10 oz.) frozen chopped spinach, thawed and squeezed dry
½ tsp. dried basil
½ tsp. dried oregano
½ tsp. salt
¼ tsp. pepper
¼ tsp. crushed red pepper flakes, optional
1 package (12 oz.) jumbo pasta shells, cooked and drained
3½ cups spaghetti sauce
   Optional: grated Parmesan cheese

1. Preheat oven to 350°. In a large bowl, combine mozzarella, ricotta, spinach, basil, oregano, salt, pepper and, if desired, crushed red pepper flakes; stuff into shells. Arrange in a greased 13x9-in. baking dish. Pour spaghetti sauce over the shells.
2. Cover and bake until heated through, 30-45 minutes. If desired, sprinkle with Parmesan cheese just before serving.
1 SERVING 314 cal., 13g fat (7g sat. fat), 44mg chol., 576mg sod., 32g carb. (9g sugars, 3g fiber), 18g pro.

"I have been making this for years and everyone—including all the grandchildren—loves this recipe. So easy, but looks like you worked for hours. Cheesy and just a wonderful taste in the mouth. I'm asked for the recipe all the time. I make this in two 8-in. pans and freeze one."

—JETCAROLINET, TASTEOFHOME.COM

5i

SPEEDY SHRIMP FLATBREADS

My husband and I are hooked on flatbread pizzas. I make at least one a week just to have something tasty around as a snack. This one came together easily because I had all the ingredients on hand.

—Cheryl Woodson, Liberty, MO

TAKES: 15 min. • **MAKES:** 2 servings

2 naan flatbreads or whole pita breads
1 pkg. (5.2 oz.) garlic-herb spreadable cheese
½ lb. peeled and deveined cooked shrimp (31-40 per lb.)
½ cup chopped oil-packed sun-dried tomatoes
¼ cup fresh basil leaves
   Lemon wedges, optional

Preheat oven to 400°. Place flatbreads on a baking sheet. Spread with cheese; top with shrimp and tomatoes. Bake until heated through, 4-6 minutes. Sprinkle with basil. If desired, serve with lemon wedges.
1 FLATBREAD 634 cal., 41g fat (24g sat. fat), 263mg chol., 1163mg sod., 38g carb. (3g sugars, 3g fiber), 33g pro.

SALMON QUICHE

Cooking is something that I've always liked doing. I pore over cookbooks the way other people read novels. This dish came from my mother—it's the kind of recipe you request after just one bite. And unlike some quiches, it's very hearty and satisfying!

—Deanna Baldwin, Bermuda Dunes, CA

PREP: 15 min. • **BAKE:** 1 hour
MAKES: 8 servings

- 1   sheet refrigerated pie crust
- 1   medium onion, chopped
- 1   Tbsp. butter
- 2   cups shredded Swiss cheese
- 1   can (14¾ oz.) salmon, drained, flaked and cartilage removed
- 5   large eggs
- 2   cups half-and-half cream
- ¼   tsp. salt
     Minced fresh parsley, optional

1. Unroll the crust into a 9-in. pie plate. Line unpricked pie crust with a double thickness of heavy-duty foil. Bake at 450° for 8 minutes. Remove foil; bake 5 minutes longer. Cool on a wire rack.
2. In a small skillet, saute onion in butter until tender. Sprinkle cheese in the crust; top with salmon and onion.
3. In a small bowl, whisk the eggs, half-and-half and salt; pour over salmon mixture. Bake at 350° for 45-50 minutes or until a knife inserted in the center comes out clean. Sprinkle with parsley if desired. Let stand 5 minutes before cutting.
1 PIECE 456 cal., 30g fat (15g sat. fat), 221mg chol., 524mg sod., 17g carb. (4g sugars, 0 fiber), 27g pro.

TILAPIA FLORENTINE

Get a little more heart-healthy fish into your weekly diet with this quick and easy entree. Topped with fresh spinach and a splash of lime, it's sure to become a favorite!

—Melanie Bachman, Ulysses, PA

TAKES: 30 min. • **MAKES:** 4 servings

- 1   pkg. (6 oz.) fresh baby spinach
- 6   tsp. canola oil, divided
- 4   tilapia fillets (4 oz. each)
- 2   Tbsp. lemon juice
- 2   tsp. garlic-herb seasoning blend
- 1   large egg, lightly beaten
- ½   cup part-skim ricotta cheese
- ¼   cup grated Parmesan cheese
      Optional: Lemon wedges and additional grated Parmesan cheese

1. Preheat oven to 375°. In a large nonstick skillet, cook spinach in 4 tsp. oil until wilted; drain. Meanwhile, place tilapia in a greased 13x9-in. baking dish. Drizzle with lemon juice and remaining 2 tsp. oil. Sprinkle with seasoning blend.
2. In a small bowl, combine the egg, ricotta cheese and spinach; spoon over fillets. Sprinkle with Parmesan cheese.
3. Bake until fish just begins to flake easily with a fork, 15-20 minutes. If desired, serve with lemon wedges and additional Parmesan cheese.
1 FILLET WITH ⅓ CUP SPINACH MIXTURE 249 cal., 13g fat (4g sat. fat), 122mg chol., 307mg sod., 4g carb. (1g sugars, 1g fiber), 29g pro.

FAVORITE DEEP-DISH PIZZA

My kids love to get pizza delivered, but it's expensive and not very healthy. I came up with a one-bowl pizza that is healthier than takeout and allows the kids to add the toppings of their choice.

—Sara Lafountain, Rockville, MD

PREP: 20 min. • **BAKE:** 20 min. • **MAKES:** 8 servings

1¾ cups whole wheat flour
1¾ cups all-purpose flour
2 pkg. (¼ oz. each) quick-rise yeast
4 tsp. sugar
1 tsp. salt
1½ cups warm water (120° to 130°)
¼ cup olive oil
1 can (8 oz.) pizza sauce
8 oz. fresh mozzarella cheese, sliced
2 cups shredded Italian cheese blend
½ tsp. dried oregano
½ tsp. Italian seasoning
   Optional: Sliced red onion, chopped green pepper, fresh oregano and crushed red pepper flakes

1. In a large bowl, combine wheat flour, 1 cup all-purpose flour, yeast, sugar and salt. Add water and oil; beat until smooth. Stir in enough remaining flour to form a soft dough. Press dough onto the bottom and up the sides of a greased 13x9-in. baking dish.

2. Spread with the pizza sauce. Top with mozzarella slices. Sprinkle with shredded cheese, oregano and Italian seasoning. If desired, top with red onion and green pepper. Bake, uncovered, at 400° for 20-25 minutes or until golden brown. Sprinkle with fresh oregano and crushed red pepper flakes on top as desired.

1 PIECE 449 cal., 20g fat (9g sat. fat), 42mg chol., 646mg sod., 47g carb. (4g sugars, 5g fiber), 19g pro.

5i
RAVIOLI CASSEROLE

The whole family will love this yummy dish that tastes like lasagna without all the fuss. Timesaving ingredients like prepared spaghetti sauce and frozen ravioli make it a cinch to put together. Children can help you assemble this one.

—Mary Ann Rothert, Austin, TX

PREP: 10 min. • **BAKE:** 30 min. • **MAKES:** 8 servings

1 pkg. (20 oz.) refrigerated cheese ravioli
3½ cups pasta sauce
2 cups small-curd 4% cottage cheese
4 cups shredded mozzarella cheese
¼ cup grated Parmesan cheese
   Minced fresh parsley, optional

1. Preheat the oven to 350°. Prepare ravioli according to package directions; drain. Spread 1 cup pasta sauce in an ungreased 13x9-in. baking dish. Layer with half the ravioli, 1¼ cups sauce, 1 cup cottage cheese and 2 cups mozzarella cheese. Repeat layers. Sprinkle with Parmesan cheese.

2. Bake, uncovered, 30-40 minutes or until bubbly. Let stand for 5-10 minutes before serving. If desired, sprinkle with fresh parsley.

1 CUP 518 cal., 25g fat (12g sat. fat), 88mg chol., 1411mg sod., 44g carb. (13g sugars, 5g fiber), 30g pro.

LIGHT-BUT-HEARTY TUNA CASSEROLE

My boyfriend grew up loving his mom's tuna casserole and says he can't even tell that this one is so light! We have it at least once a month. I usually serve it with a salad, but it has enough veggies to stand on its own.

—Heidi Carofano, Brooklyn, NY

PREP: 20 min. • **BAKE:** 25 min. • **MAKES:** 4 servings

- 3 cups uncooked yolk-free noodles
- 1 can (10¾ oz.) reduced-fat reduced-sodium condensed cream of mushroom soup, undiluted
- ½ cup fat-free milk
- 2 Tbsp. reduced-fat mayonnaise
- ½ tsp. ground mustard
- 1 jar (6 oz.) sliced mushrooms, drained
- 1 can (5 oz.) albacore white tuna in water
- ¼ cup chopped roasted sweet red pepper

TOPPING
- ¼ cup dry bread crumbs
- 1 Tbsp. butter, melted
- ½ tsp. paprika
- ¼ tsp. Italian seasoning
- ¼ tsp. pepper

1. Preheat oven to 400°. Cook noodles according to package directions.

2. In a large bowl, combine soup, milk, mayonnaise and mustard. Stir in the mushrooms, tuna and red pepper. Drain noodles; add to soup mixture and stir until blended. Transfer to a greased 8-in. square baking dish.

3. Combine topping ingredients; sprinkle over casserole. Bake 25-30 minutes or until bubbly.

1½ CUPS 322 cal., 9g fat (3g sat. fat), 32mg chol., 843mg sod., 39g carb. (7g sugars, 4g fiber), 18g pro.

PUMP UP THE VEGGIES

Love mushrooms? Instead of the jarred ones called for in this recipe, stir ½ lb. of sliced white or baby portobello mushrooms into the egg noodles during the last 5 minutes of cooking.

OVER-THE-RAINBOW
MINESTRONE, 218

209

194

179

SLOW COOKER

MOROCCAN APRICOT CHICKEN

Chili sauce, apricots and Moroccan seasoning create an incredible sauce for slow-cooked chicken thighs. Traditional Moroccan apricot chicken typically includes chili pepper paste, but I use chili sauce in my version.

—Arlene Erlbach, Morton Grove, IL

PREP: 25 min. • **COOK:** 4¼ hours • **MAKES:** 6 servings

1 tsp. olive oil
½ cup slivered almonds
6 bone-in chicken thighs (about 2¼ lbs.)
¾ cup chili sauce
½ cup apricot preserves
½ cup dried apricots, quartered
4 tsp. Moroccan seasoning (ras el hanout)
1 Tbsp. vanilla extract
1½ tsp. garlic powder
1 can (15 oz.) garbanzo beans or chickpeas, rinsed and drained
¼ cup orange juice
Chopped fresh parsley, optional

1. In a large skillet, heat oil over medium heat. Add almonds; cook and stir until lightly browned, 2-3 minutes. Remove with a slotted spoon; drain on paper towels. In the same skillet, brown the chicken on both sides. Remove from heat. Transfer chicken to a 4- or 5-qt. slow cooker. Stir chili sauce, preserves, apricots, Moroccan seasoning, vanilla and garlic powder into drippings. Pour over chicken.

2. Cook, covered, on low 4-4½ hours or until a thermometer inserted in chicken reads 170°-175°. Stir in garbanzo beans and orange juice. Cook, covered, on low until heated through, 15-30 minutes longer. Serve with almonds. If desired, sprinkle with parsley.

1 CHICKEN THIGH WITH ¾ CUP GARBANZO BEAN MIXTURE 482 cal., 21g fat (4g sat. fat), 81mg chol., 633mg sod., 47g carb. (27g sugars, 5g fiber), 28g pro.

"I made a quick version of this with boneless chicken thighs on the stovetop and it was SO easy and delicious. I love that you could also easily omit the chicken and double the chickpeas for a vegan version. It's definitely going in the regular rotation!"

—LEANNA321, TASTEOFHOME.COM

SWEET & SPICY PINEAPPLE CHICKEN SANDWICHES

My kids often ask for chicken sloppy joes, and this version has a bonus of sweet pineapple. It is a perfect recipe to double for a potluck. Try topping the sandwiches with smoked Gouda cheese.

—Nancy Heishman, Las Vegas, NV

PREP: 15 min. • **COOK:** 2¾ hours • **MAKES:** 8 servings

2½ lbs. boneless skinless chicken breasts
1 bottle (18 oz.) sweet and spicy barbecue sauce, divided
2 Tbsp. honey mustard
1 can (8 oz.) unsweetened crushed pineapple, undrained
8 hamburger buns, split and toasted
Optional: Bibb lettuce leaves and thinly sliced red onion

1. Place chicken breasts in a 4-qt. slow cooker. Combine ¼ cup barbecue sauce and the mustard; pour over chicken. Cover and cook on low 2½-3 hours or until chicken is tender.
2. Remove chicken; discard liquid. Shred the chicken with 2 forks; return to slow cooker. Add the crushed pineapple and remaining barbecue sauce; cover and cook on high for 15 minutes.
3. Serve on toasted buns. If desired, add lettuce and onion.

FREEZE OPTION Place shredded chicken in freezer containers. Cool and freeze. To use, partially thaw in refrigerator overnight. Heat through in a covered saucepan, stirring occasionally; add broth or water if necessary.
1 SANDWICH 415 cal., 6g fat (1g sat. fat), 78mg chol., 973mg sod., 56g carb. (30g sugars, 2g fiber), 34g pro.

TURKEY TACO MACARONI

Ground turkey and taco seasoning make for a nice twist on a classic dish. If you love cheese, feel free to add more. When we're in the mood to toss in some veggies, green peppers are terrific additions.

—Barb Kondolf, Hamlin, NY

PREP: 15 min. • **COOK:** 3 hours + standing • **MAKES:** 10 servings

2 Tbsp. canola oil, divided
4 cups uncooked elbow macaroni
2 lbs. ground turkey
1 medium onion, chopped
4 cans (8 oz. each) tomato sauce
1 cup water
1 cup salsa
1 envelope taco seasoning
2 cups shredded cheddar cheese

1. In a large skillet, heat 1 Tbsp. oil over medium heat. Add pasta; cook and stir 2-3 minutes or until pasta is toasted. Transfer to a 5-qt. slow cooker. In the same skillet, heat remaining 1 Tbsp. oil over medium-high heat. Add turkey and onion; cook and stir until turkey is no longer pink, breaking it into crumbles, 6-8 minutes.

2. Transfer to slow cooker. Stir in tomato sauce, water, salsa and taco seasoning. Cover and cook on low 3-4 hours or until pasta is tender.
3. Remove insert; top with cheese. Let stand, covered, 15 minutes.
1 CUP 402 cal., 19g fat (6g sat. fat), 83mg chol., 1063mg sod., 32g carb. (4g sugars, 3g fiber), 29g pro.

SWEET & SPICY PINEAPPLE CHICKEN SANDWICHES

CURRY COCONUT CHICKEN

My husband and I love this yummy dish! It's a breeze to prepare in the slow cooker, and it tastes just like a meal you'd have at your favorite Indian or Thai restaurant.

—Andi Kauffman, Beavercreek, OR

PREP: 20 min. • **COOK:** 4 hours • **MAKES:** 2 servings

1 medium potato, peeled and cubed
¼ cup chopped onion
2 boneless skinless chicken breast halves (4 oz. each)
½ cup light coconut milk
2 tsp. curry powder
1 garlic clove, minced
½ tsp. reduced-sodium chicken bouillon granules
⅛ tsp. salt
⅛ tsp. pepper
1 cup hot cooked rice
1 green onion, thinly sliced
    Optional: Raisins, shredded coconut and chopped unsalted peanuts

1. Place potatoes and onion in a 1½- or 2-qt. slow cooker. In a large skillet coated with cooking spray, brown chicken on both sides. Transfer to slow cooker.

2. In a small bowl, combine the coconut milk, curry, garlic, bouillon, salt and pepper; pour over chicken. Cover and cook on low 4-5 hours or until meat is tender.

3. Serve chicken and sauce with rice; sprinkle with green onion. If desired, garnish with raisins, coconut and peanuts.

1 SERVING 353 cal., 7g fat (4g sat. fat), 63mg chol., 266mg sod., 42g carb. (3g sugars, 3g fiber), 27g pro.

DIY CURRY POWDER

Many cooks prefer making their own curry powder. Here's a basic recipe you can start with, then customize as you see fit. In a spice grinder or with a mortar and pestle, combine the seeds from 3 cardamom pods, 2 tsp. each ground coriander and cumin, 1 tsp. ground turmeric, ½ tsp. chili powder, ½ tsp. pepper and ⅛ tsp. ground fennel seed. Grind until mixture has a fine powderlike consistency. Store in an airtight container for up to a year.

CHICKEN & RED POTATOES

Try this juicy and tender chicken-and-potato dish with scrumptious gravy tonight! Just fix it earlier in the day, then forget about it until mealtime.

—Michele Trantham, Waynesville, NC

- -

PREP: 20 min. • **COOK:** 3½ hours • **MAKES:** 4 servings

- -

3 Tbsp. all-purpose flour
4 boneless skinless chicken breast halves (6 oz. each)
2 Tbsp. olive oil
4 medium red potatoes, cut into wedges
2 cups fresh baby carrots, halved lengthwise
1 can (4 oz.) mushroom stems and pieces, drained
4 canned whole green chiles, cut into ½-in. slices
1 can (10¾ oz.) condensed cream of onion soup, undiluted
¼ cup 2% milk
½ tsp. chicken seasoning
¼ tsp. salt
¼ tsp. dried rosemary, crushed
¼ tsp. pepper

1. Place flour in a large bowl or dish. Add chicken, 1 piece at a time; toss to coat. In a large skillet, brown chicken in oil on both sides.

2. Meanwhile, place the potatoes, carrots, mushrooms and chiles in a greased 5-qt. slow cooker. In a small bowl, combine remaining ingredients. Pour half of soup mixture over the vegetables.

3. Transfer chicken to slow cooker; top with remaining soup mixture. Cover and cook on low for 3½-4 hours or until a thermometer inserted in the chicken reads 165°.

NOTE This recipe was tested with McCormick's Montreal Chicken Seasoning. Look for it in the spice aisle.

1 CHICKEN BREAST HALF WITH 1½ CUPS VEGETABLES 451 cal., 15g fat (3g sat. fat), 105mg chol., 1046mg sod., 38g carb. (8g sugars, 4g fiber), 40g pro.

BUFFALO CHICKEN CHILI

This Buffalo chicken chili is rich in the best way. The cream cheese, blue cheese and tangy hot sauce join forces for a dinner recipe everyone will love.

—Peggy Woodward, Shullsburg, WI

PREP: 10 min. • **COOK:** 5½ hours
MAKES: 6 servings (about 2 qt.)

- 1 can (15½ oz.) navy beans, rinsed and drained
- 1 can (14½ oz.) chicken broth
- 1 can (14½ oz.) fire-roasted diced tomatoes
- 1 can (8 oz.) tomato sauce
- ½ cup Buffalo wing sauce
- ½ tsp. onion powder
- ½ tsp. garlic powder
- 1 lb. boneless skinless chicken breast halves
- 1 pkg. (8 oz.) cream cheese, cubed and softened
  Optional toppings: Crumbled blue cheese, chopped celery and chopped green onions

1. In a 4- or 5-qt. slow cooker, combine first 7 ingredients. Add chicken. Cover and cook on low 5-6 hours or until chicken is tender.

2. Remove chicken; shred with 2 forks. Return to slow cooker. Stir in cream cheese. Cover and cook on low until cheese is melted, about 30 minutes. Stir until blended. Serve with toppings as desired.

1¼ CUPS 337 cal., 16g fat (8g sat. fat), 80mg chol., 1586mg sod., 25g carb. (5g sugars, 5g fiber), 25g pro.

SLOW-COOKER CHICKEN TIKKA MASALA

Just a small dash of garam marsala adds lots of flavor. The bright red sauce coats the caramelized chicken beautifully.

—Anwar Khan, Iriving, TX

PREP: 25 min. • **COOK:** 3 hours 10 min. • **MAKES:** 4 servings

1   can (15 oz.) tomato puree
1   small onion, grated
3   garlic cloves, minced
2   Tbsp. tomato paste
1   tsp. grated lemon zest
1   Tbsp. lemon juice
1   tsp. hot pepper sauce
1   Tbsp. canola oil
1   tsp. curry powder
1   tsp. salt
¼   tsp. pepper
¼   tsp. garam masala
4   bone-in chicken thighs
3   Tbsp. plain Greek yogurt, plus more for topping
1   Tbsp. unsalted butter, melted
    Optional: Chopped cilantro and grated lemon zest
    Hot cooked rice

1. Combine first 12 ingredients in a 3- or 4-qt. slow cooker. Add chicken thighs and stir gently to coat. Cook, covered, on low 3-4 hours or until chicken is tender.

2. Preheat broiler. Using a slotted spoon, transfer chicken to a broiler-safe baking pan lined with foil. Broil 4-6 in. from heat for 3-4 minutes on each side or until lightly charred.

3. Meanwhile, transfer cooking juices from the slow cooker to a saucepan. Cook, uncovered, over medium-high heat until slightly thickened, 6-8 minutes. Remove from heat and gently stir in yogurt and butter. Serve chicken with sauce. If desired, garnish with chopped cilantro, lemon zest and additional yogurt. Serve with hot cooked rice.

1 CHICKEN THIGH 364 cal., 22g fat (7g sat. fat), 91mg chol., 705mg sod., 12g carb. (4g sugars, 3g fiber), 25g pro.

DID YOU KNOW?

Although tikka masala is inspired by Indian cuisine, it's far more popular in Great Britain, where it is rumored to have originated.

MEXICAN CHICKEN CHILI

Corn and black beans give this satisfying chili Mexican flair the whole family will love. Adjust the cayenne if you have small children or are looking for a little less zip.

—Stephanie Rabbitt-Schapp, Cincinnati, OH

PREP: 30 min. • **COOK:** 5 hours. • **MAKES:** 6 servings (2 qt.)

- 1   lb. boneless skinless chicken breasts, cubed
- 1   Tbsp. canola oil
- 2   cans (14½ oz. each) diced tomatoes, undrained
- 2   cups frozen corn
- 1   can (15 oz.) black beans, rinsed and drained
- 1   can (14½ oz.) reduced-sodium chicken broth
- 1   can (4 oz.) chopped green chiles
- 2   Tbsp. chili powder
- 1   Tbsp. ground cumin
- ½   tsp. salt
- ¼   tsp. cayenne pepper

In a large skillet, brown chicken in oil. Transfer to a 5-qt. slow cooker. Stir in remaining ingredients. Cover and cook on low until chicken is no longer pink, 5-6 hours.

1⅓ CUPS 254 cal., 5g fat (1g sat. fat), 42mg chol., 843mg sod., 31g carb. (6g sugars, 8g fiber), 23g pro.

ITALIAN TURKEY SANDWICHES

I hope you enjoy these tasty turkey sandwiches as much as our family does. The recipe makes plenty, so it's great for potlucks. Plus, the leftovers are just as good.

—Carol Riley, Ossian, IN

PREP: 10 min. • **COOK:** 5 hours • **MAKES:** 12 sandwiches

- 1   bone-in turkey breast (6 lbs.), skin removed
- 1   medium onion, chopped
- 1   small green pepper, chopped
- ¼   cup chili sauce
- 3   Tbsp. white vinegar
- 2   Tbsp. dried oregano or Italian seasoning
- 4   tsp. beef bouillon granules
- 12 kaiser or hard rolls, split

1. Place turkey breast in a greased 5-qt. slow cooker. Add onion and green pepper.
2. Combine chili sauce, vinegar, oregano and bouillon; pour over the turkey and vegetables. Cover and cook on low until turkey is tender, 5-6 hours.
3. Shred turkey with 2 forks and return to the slow cooker; heat through. Spoon ½ cup onto each roll.
FREEZE OPTION Place the cooled meat and its juices in freezer containers. To use, partially thaw in the refrigerator overnight. Microwave, covered, on high in a microwave-safe dish until heated through, stirring gently; add water if necessary.

1 SANDWICH 374 cal., 4g fat (1g sat. fat), 118mg chol., 724mg sod., 34g carb. (3g sugars, 2g fiber), 49g pro. **DIABETIC EXCHANGES** 6 lean meat, 2 starch.

"Absolutely delicious! I had a boneless turkey breast that was 3 lbs., so I cut all ingredients in half and cooked on low for 3 hours in my 4-qt. crockpot. The meat turned out perfect. My family has already requested that I make it again."

—LMMANDA, TASTEOFHOME.COM

MEXICAN CHICKEN CHILI

SLOW-COOKER RANCH CHICKEN

This is a fabulous recipe that we have passed around to all our friends, especially those who have young children. It's wonderful for a cold winter night or a hot summer day when you don't want to turn on the oven. Serve it as a weeknight family dinner or for a large group.

—Sonya Stark, West Jordan, UT

PREP: 10 min. • **COOK:** 7 hours • **MAKES:** 8 servings

¾ cup chicken broth
1 envelope ranch salad dressing mix
2 lbs. boneless skinless chicken breast halves
1 can (10½ oz.) condensed cream of chicken soup, undiluted
1 pkg. (8 oz.) cream cheese, cubed and softened
Hot cooked noodles or rice
Optional: Shredded cheddar cheese, crumbled cooked bacon and chopped green onions

1. In a 4- or 5-qt. slow cooker, combine broth and dressing mix; add chicken. Cover and cook on low for 6 hours. Remove chicken to cutting board; shred with 2 forks and return to slow cooker.
2. Stir in soup and cream cheese. Cover and cook on low until cream cheese is melted, about 30 minutes. Serve over noodles or rice. Add optional toppings as desired.

⅔ CUP 267 cal., 15g fat (7g sat. fat), 94mg chol., 776mg sod., 7g carb. (1g sugars, 1g fiber), 25g pro.

RANCH CHICKEN TIPS

Can you put frozen chicken in the slow cooker?
No, it's not safe to put frozen chicken in the slow cooker. The slow heat can keep the meat at unsafe temperatures, encouraging bacteria growth. Thaw the chicken overnight in the fridge or, for quicker thawing, under cold running water.

Can you cook this recipe on high for less time?
Yes, you can cook it on high for a faster meal. Cook the chicken, broth and dressing mix on high for 3 hours, then continue with the recipe as directed.

Can you make ranch chicken on the stove?
Yes, though the chicken might not be as tender as it would get in a slow cooker. In a medium saucepan, simmer the chicken with broth and ranch dressing mix, covered, until cooked through. Shred the chicken, add condensed soup and cream cheese, and cook on low until the cheese melts, stirring occasionally.

What can you serve with Slow-Cooker Ranch Chicken?
Pair it with fresh sides like steamed broccoli with lemon or a simple salad. Garlic bread also makes a great addition for sopping up the creamy sauce.

SLOW-COOKED LEMON CHICKEN ORZO

This lemon chicken orzo is reminiscent of what you get at a Greek restaurant. The only challenge is waiting the two hours while it's cooking!

—Laura Wilhelm, Los Angeles County, CA

PREP: 20 min. • **COOK:** 2 hours • **MAKES:** 4 servings

2 Tbsp. canola oil
1 lb. boneless skinless chicken thighs, cut into 1-in. pieces
1½ cups chicken stock
2 tsp. Greek seasoning
½ tsp. garlic powder
1 cup uncooked orzo pasta
⅓ cup chopped pitted Greek olives
¼ cup julienned soft sun-dried tomatoes (not packed in oil)
2 cups fresh baby spinach
½ cup crumbled garlic and herb feta cheese
1 medium lemon, zested and juiced
1 Tbsp. snipped fresh dill
1 tsp. lemon-pepper seasoning, optional

1. In a large skillet, heat oil over medium-high heat. Brown chicken in batches. Transfer to a 4-qt. slow cooker. Add the stock, Greek seasoning and garlic powder to skillet, scraping up any brown bits from pan; add to slow cooker. Cover and cook on high 1½ hours.

2. Stir in orzo, olives and sun-dried tomatoes into slow cooker, making sure orzo is submerged in liquid. Cover and cook on high until orzo is tender and liquid is absorbed, about 30 minutes. Add spinach, feta, lemon juice and zest, dill and, if desired, lemon pepper to slow cooker. Stir until spinach is wilted.

1 SERVING 512 cal., 22g fat (5g sat. fat), 86mg chol., 1107mg sod., 44g carb. (4g sugars, 3g fiber), 32g pro.

HOW TO GET THE MOST JUICE

Next time you need to squeeze fresh lemon juice, warm the fruit in the microwave for 7-10 seconds first. Then roll the lemon back and forth under your palm on the counter, giving it firm pressure.

Besides yielding more juice, the fruit will also be easier to squeeze. This technique works for limes and other citrus too.

ITALIAN SAUSAGE PIZZA SOUP

My mom's friend shared this recipe with her more than 50 years ago. I've tweaked it over the years, and it's still a family favorite. Warm garlic bread is heavenly on the side.

—Joan Hallford, North Richland Hills, TX

PREP: 15 min. • **COOK:** 6 hours
MAKES: 12 servings (3 qt.)

- 1   lb. Italian turkey sausage links
- 1   medium onion, chopped
- 1   medium green pepper, cut into strips
- 1   medium sweet red or yellow pepper, cut into strips
- 1   can (15 oz.) cannellini beans, rinsed and drained
- 1   can (14½ oz.) diced tomatoes, undrained
- 1   jar (14 oz.) pizza sauce
- 2   tsp. Italian seasoning
- 2   garlic cloves, minced
- 2   cans (14½ oz. each) beef broth
- 1   pkg. (5 oz.) Caesar salad croutons
     Shredded part-skim mozzarella cheese

1. Remove casings from sausage. In a large skillet over medium-high heat, cook and crumble sausage until no longer pink. Add onion and peppers; cook until crisp-tender. Drain; transfer to a 6-qt. slow cooker.
2. Add the next 5 ingredients; pour in the broth. Cook, covered, on low until vegetables are tender, 6-8 hours. Serve with croutons and cheese.

1 CUP 158 cal., 5g fat (1g sat. fat), 15mg chol., 828mg sod., 19g carb. (4g sugars, 4g fiber), 9g pro.

TACO BOWLS

We love this delicious taco-style dish because of its simple prep. Each serving is so easy to customize to everyone's individual tastes thanks to the toppings. It's become a regular when we're entertaining.

—Hope Wasylenki, Gahanna, OH

PREP: 15 min. • **COOK:** 7 hours • **MAKES:** 10 servings

1 boneless beef chuck roast (2½ lbs.), cut in half
¼ cup beef broth
1 Tbsp. canola oil
1 small onion, finely chopped
1 jalapeno pepper, seeded and finely chopped
1 garlic clove, minced
3 tsp. chili powder
1½ tsp. ground cumin
Dash salt
2 cups canned crushed tomatoes in puree
1 cup salsa verde
5 cups hot cooked brown rice
1 can (15 oz.) black beans, rinsed, drained and warmed
1 cup pico de gallo
Optional: Reduced-fat sour cream, shredded cheddar cheese, sliced avocado, lime wedges and warmed corn tortillas

1. Place beef and broth in a 5-qt. slow cooker. Cook, covered, on low 6-8 hours or until meat is tender.
2. Remove beef; discard juices. Return beef to slow cooker; shred with 2 forks.
3. In a large skillet, heat oil over medium heat; saute the onion and jalapeno until softened, 3-4 minutes. Add garlic and seasonings; cook and stir 1 minute. Stir in tomatoes and salsa; bring to a boil. Add to the beef, stirring to combine. Cook, covered, on high for 1 hour or until flavors are blended.
4. For each serving, place ½ cup rice in a soup bowl. Top with beef mixture, beans and pico de gallo. Serve with optional ingredients as desired.

FREEZE OPTION Freeze cooled meat mixture in freezer containers. To use, partially thaw in refrigerator overnight. Heat through in a saucepan, stirring occasionally.

NOTE Wear disposable gloves when cutting hot peppers; the oils can burn skin. Avoid touching your face.

1 SERVING 389 cal., 13g fat (5g sat. fat), 74mg chol., 550mg sod., 38g carb. (4g sugars, 5g fiber), 28g pro. **DIABETIC EXCHANGES** 3 lean meat, 2½ starch, ½ fat.

"A good-tasting meal! This can easily be converted into a stovetop recipe using ground beef instead of pot roast. Make sure you use some or all of the suggested fixings—they add some great flavors and textures!"

—NH-RESCUE, TASTEOFHOME.COM

SLOW-COOKER SHORT RIB RAGU

An irresistible sauce gives this beef another dimension of flavor. Nearly any starchy side, such as potatoes or polenta, will work in place of the pasta. Short ribs are my crowd-pleaser weekend meal for all occasions.

—Missy Raho, Morristown, NJ

PREP: 30 min. • **COOK:** 7 hours • **MAKES:** 12 servings

1 Tbsp. olive oil
2 lbs. boneless beef short ribs, cut into 2-in. pieces
8 oz. sliced mushrooms
1 small onion, chopped
2 small carrots, peeled and chopped
2 bay leaves
1 can (12 oz.) tomato paste
½ cup dry red wine
3 garlic cloves, minced
1 Tbsp. Italian seasoning
1 tsp. crushed red pepper flakes
½ tsp. salt
½ tsp. pepper
1 can (28 oz.) diced tomatoes, undrained
1 lb. pappardelle
Grated or shaved Parmesan cheese, optional

1. In a large skillet, heat the oil over medium-high heat; brown the meat in batches. Transfer meat to a 5- or 6-qt. slow cooker. Add mushrooms, onion, carrots and bay leaves.
2. Add tomato paste, wine, garlic and seasonings to the skillet. Cook and stir over medium heat until fragrant and slightly darkened, 2-4 minutes. Stir in diced tomatoes until blended. Transfer mixture to slow cooker; cover. Cook on low until the beef is tender, 7-9 hours. Discard bay leaves.
3. Cook pasta according to the package directions for al dente. Serve ragu over pasta. If desired, serve with Parmesan cheese.

¾ CUP RAGU OVER ¾ CUP PASTA
302 cal., 8g fat (3g sat. fat), 31mg chol., 328mg sod., 39g carb. (7g sugars, 4g fiber), 18g pro.

SLOW-COOKER
KOREAN BEEF

SLOW-COOKER KOREAN BEEF

My husband and I recently discovered a love for Korean food. I developed this recipe to give us the flavors we enjoy in an ordinary cut of meat.

—Lisa Renshaw, Kansas City, MO

PREP: 15 min. • COOK: 9½ hours • MAKES: 10 servings

½ cup packed brown sugar
⅓ cup gluten-free tamari soy sauce
¼ cup Sriracha chili sauce
3 Tbsp. minced garlic
3 Tbsp. minced fresh gingerroot
2 Tbsp. rice vinegar
1 Tbsp. fish sauce or additional soy sauce
1 Tbsp. sesame oil
½ tsp. crushed red pepper flakes
1 boneless beef chuck roast (4 lbs.)
1 medium onion, chopped
4 Tbsp. cornstarch
¼ cup reduced-sodium beef broth
Optional: Hot cooked rice and sliced green onions

1. In a small bowl, whisk the first 9 ingredients. Place the roast and onion in a 5- or 6-qt. slow cooker; top with the brown sugar mixture. Cook, covered, on low until the beef is tender, 9-10 hours.
2. In a small bowl, mix cornstarch and broth until smooth; gradually stir into the slow cooker. Cook, covered, on high until the sauce is thickened, about 30 minutes. If desired, serve with rice and top with sliced green onion.

FREEZE OPTION Place beef in a 13x9-in. baking dish; top with sauce. Cool; cover and freeze. To use, partially thaw in the refrigerator overnight. Remove from refrigerator 30 minutes before baking. Preheat oven to 350°. Reheat the beef, covered, until a thermometer inserted in center reads 165°, 25-30 minutes.
5 OZ. COOKED BEEF 402 cal., 18g fat (7g sat. fat), 118mg chol., 966mg sod., 19g carb. (14g sugars, 0 fiber), 37g pro.

5i

SLOW-COOKED SWISS STEAK

I like to flour and season the steaks and refrigerate them overnight. The next morning, I put all the ingredients in the slow cooker, and return home to a delicious dinner.

—Sarah Burks, Wathena, KS

PREP: 10 min. • COOK: 6 hours • MAKES: 6 servings

2 Tbsp. all-purpose flour
½ tsp. salt
¼ tsp. pepper
1½ lbs. beef round steak, cut into 6 pieces
1 medium onion, cut into ¼-in. slices
1 celery rib, cut into ½-in. slices
2 cans (8 oz. each) tomato sauce

1. In a bowl or shallow dish, combine the flour, salt and pepper. Add steak and turn to coat.
2. Place the onion in a greased 3-qt. slow cooker. Top with steak, celery and tomato sauce. Cover and cook on low for 6-8 hours or until meat is tender.

1 SERVING 171 cal., 4g fat (1g sat. fat), 64mg chol., 409mg sod., 6g carb. (2g sugars, 1g fiber), 27g pro. **DIABETIC EXCHANGES** 3 lean meat, 1 vegetable.

POLYNESIAN ROAST BEEF

This marvelous recipe from my sister has been a family favorite for years. Pineapple and peppers add a perfect contrast to the rich and savory beef.

—Annette Mosbarger, Peyton, CO

PREP: 15 min. • **COOK:** 7 hours
MAKES: 10 servings

- 1 beef top round roast (3¼ lbs.)
- 2 Tbsp. browning sauce, optional
- ¼ cup all-purpose flour
- 1 tsp. salt
- ¼ tsp. pepper
- 1 medium onion, sliced
- 1 can (8 oz.) unsweetened sliced pineapple
- ¼ cup packed brown sugar
- 2 Tbsp. cornstarch
- ¼ tsp. ground ginger
- ½ cup beef broth
- ¼ cup reduced-sodium soy sauce
- ½ tsp. minced garlic
- 1 medium green pepper, sliced

1. Cut roast in half; brush with browning sauce if desired. Combine the flour, salt and pepper; rub over meat. Place onion in a 3-qt. slow cooker; top with roast.
2. Drain pineapple, reserving the juice; refrigerate the pineapple slices. In a small bowl, combine the brown sugar, cornstarch and ginger; whisk in the broth, soy sauce, garlic and reserved pineapple juice until smooth. Pour over meat. Cook, covered, on low for 6 hours.
3. Add the pineapple and green pepper. Cook until tender, 1-2 hours longer.
4 OZ. COOKED BEEF 253 cal., 5g fat (2g sat. fat), 82mg chol., 560mg sod., 16g carb. (10g sugars, 1g fiber), 34g pro.

SMOTHERED ROUND STEAK

Try affordable round steak and gravy served over egg noodles for a hearty meal. Packed with veggies, this meaty slow-cooker creation will take the worry out of wondering what's for dinner.

—Kathy Garrett, Camden, WV

PREP: 15 min. • **COOK:** 6 hours
MAKES: 4 servings

- 1½ lbs. beef top round steak, cut into strips
- ⅓ cup all-purpose flour
- ½ tsp. salt
- ¼ tsp. pepper
- 1 large onion, sliced
- 1 large green pepper, sliced
- 1 can (14½ oz.) diced tomatoes, undrained
- 1 jar (4 oz.) sliced mushrooms, drained
- 3 Tbsp. reduced-sodium soy sauce
- 2 Tbsp. molasses
  Hot cooked egg noodles, optional

1. In a 3-qt. slow cooker, toss the beef with flour, salt and pepper. Stir in all the remaining ingredients except noodles.
2. Cook, covered, on low until the meat is tender, 6-8 hours. If desired, serve with noodles.
1¼ CUPS BEEF MIXTURE 335 cal., 6g fat (2g sat. fat), 95mg chol., 1064mg sod., 28g carb. (14g sugars, 4g fiber), 42g pro.

CHICAGO-STYLE BEEF ROLLS

I have fond memories of eating these big, messy sandwiches at a neighbor's house when I was growing up. Freeze any extras and save for another meal!

—Trisha Kruse, Eagle, ID

PREP: 20 min. • **COOK:** 8 hours • **MAKES:** 16 servings

- 1 boneless beef chuck roast (4 to 5 lbs.)
- 1 Tbsp. olive oil
- 3 cups beef broth
- 1 medium onion, chopped
- 1 pkg. Italian salad dressing mix
- 3 garlic cloves, minced
- 1 Tbsp. Italian seasoning
- ½ tsp. crushed red pepper flakes
- 16 hoagie buns, split
  Optional: Sliced pepperoncini and pickled red pepper rings

1. Brown the roast in oil on all sides in a large skillet; drain. Transfer beef to a 5-qt. slow cooker. Combine the broth, onion, dressing mix, garlic, Italian seasoning and pepper flakes in a large bowl; pour over roast.

2. Cover and cook on low for 8-10 hours or until tender. Remove meat; cool slightly. Skim fat from cooking juices. Shred beef with 2 forks and return to slow cooker; heat through. Using a slotted spoon, place ½ cup on each roll. Serve with pepperoncini and pepper rings if desired.

1 SANDWICH 418 cal., 16g fat (5g sat. fat), 74mg chol., 771mg sod., 36g carb. (6g sugars, 1g fiber), 31g pro.

"Very good and easy to throw together. I did not brown the meat before putting it in the crockpot, but it was still yummy."

—ALLISONO, TASTEOFHOME.COM

SLOW-COOKER MONGOLIAN BEEF

This dish uses inexpensive ingredients to offer big flavor in a small amount of time. The slow cooker makes easy work of it as well—easier than getting takeout!

—*Taste of Home* Test Kitchen

PREP: 10 min. • **COOK:** 4¼ hours • **MAKES:** 4 servings

- ¾ cup reduced-sodium chicken broth
- 2 Tbsp. reduced-sodium soy sauce
- 1 Tbsp. hoisin sauce
- 2 tsp. minced fresh gingerroot
- 2 tsp. sesame oil
- 1 tsp. minced garlic
- ½ tsp. salt
- ¼ tsp. crushed red pepper flakes
- 1 lb. beef flank steak, cut into thin strips

- 2 Tbsp. cornstarch
- 2 Tbsp. water
- 2 cups hot cooked rice
- 5 green onions, cut into 1-in. pieces
  Sesame seeds, optional

1. In a 4- or 5-qt. slow cooker, combine the first 8 ingredients. Add the beef and toss to coat. Cook, covered, on low 4-5 hours or until meat is tender.

2. In a small bowl, mix cornstarch and water until smooth; gradually stir into beef. Cook, covered, on high until sauce is thickened, 15-30 minutes. Serve over hot cooked rice. Sprinkle with green onion and, if desired, sesame seeds.

1 SERVING 329 cal., 11g fat (4g sat. fat), 54mg chol., 530mg sod., 30g carb. (2g sugars, 1g fiber), 26g pro.

CHICAGO-STYLE
BEEF ROLLS

SLOW-COOKER CUBED STEAK

Easy and inexpensive, this recipe is perfect for those busy nights when you want something delicious yet simple. Tender steak is covered in a thick gravy sauce that uses cream of mushroom soup, beef broth and onion soup mix to give it that comforting taste.

—Julie Andrews, Rockford, MI

PREP: 10 min. • **COOK:** 1½ hours
MAKES: 4 servings

- 2 cans (10½ oz. each) condensed cream of mushroom soup, undiluted
- 1½ cups beef broth, divided
- 1 envelope (1 oz.) onion soup mix
- 4 beef cubed steaks (6 oz. each)
- 2 Tbsp. cornstarch
  Cooked egg noodles or mashed potatoes, optional

1. In a 6-qt. slow cooker, stir together soup, 1 cup broth and onion soup mix until combined. Add the cubed steaks. Cook on high 3 hours or low 6 hours.
2. In a small bowl, whisk together the remaining ½ cup broth and cornstarch until dissolved. Stir in the cornstarch mixture; cook until sauce is thickened, 30-35 minutes longer. Serve over egg noodles or mashed potatoes, if desired.
1 STEAK WITH GRAVY 381 cal., 13g fat (3g sat. fat), 101mg chol., 2118mg sod., 20g carb. (2g sugars, 3g fiber), 41g pro.

SLOPPY JOE TATER TOT CASSEROLE

This simple casserole is an easy dinner for both you and the kids. Serve with carrot and celery sticks for a fuss-free feast. You can also stir in some spicy brown mustard if the adults want a bit more zing.

—Laura Wilhelm, West Hollywood, CA

PREP: 20 min. • **COOK:** 4 hours + standing • **MAKES:** 10 servings

1 bag (32 oz.) frozen Tater Tots, divided
2 lbs. ground beef or turkey
1 can (15 oz.) tomato sauce
1 bottle (8 oz.) sweet chili sauce
2 Tbsp. packed brown sugar
1 Tbsp. Worcestershire sauce
1 Tbsp. dried minced garlic
1 Tbsp. dried minced onion
½ tsp. salt
½ tsp. pepper
1¼ cups shredded Colby-Monterey Jack cheese
¼ tsp. paprika

1. Place half the Tater Tots in the bottom of a 5-qt. slow cooker.

2. In a large skillet, cook the beef over medium-high heat until no longer pink, 5-6 minutes, breaking into crumbles; drain. Stir in the next 8 ingredients; reduce heat and simmer 2-3 minutes. Place the beef mixture in slow cooker; top with the remaining Tater Tots. Cook, covered, on low 4 hours.

3. Top with the cheese and sprinkle with paprika. Let stand, uncovered, 15 minutes before serving.

1 CUP 466 cal., 24g fat (9g sat. fat), 69mg chol., 1332mg sod., 41g carb. (18g sugars, 4g fiber), 22g pro.

SLOW-COOKER ENCHILADAS

When you crave southwestern food but don't want to spend time preparing it in the evening, this recipe will come in handy. It's a sensational supper for busy weeknights.

—Mary Luebbert, Benton, KS

PREP: 30 min. • **COOK:** 5 hours • **MAKES:** 4 servings

1 lb. ground beef
1 cup chopped onion
½ cup chopped green pepper
1 can (16 oz.) pinto or kidney beans, rinsed and drained
1 can (15 oz.) black beans, rinsed and drained
1 can (10 oz.) diced tomatoes and green chiles, undrained
⅓ cup water
1 tsp. chili powder
½ tsp. ground cumin
½ tsp. salt
¼ tsp. pepper
1 cup shredded sharp cheddar cheese
1 cup shredded Monterey Jack cheese
6 flour tortillas (6 in.)
Optional: Chopped tomatoes, minced fresh cilantro and sliced avocado

1. In a large skillet, cook the beef, onion and green pepper until meat is no longer pink; drain. Add the next 8 ingredients; bring to a boil. Reduce heat; cover and simmer 10 minutes. In a bowl, combine cheeses.

2. In a 5-qt. slow cooker, layer about ¾ cup beef mixture, 1 tortilla and about ⅓ cup cheese. Repeat layers 5 times. Cover and cook on low for 5-7 hours or until heated through. If desired, serve with optional toppings.

1 SERVING 734 cal., 32g fat (16g sat. fat), 111mg chol., 1672mg sod., 62g carb. (6g sugars, 11g fiber), 49g pro.

ENCHILADA TIPS

Can you use corn tortillas for these enchiladas?
Yes, corn tortillas will work in this dish. You'll need more than 6, though, to account for corn tortillas' smaller size.

Can you use enchilada sauce in this slow-cooker recipe?
Absolutely! Substitute a 15-oz. can red enchilada sauce or 1¾ cups homemade enchilada sauce for the diced tomatoes, green chiles and spices. Adjust the seasoning to your taste.

What do you serve with Slow-Cooker Enchiladas?
Top them with sour cream, tomatoes, avocados, cilantro, green onions or sliced olives. Pair with refried beans, rice or green salad.

SLOW-COOKER GUINNESS BEEF STEW

Make this traditional Irish stew in your slow cooker! Cooking low and slow creates very tender beef and a robust flavor. The best part is that it's ready to eat after you get home from a long day.

—*Taste of Home* Test Kitchen

PREP: 30 min. • **COOK:** 7 hours • **MAKES:** 11 servings

1½ lbs. potatoes (about 3 medium), peeled and cut into 1-in. cubes
3 medium carrots, thinly sliced
2 medium onions, chopped
2 medium parsnips, peeled and thinly sliced
2 celery ribs, cut into 1-in. pieces
1 boneless beef chuck roast (3 lbs.), cut into 2-in. pieces
½ cup all-purpose flour
1¾ tsp. salt
¾ tsp. pepper
2 Tbsp. olive oil
1 can (6 oz.) tomato paste
2 garlic cloves, minced
1 bottle (12 oz.) Guinness stout or beef broth
1 can (14½ oz.) beef broth
2 tsp. minced fresh thyme or ½ tsp. dried thyme
Minced fresh parsley

1. Place the first 5 ingredients in a 5- or 6-qt. slow cooker.
2. Toss beef with flour, salt and pepper. In a large skillet, heat oil over medium-high heat. Brown the beef in batches. Transfer the beef to slow cooker with a slotted spoon. Reduce heat to medium. To same skillet, add tomato paste and garlic. Cook and stir 1 minute.
3. Add beer to skillet, stirring to loosen browned bits from pan. Transfer to slow cooker. Stir in broth and thyme.
4. Cook, covered, on low until the beef and vegetables are tender, 7-8 hours. Garnish with parsley.

1 CUP 342 cal., 14g fat (5g sat. fat), 80mg chol., 589mg sod., 25g carb. (5g sugars, 3g fiber), 28g pro. **DIABETIC EXCHANGES** 4 lean meat, 1½ starch, ½ fat.

SLOW-COOKED PEPPER STEAK

After a long day working in our greenhouse, raising bedding plants, I enjoy coming in to this hearty beef dish for supper. It's one of my favorite meals.

—Sue Gronholz, Beaver Dam, WI

PREP: 20 min. • **COOK:** 6½ hours • **MAKES:** 6 servings

1½ lbs. beef top round steak
2 Tbsp. canola oil
1 cup chopped onion
¼ cup reduced-sodium soy sauce
1 garlic clove, minced
1 tsp. sugar
½ tsp. salt
¼ tsp. ground ginger
¼ tsp. pepper
4 medium tomatoes, cut into wedges or 1 can (14½ oz.) diced tomatoes, undrained
1 large green pepper, cut into strips
1 Tbsp. cornstarch
½ cup cold water
Hot cooked noodles or rice

1. Cut beef into 3x1-in. strips. In a large skillet, brown beef in oil. Transfer to a 3-qt. slow cooker. Combine the onion, soy sauce, garlic, sugar, salt, ginger and pepper; pour over beef. Cover and cook on low until meat is tender, for 5-6 hours. Add tomatoes and green pepper; cook on low until the vegetables are tender, about 1 hour longer.

2. Combine cornstarch and cold water until smooth; gradually stir into slow cooker. Cover and cook on high until thickened, 20-30 minutes. Serve with noodles or rice.

FREEZE OPTION Freeze cooled beef mixture in freezer containers. To use, partially thaw in refrigerator overnight. Heat through in a covered saucepan, stirring gently. Add broth or water if necessary.

1 CUP BEEF MIXTURE 232 cal., 8g fat (2g sat. fat), 64mg chol., 639mg sod., 11g carb. (5g sugars, 2g fiber), 28g pro.
DIABETIC EXCHANGES 4 lean meat, 1 vegetable, 1 fat.

"This is wonderful! I used a round roast, as that is what I had on hand, and canned diced tomatoes. It turned out so good. I will make this again. Served mine with buttered noodles. Yummy!"

—LUIGIMON, TASTEOFHOME.COM

SLOW-COOKED REUBEN BRATS

Sauerkraut gives these beer-simmered brats a big flavor boost, but it's the special chili sauce and melted cheese that put them over the top. Top your favorite burger with some of the chili sauce; you won't be sorry.

—Alana Simmons, Johnstown, PA

PREP: 30 min. • **COOK:** 7¼ hours • **MAKES:** 10 servings

10   uncooked bratwurst links
3   bottles (12 oz. each) light beer or nonalcoholic beer
1   large sweet onion, sliced
1   can (14 oz.) sauerkraut, rinsed and well-drained
¾   cup mayonnaise
¼   cup chili sauce
2   Tbsp. ketchup
1   Tbsp. finely chopped onion
2   tsp. sweet pickle relish
1   garlic clove, minced
⅛   tsp. pepper
10   hoagie buns, split
10   slices Swiss cheese

1. In a large skillet, brown bratwurst in batches; drain. In a 5-qt. slow cooker, combine beer, sliced onion and sauerkraut; add bratwurst. Cook, covered, on low 7-9 hours or until sausages are cooked through.

2. Preheat oven to 350°. In a small bowl, mix mayonnaise, chili sauce, ketchup, chopped onion, relish, garlic and pepper until blended. Spread over cut sides of buns; top with cheese, bratwurst and sauerkraut mixture. Place on an ungreased baking sheet. Bake 8-10 minutes or until cheese is melted.

1 SANDWICH 733 cal., 50g fat (16g sat. fat), 94mg chol., 1643mg sod., 45g carb. (10g sugars, 2g fiber), 26g pro.

"Amazing! I loved them. I get so tired of hamburgers and hot dogs camping in the summer. I can't wait to share this recipe. Really enjoyed the Reuben sauce too. No more thousand island dressing from a bottle!"

—KENNEDY22, TASTEOFHOME.COM

BARBECUE PORK COBB SALAD

My lunchtime salad gets way more interesting topped with barbecue pork, cheddar cheese and creamy avocado. It's as satisfying as it is delicious.

—Shawn Carleton, San Diego, CA

PREP: 30 min. • **COOK:** 4 hours • **MAKES:** 6 servings

1¼ cups barbecue sauce
½ tsp. garlic powder
¼ tsp. paprika
1½ lbs. pork tenderloin
12 cups chopped romaine
3 plum tomatoes, chopped
2 avocados, peeled and chopped
2 small carrots, thinly sliced
1 medium sweet red or green pepper, chopped
3 hard-boiled large eggs, chopped
1½ cups shredded cheddar cheese
Salad dressing of your choice

1. In a greased 3-qt. slow cooker, mix barbecue sauce, garlic powder and paprika. Add pork; turn to coat. Cook, covered, on low 4-5 hours or until pork is tender.
2. Remove pork from slow cooker; shred into bite-sized pieces. In a bowl, toss pork with 1 cup barbecue sauce mixture. Place romaine on a large serving platter; arrange pork, tomatoes, avocado, carrots, chopped pepper, eggs and cheese over romaine. Drizzle with dressing.

FREEZE OPTION Place shredded pork in freezer containers. Cool and freeze. To use, partially thaw in refrigerator overnight. Heat through in a covered saucepan, stirring gently. Add broth or water if necessary.
1 SERVING 492 cal., 24g fat (9g sat. fat), 185mg chol., 868mg sod., 35g carb. (23g sugars, 7g fiber), 35g pro.

ALL-DAY RED BEANS & RICE

My family loves New Orleans-style cooking, so I make this dish often. I appreciate how simple it is, and the smoky ham flavor is scrumptious.

—Celinda Dahlgren, Napa, CA

PREP: 40 min. + soaking • **COOK:** 8½ hours • **MAKES:** 6 servings

1 cup dried red beans
2 smoked ham hocks
1 medium onion, chopped
1½ tsp. minced garlic
1 tsp. ground cumin
3 cups water
1 medium tomato, chopped
1 medium green pepper, chopped
1 tsp. salt
4 cups hot cooked rice

1. Rinse and sort beans. Place in a large saucepan; add water to cover by 2 in. Let soak, covered, overnight.
2. Drain and rinse beans, discarding liquid. Transfer beans to a 3-qt. slow cooker; add ham hocks, onion, garlic, cumin and 3 cups water. Cover and cook on low until beans are tender, 8-10 hours.

3. Remove ham hocks; cool slightly. Remove meat from bones. Finely chop meat and return to slow cooker; discard bones. Stir in the tomato, green pepper and salt; cover and cook on high until pepper is tender, about 30 minutes. Serve with rice.
⅔ CUP BEAN MIXTURE WITH ⅔ CUP RICE 297 cal., 7g fat (3g sat. fat), 33mg chol., 441mg sod., 50g carb. (3g sugars, 12g fiber), 17g pro

BARBECUE PORK COBB SALAD

ITALIAN PORK CHOP DINNER

My family loves this meal after church services. I serve it with spaghetti, salad and garlic bread.

—Martina Williams, Grovetown, GA

PREP: 30 min. • **COOK:** 4 hours • **MAKES:** 6 servings

6 bacon strips, diced
½ lb. fresh mushrooms, sliced
1 medium onion, finely chopped
1 garlic clove, minced
¾ cup all-purpose flour
4 tsp. Italian seasoning, divided
¼ tsp. salt
¼ tsp. garlic powder
⅛ tsp. pepper
   Dash cayenne pepper
6 bone-in pork loin chops (1 in. thick)
1 can (14½ oz.) diced tomatoes, undrained
1 can (14½ oz.) chicken broth
1 can (6 oz.) tomato paste
1 pkg. (10 oz.) frozen peas, thawed
   Hot cooked pasta

1. In a large skillet, cook the bacon over medium heat until crisp. Using a slotted spoon, remove to paper towels. In the drippings, saute mushrooms, onion and garlic until tender. Transfer to a 5-qt. slow cooker with a slotted spoon. In a shallow bowl, combine the flour, 3 tsp. Italian seasoning, salt, garlic powder, pepper and cayenne; coat pork chops with flour mixture.

2. In the same skillet, brown the pork chops; transfer to the slow cooker. Top with tomatoes and bacon. Combine the broth, tomato paste and remaining Italian seasoning; add to slow cooker.

3. Cover and cook on low until pork is tender, 4-6 hours; add peas during the last 30 minutes. Serve with pasta.

1 PORK CHOP 528 cal., 23g fat (8g sat. fat), 124mg chol., 842mg sod., 31g carb. (8g sugars, 5g fiber), 48g pro.

MAKE IT YOUR OWN

This dish is a version of cacciatore, a hearty Italian stew that contains tomatoes, mushrooms and sometimes wine, bell peppers and potatoes. Add any of those ingredients you like to create your signature cacciatore. Cacciatore translates to "hunter" in Italian, and cooking meat *alla cacciatore* means braising it in a tomato sauce with veggies to create a comforting one-pot meal.

COUNTRY FRENCH PORK WITH PRUNES & APPLES

The classic flavors of herbes de Provence, apples and dried plums make this easy slow-cooked pork taste like a hearty meal at a French country cafe. For a traditional pairing, serve the pork with braised lentils.

—Suzanne Banfield, Basking Ridge, NJ

PREP: 20 min. • **COOK:** 4 hours + standing • **MAKES:** 10 servings

- 2 Tbsp. all-purpose flour
- 1 Tbsp. herbes de Provence
- 1½ tsp. salt
- ¾ tsp. pepper
- 1 boneless pork loin roast (3 to 4 lbs.)
- 2 Tbsp. olive oil
- 2 medium onions, halved and thinly sliced
- 1 cup apple cider or unsweetened apple juice
- 1 cup beef stock
- 2 bay leaves
- 2 large tart apples, peeled, cored and chopped
- 1 cup pitted dried plums (prunes)

1. Mix flour, herbes de Provence, salt and pepper; rub over pork. In a large skillet, heat oil over medium-high heat. Brown roast on all sides. Place roast in a 5- or 6-qt. slow cooker. Add onions, apple cider, beef stock and bay leaves.

2. Cook, covered, on low 3 hours. Add apples and plums. Cook, covered, on low 1-1½ hours longer or until apples and pork are tender. Remove roast, onions, apples and plums to a serving platter, discarding bay leaves; tent with foil. Let stand 15 minutes before slicing.
4 OZ. COOKED PORK WITH ¾ CUP FRUIT MIXTURE 286 cal., 9g fat (3g sat. fat), 68mg chol., 449mg sod., 22g carb. (13g sugars, 2g fiber), 28g pro.

5i
SLOW-COOKER BARBECUE PULLED PORK SANDWICHES

Foolproof and wonderfully delicious describes my barbecue pork recipe. Just four ingredients and a slow cooker make a fabulous dish with little effort from you.

—Sarah Johnson, Chicago, IL

PREP: 15 min. • **COOK:** 7 hours • **MAKES:** 6 servings

- 1 lemon-garlic pork loin fillet (about 1⅓ lbs.)
- 1 can (12 oz.) Dr Pepper
- 1 bottle (18 oz.) barbecue sauce
- 6 hamburger buns, split

1. Place pork in a 3-qt. slow cooker. Pour Dr Pepper over top. Cover and cook on low 7-9 hours or until meat is tender.

2. Remove meat; cool slightly. Discard cooking juices. Shred meat with 2 forks and return to slow cooker. Stir in barbecue sauce; heat through. Serve on buns.
1 SANDWICH 348 cal., 8g fat (2g sat. fat), 45mg chol., 1695mg sod., 43g carb. (22g sugars, 2g fiber), 25g pro.

HOISIN PORK WRAPS

For a casual get-together, set a buffet with the pork, tortillas and the red cabbage slaw and have your guests make their own wraps.

—Linda Woo, Derby, KS

PREP: 25 min. • **COOK:** 7 hours
MAKES: 15 servings

- 1 boneless pork loin roast (3 lbs.)
- 1 cup hoisin sauce, divided
- 1 Tbsp. minced fresh gingerroot
- 6 cups shredded red cabbage
- 1½ cups shredded carrots
- ¼ cup thinly sliced green onions
- 3 Tbsp. rice vinegar
- 4½ tsp. sugar
- 15 flour tortillas (8 in.), warmed

1. Cut roast in half. Combine ⅓ cup hoisin sauce and ginger; rub over pork. Transfer to a 4- or 5-qt. slow cooker. Cover and cook on low for 7-8 hours or until pork is tender.

2. Meanwhile, in a large bowl, combine the cabbage, carrots, onions, vinegar and sugar. Chill until serving.

3. Shred meat with 2 forks and return to slow cooker; heat through. Place 2 tsp. remaining hoisin sauce down the center of each tortilla; top with ⅓ cup shredded pork and ⅓ cup coleslaw. Roll up.

1 WRAP 314 cal., 8g fat (2g sat. fat), 46mg chol., 564mg sod., 37g carb. (7g sugars, 1g fiber), 23g pro. **DIABETIC EXCHANGES** 2½ starch, 2 lean meat.

PENNSYLVANIA POT ROAST

This heartwarming one-dish meal is adapted from a Pennsylvania Dutch recipe. I start the pot roast cooking before I leave for church, adding the vegetables when I get home. Then I just sit back and relax until it's done.

—Donna Wilkinson, Monrovia, MD

PREP: 10 min. • **COOK:** 5 hours • **MAKES:** 6 servings

1 boneless pork shoulder butt roast (2½ to 3 lbs.), halved
1½ cups beef broth
½ cup sliced green onions
1 tsp. dried basil
1 tsp. dried marjoram
½ tsp. salt
½ tsp. pepper
1 bay leaf
6 medium red potatoes, cut into 2-in. chunks
4 medium carrots, cut into 2-in. chunks
½ lb. medium fresh mushrooms, halved
¼ cup all-purpose flour
½ cup cold water
¼ tsp. browning sauce
Additional sliced green onions, optional

1. Place roast in a 5-qt. slow cooker; add broth, onions and seasonings. Cook, covered, on high for 4 hours. Add potatoes, carrots and mushrooms. Cook, covered, on high 1 hour longer or until vegetables are tender. Remove meat and vegetables; keep warm. Discard bay leaf.
2. In a saucepan, combine flour and cold water until smooth; stir in 1½ cups cooking juices. Bring to a boil. Cook and stir until thickened, 2 minutes; add browning sauce. Serve gravy with roast and vegetables and, if desired, top with additional green onions.

1 SERVING 331 cal., 12g fat (4g sat. fat), 78mg chol., 490mg sod., 28g carb. (5g sugars, 4g fiber), 26g pro.

"My husband and I really enjoyed this dinner! I added 1 cup of celery to the recipe; we couldn't do a roast without celery. Everything was so tender and delicious, we would definitely make it again!"

—NOTASTEELERFAN, TASTEOFHOME.COM

HOW TO SPEED-PEEL CARROTS

Hold the carrot at a 45° angle with the tip resting on the counter or a cutting board. Start the peeler at the middle of the carrot, stroking downward toward the counter. Immediately switch directions and peel upward but only to the middle of the carrot, rotating the carrot as you go. Continue zig-zagging until bottom half of carrot is peeled.

.Flip the carrot so its top rests on the counter (shown) and repeat.

ITALIAN SHREDDED PORK STEW

Need a warm meal for a chilly night? Throw together this stew that's brightened with sweet potatoes, kale and Italian seasoning. The shredded pork is so tender, you're going to want to make this dish all season long.

—Robin Jungers, Campbellsport, WI

PREP: 20 min. • **COOK:** 8 hours
MAKES: 9 servings (about 3½ qt.)

2 medium sweet potatoes, peeled and cubed
2 cups chopped fresh kale
1 large onion, chopped
3 garlic cloves, minced
1 boneless pork shoulder butt roast (2½ to 3½ lbs.)
1 can (14 oz.) cannellini beans, rinsed and drained
1½ tsp. Italian seasoning
½ tsp. salt
½ tsp. pepper
3 cans (14½ oz. each) chicken broth
Sour cream, optional

1. Place the sweet potatoes, kale, onion and garlic in a 5-qt. slow cooker. Place roast on vegetables. Add the beans and seasonings. Pour broth over top. Cook, covered, on low until meat is tender, 8-10 hours.
2. Remove meat; cool slightly. Skim fat from cooking juices. Shred pork with 2 forks and return to slow cooker; heat through. If desired, garnish with sour cream.
1½ CUPS 283 cal., 13g fat (5g sat. fat), 78mg chol., 860mg sod., 15g carb. (4g sugars, 3g fiber), 24g pro.

PORK CHOP POTATO DINNER

This meal of tender pork chops with creamy, cheesy potatoes is a snap to assemble—and my family loves it!

—Dawn Huizinga, Owatonna, MN

PREP: 10 min. • **COOK:** 5¼ hours
MAKES: 6 servings

- 6 bone-in pork loin chops (8 oz. each)
- 1 Tbsp. canola oil
- 1 pkg. (30 oz.) frozen shredded hash brown potatoes, thawed
- 1½ cups shredded cheddar cheese, divided
- 1 can (10¾ oz.) condensed cream of celery soup, undiluted
- ½ cup 2% milk
- ½ cup sour cream
- ½ tsp. seasoned salt
- ⅛ tsp. pepper
- 1 can (2.8 oz.) French-fried onions, divided

1. In a large skillet, brown chops in oil on both sides; set aside. In a large bowl, combine the potatoes, 1 cup cheese, soup, milk, sour cream, seasoned salt and pepper. Stir in half of the onions.
2. Transfer to a greased 5-qt. slow cooker; top with pork chops. Cover and cook on low for 5-6 hours or until meat is tender. Sprinkle with remaining cheese and onions. Cover and cook 15 minutes longer or until cheese is melted.
1 SERVING 621 cal., 32g fat (15g sat. fat), 137mg chol., 896mg sod., 37g carb. (3g sugars, 2g fiber), 43g pro.

SLOW-COOKED SWEET & SOUR PORK

Even though a co-worker gave me this recipe more than 20 years ago, my family still enjoys it today.

—Martha Nickerson, Hancock, ME

PREP: 20 min. • **COOK:** 6½ hours • **MAKES:** 6 servings

2   Tbsp. plus 1½ tsp. paprika
1½ lbs. boneless pork loin roast, cut into 1-in. strips
1   Tbsp. canola oil
1   can (20 oz.) unsweetened pineapple chunks
1   medium onion, chopped
1   medium green pepper, chopped
¼   cup cider vinegar
3   Tbsp. brown sugar
3   Tbsp. reduced-sodium soy sauce
1   Tbsp. Worcestershire sauce
½   tsp. salt
2   Tbsp. cornstarch
¼   cup cold water
     Optional: Hot cooked rice and thinly sliced green onions

1. Place paprika in a shallow bowl. Add pork, a few pieces at a time, and turn to coat. In a nonstick skillet, brown pork in oil in batches over medium-high heat. Transfer to a 3-qt. slow cooker.

2. Drain pineapple, reserving juice; refrigerate the pineapple. Add the pineapple juice, onion, green pepper, vinegar, brown sugar, soy sauce, Worcestershire sauce and salt to slow cooker. Cover and cook on low for 6-8 hours or until meat is tender.

3. Combine cornstarch and water until smooth; stir into pork mixture. Add pineapple. Cover and cook 30 minutes longer or until sauce is thickened. If desired, serve over rice and sprinkle with green onions.

1 CUP 281 cal., 8g fat (2g sat. fat), 57mg chol., 551mg sod., 27g carb. (20g sugars, 2g fiber), 24g pro.

"We make this dish when we go camping. Start it in the morning ... go for a bike ride or hike ... when we return, I just steam some rice and dinner is served! Fast, easy and delicious!"

—PAMELASCHMALE, TASTEOFHOME.COM

BAJA PORK TACOS

This delicious recipe is my copycat version of the most excellent Mexican food we ever had in Flagstaff, Arizona. The original recipe used beef instead of pork, but this comes mighty close to the same taste.

—Ariella Winn, Mesquite, TX

PREP: 10 min. • **COOK:** 8 hours • **MAKES:** 12 servings

- 1 boneless pork sirloin roast (3 lbs.)
- 5 cans (4 oz. each) chopped green chiles
- 2 Tbsp. reduced-sodium taco seasoning
- 3 tsp. ground cumin
- 24 corn tortillas (6 in.), warmed
- 3 cups shredded lettuce
- 1½ cups shredded part-skim mozzarella cheese

1. Cut roast in half; place in a 3- or 4-qt. slow cooker. Mix chiles, taco seasoning and cumin; spoon over pork. Cook, covered, on low 8-10 hours or until meat is tender.
2. Remove pork; cool slightly. Skim fat from cooking juices. Shred meat with 2 forks. Return to slow cooker; heat through. Serve in tortillas with lettuce and cheese.

FREEZE OPTION Place cooled pork mixture in freezer containers; freeze up to 3 months. To use, partially thaw in refrigerator overnight. Heat through in a covered saucepan, stirring gently; add broth if necessary.

2 TACOS 320 cal., 11g fat (4g sat. fat), 77mg chol., 434mg sod., 26g carb. (1g sugars, 4g fiber), 30g pro. **DIABETIC EXCHANGES** 3 medium-fat meat, 2 starch.

SUNDAY POT ROAST

With the help of a slow cooker, you can prepare a down-home dinner any day of the week, not just on Sundays. The roast turns out tender and savory every time.

—Brandy Schaefer, Glen Carbon, IL

PREP: 10 min. + chilling • **COOK:** 8 hours • **MAKES:** 14 servings

- 1 tsp. dried oregano
- ½ tsp. onion salt
- ½ tsp. caraway seeds
- ½ tsp. pepper
- ¼ tsp. garlic salt
- 1 boneless pork loin roast (3½ to 4 lbs.), trimmed
- 6 medium carrots, peeled and cut into 1½-in. pieces
- 3 large potatoes, peeled and quartered
- 3 small onions, quartered
- 1½ cups beef broth
- ⅓ cup all-purpose flour
- ⅓ cup cold water
- ¼ tsp. browning sauce, optional

1. Combine first 5 ingredients; rub over roast. Cover; refrigerate overnight.
2. Place carrots, potatoes and onions in a 6-qt. slow cooker; add broth. Place roast in slow cooker. Cook, covered, on low until meat and vegetables are tender, 8-10 hours.
3. Transfer roast and vegetables to a serving platter; tent with foil. Pour cooking juices into a small saucepan. Mix flour and water until smooth; stir into pan. Bring to a boil; cook and stir until thickened, about 2 minutes. If desired, add browning sauce. Serve roast with gravy and vegetables.

1 SERVING 217 cal., 5g fat (2g sat. fat), 57mg chol., 230mg sod., 17g carb. (3g sugars, 2g fiber), 24g pro. **DIABETIC EXCHANGES** 3 lean meat, 1½ starch.

"Made this beautiful slow-cooker dinner as written. House smelled divine, and the dish tasted even more divine!"

—CYNANDTOM, TASTEOFHOME.COM

BAJA PORK TACOS

SLOW-COOKER BAKED ZITI

I don't know one family that doesn't have some crazy, hectic evening. This recipe is a quick and easy fix for a busy weeknight dinner.

—Christy Addison, Clarksville, OH

PREP: 10 min. • **COOK:** 2 hours • **MAKES:** 6 servings

- 1 container (15 oz.) whole-milk ricotta cheese
- 1 large egg, beaten
- 1 tsp. dried basil
- ½ tsp. crushed red pepper flakes, optional
- 1 jar (24 oz.) meatless pasta sauce
- 2 cups uncooked ziti
- ¼ cup water
- 2 cups shredded mozzarella cheese
- ¼ cup minced fresh basil
  Grated Parmesan cheese, optional

1. In a small bowl, stir together ricotta cheese, egg, basil and, if desired, red pepper flakes. Pour pasta sauce into a 5-qt. slow cooker. Evenly top sauce with pasta; pour water over top. Drop the ricotta cheese mixture by heaping tablespoonfuls over pasta. Sprinkle with mozzarella cheese.

2. Cook, covered, on high until heated through and pasta is tender, 2-2½ hours. Top with the fresh basil and, if desired, Parmesan cheese and additional red pepper flakes. Serve immediately.

1½ CUPS 379 cal., 17g fat (10g sat. fat), 89mg chol., 886mg sod., 36g carb. (13g sugars, 3g fiber), 23g pro.

ZITI SUBSTITUTE

Many short pasta shapes will work fine here instead of ziti. Try fusilli, rigatoni, penne, radiatore or casarecce.

SWEET POTATO LENTIL STEW

Years ago, I first experienced the spicy flavor and wonderful aroma of this hearty dish. You can serve the stew alone or as a topper for meat or poultry.

—Heather Gray, Little Rock, AR

PREP: 15 min. • **COOK:** 5 hours • **MAKES:** 6 servings

- 1¼ lbs. sweet potatoes (about 2 medium), peeled and cut into 1-in. pieces
- 1½ cups dried lentils, rinsed
- 3 medium carrots, cut into 1-in. pieces
- 1 medium onion, chopped
- 4 garlic cloves, minced
- ½ tsp. ground cumin
- ¼ tsp. ground ginger
- ¼ tsp. cayenne pepper
- 1 carton (32 oz.) vegetable broth
- ¼ cup minced fresh cilantro

In a 3-qt. slow cooker, combine the first 9 ingredients. Cook, covered, on low for 5-6 hours or until the vegetables and lentils are tender. Stir in cilantro.

1⅓ CUPS 290 cal., 1g fat (0 sat. fat), 0 chol., 662mg sod., 58g carb. (16g sugars, 15g fiber), 15g pro.

OVER-THE-RAINBOW MINESTRONE

This vegetarian soup features a rainbow of veggies. You can use any multicolored pasta in place of the spirals.

—Crystal Schlueter, Northglenn, CO

PREP: 20 min. • **COOK:** 6 hours 20 min. • **MAKES:** 10 servings (3¾ qt.)

½ lb. Swiss chard
2 Tbsp. olive oil
1 medium red onion, finely chopped
6 cups vegetable broth
2 cans (14½ oz. each) fire-roasted diced tomatoes, undrained
1 can (16 oz.) kidney beans, rinsed and drained
1 can (15 oz.) garbanzo beans or chickpeas, rinsed and drained
1 medium yellow summer squash or zucchini, halved and cut into ¼-in. slices
1 medium sweet red or yellow pepper, finely chopped
1 medium carrot, finely chopped
2 garlic cloves, minced
1½ cups uncooked spiral pasta or small pasta shells
¼ cup prepared pesto
Optional toppings: Additional prepared pesto, shredded Parmesan cheese, crushed red pepper flakes and minced fresh basil

1. Cut stems from chard; chop the stems and leaves separately. Reserve leaves for adding later. In a large skillet, heat oil over medium heat. Add onion and chard stems; cook and stir until tender, 3-5 minutes. Transfer mixture to a 6-qt. slow cooker.
2. Stir in broth, tomatoes, kidney beans, garbanzo beans, squash, pepper, carrot and garlic. Cook, covered, on low until vegetables are tender, 6-8 hours.
3. Stir in the pasta and reserved chard leaves. Cook, covered, on low until pasta is tender, 20-25 minutes longer; stir in pesto. If desired, serve with additional pesto, Parmesan cheese, red pepper flakes and fresh basil.

1½ CUPS 231 cal., 7g fat (1g sat. fat), 2mg chol., 1015mg sod., 34g carb. (7g sugars, 6g fiber), 9g pro.

"My husband and I both loved this soup. I cooked it on the stove, bringing it to a boil, then covering and simmering on medium-low heat for 20 minutes. I added the pasta and chard leaves and cooked an additional 10 minutes. The addition of pesto is brilliant."

—KARISANN, TASTEOFHOME.COM

SLAMMIN' LAMB

This meat is easy, flavorful and best when marinated overnight. You can even mix it up and freeze it until you want to throw it in the cooker! Make sure you have lots of pita bread on hand to soak up the juices.

—Ruth Hartunian-Alumbaugh,
  Willimantic, CT

PREP: 20 min. + marinating
COOK: 4 hours • **MAKES:** 6 servings

  2   small garlic bulbs
  ¾   cup plus 2 Tbsp. minced fresh mint, divided
  ½   cup balsamic vinegar
  ¼   cup olive oil
  2   lbs. boneless lamb, cut into 1-in. cubes
       Hot cooked rice or pita bread, optional

1. Remove papery outer skin from garlic bulbs; cut off tops of bulbs, exposing individual cloves. Peel and halve cloves. In a large dish, combine garlic, ¾ cup mint, vinegar and olive oil. Add lamb; turn to coat. Cover and refrigerate up to 24 hours.
2. Transfer lamb and marinade to a 3-qt. slow cooker. Cook, covered, on low until meat is tender, 4-5 hours. Sprinkle with remaining mint. Serve with hot cooked rice or pita bread as desired.
1 SERVING 323 cal., 17g fat (4g sat. fat), 98mg chol., 102mg sod., 10g carb. (6g sugars, 1g fiber), 31g pro.

SLOW-COOKER TUNA NOODLE CASSEROLE

We tweaked this family-friendly classic to work for the slow cooker. It's easy, wholesome and totally homemade!

—*Taste of Home* Test Kitchen

PREP: 25 min. • **COOK:** 4 hours + standing • **MAKES:** 10 servings

¼ cup butter, cubed
½ lb. sliced fresh mushrooms
1 medium onion, chopped
1 medium sweet pepper, chopped
1 tsp. salt, divided
1 tsp. pepper, divided
2 garlic cloves, minced
¼ cup all-purpose flour
2 cups reduced-sodium chicken broth
2 cups half-and-half cream
4 cups uncooked egg noodles (about 6 oz.)
3 cans (5 oz. each) light tuna in water, drained
2 Tbsp. lemon juice
2 cups shredded Monterey Jack cheese
2 cups frozen peas, thawed
2 cups crushed potato chips

1. In a large skillet, melt butter over medium-high heat. Add mushrooms, onion, sweet pepper, ½ tsp. salt and ½ tsp. pepper; cook and stir until tender, 6-8 minutes. Add garlic; cook 1 minute longer. Stir in the flour until blended. Gradually whisk in broth. Bring to a boil, stirring constantly; cook and stir until thickened, 1-2 minutes.

2. Transfer to a 5-qt. slow cooker. Stir in cream and noodles. Cook, covered, on low until the noodles are tender, 4-5 hours. Meanwhile, in a small bowl, combine the tuna, lemon juice and remaining salt and pepper.

3. Remove insert from the slow cooker. Stir cheese, tuna mixture and peas into noodle mixture. Let stand, uncovered, 20 minutes. Just before serving, sprinkle with potato chips.

1 CUP 393 cal., 21g fat (12g sat. fat), 84mg chol., 752mg sod., 28g carb. (5g sugars, 3g fiber), 22g pro.

"This was great! Total throwback to childhood. I cut the salt, cheese and potato chips in half, and it worked out just fine."

—POLS005, TASTEOFHOME.COM

SLOW-COOKER FRITTATA PROVENCAL

This recipe means that a delectable dinner is ready when I walk in the door from work. The meatless slow cooker meal also makes an elegant brunch for lazy weekend mornings.

—Connie Eaton, Pittsburgh, PA

PREP: 30 min. • **COOK:** 3 hours • **MAKES:** 6 servings

- ½ cup water
- 1 Tbsp. olive oil
- 1 medium Yukon Gold potato, peeled and sliced
- 1 small onion, thinly sliced
- ½ tsp. smoked paprika
- 12 large eggs
- 1 tsp. minced fresh thyme or ¼ tsp. dried thyme
- 1 tsp. hot pepper sauce
- ½ tsp. salt
- ¼ tsp. pepper
- 1 log (4 oz.) fresh goat cheese, coarsely crumbled
- ½ cup chopped soft sun-dried tomatoes (not packed in oil)

1. Layer two 24-in. pieces of aluminum foil; starting with a long side, fold up foil to create a 1-in.-wide strip. Shape strip into a coil to make a rack for bottom of a 6-qt. oval slow cooker. Add water to slow cooker; set foil rack in water.

2. In a large skillet, heat oil over medium-high heat. Add potato and onion; cook and stir until potato is lightly browned, 5-7 minutes. Stir in paprika. Transfer to a greased 1½-qt. baking dish (dish must fit in slow cooker).

3. In a large bowl, whisk eggs, thyme, pepper sauce, salt and pepper; stir in 2 oz. cheese. Pour over potato mixture. Top with tomatoes and remaining goat cheese. Place dish on foil rack.

4. Cook, covered, on low until eggs are set and a knife inserted in center comes out clean, 3-4 hours.

1 SERVING 245 cal., 14g fat (5g sat. fat), 385mg chol., 338mg sod., 12g carb. (4g sugars, 2g fiber), 15g pro. **DIABETIC EXCHANGES** 2 medium-fat meat, 1 starch, ½ fat.

"I cut the recipe in half, but used 8 eggs. It turned out so well. Three hours in the slow cooker (on low) was perfect. I deleted the salt, but otherwise made it as shown. So good!"

—MKFRAZIER, TASTEOFHOME.COM

VEGETARIAN RED BEAN CHILI

This vegetarian chili recipe is healthy and tastes wonderful. Even meat lovers would like it! I like to top my bowl with shredded cheddar cheese.

—Connie Barnett, Athens, GA

PREP: 10 min. • **COOK:** 5 hours • **MAKES:** 6 servings (2 qt.)

1 can (16 oz.) red beans, rinsed and drained
2 cans (8 oz. each) no-salt-added tomato sauce
2 cups water
1 can (14½ oz.) diced tomatoes, undrained
1 pkg. (12 oz.) frozen vegetarian meat crumbles
1 large onion, chopped
1 to 2 Tbsp. chili powder
1 Tbsp. ground cumin
2 garlic cloves, minced
1 tsp. pepper
½ tsp. salt
½ tsp. cayenne pepper
   Optional: Sour cream and shredded cheddar cheese

In a 4-qt. slow cooker, combine first 12 ingredients. Cover and cook on low until heated through, 5-6 hours. Serve with sour cream and cheddar cheese if desired.

FREEZE OPTION Freeze cooled chili in freezer containers. To use, partially thaw in refrigerator overnight. Heat through in a saucepan, stirring occasionally; add broth if necessary.

NOTE Vegetarian meat crumbles are a nutritious pro source made from soy. Look for them in the natural foods freezer section.

1⅓ CUPS 201 cal., 3g fat (0 sat. fat), 0 chol., 1035mg sod., 27g carb. (5g sugars, 9g fiber), 17g pro.

LENTIL RED BEAN CHILI Substitute 1½ cups cooked green lentils for the vegetarian meat crumbles. Decrease cumin to 1½ tsp.; add ¼ tsp. smoked paprika.

RED BEAN CHILI TIPS

Can you cook this chili on the stovetop?
Yes! Use a Dutch oven to simmer the chili, uncovered, 20–25 minutes or until the onion is tender and the flavors are blended.

What are some other good toppings for red bean chili?
Try tomatoes, radishes, green onions, cilantro or crispy air-fryer tortilla chips for added flavor and texture.

What can you use in chili instead of vegetarian meat crumbles?
Besides the lentil option provided, consider using 1 lb. cooked and crumbled ground beef, chicken, or turkey. Or substitute other types of canned beans, rinsed and drained.

How do you store leftover chili?
Refrigerate for 4-5 days in a covered container or freeze for up to 3 months.

SLOW-COOKED BALSAMIC LENTIL SOUP

Balsamic vinegar and honey give this healthy soup a tangy and slightly sweet flavor. Since this soup is slow-cooked, the vegetables and lentils retain their texture and don't turn into mush.

—Colleen Delawder, Herndon, VA

PREP: 15 min. • **COOK:** 5 hours.
MAKES: 8 servings

- 1 carton (32 oz.) reduced-sodium chicken broth
- 3 celery ribs, chopped
- 2 medium carrots, chopped
- 2 medium red potatoes, cut into ½-in. cubes
- 1 cup chopped sweet onion
- 1 cup dried red lentils, rinsed
- 1 Tbsp. honey
- 2 tsp. Italian seasoning
- ½ tsp. salt
- ½ tsp. pepper
- ¼ tsp. crushed red pepper flakes
- ¼ tsp. garlic powder
- ¼ cup balsamic vinegar
  Optional: Shaved Parmesan cheese, fresh parsley, balsamic glaze drizzle

In a 3- or 4-qt. slow cooker, combine the first 12 ingredients. Cook, covered, on low until vegetables and lentils are tender, 5-6 hours. Stir in vinegar. Garnish as desired.

1 CUP 145 cal., 0 fat (0 sat. fat), 0 chol., 459mg sod., 28g carb. (7g sugars, 4g fiber), 8g pro. **DIABETIC EXCHANGES** 2 starch.

MOROCCAN LAMB WRAPS

I am a huge fan of both lamb and lettuce wraps. This combination—with creamy dressing and crunchy cucumber—makes a tasty slow-cooked dish. The wine and chili powder add more flavor elements.

—Arlene Erlbach, Morton Grove, IL

PREP: 25 min. • **COOK:** 5 hours
MAKES: 8 servings

- 2 lbs. lamb stew meat
- 1 cup chunky salsa
- ⅓ cup apricot preserves
- 6 Tbsp. dry red wine, divided
- 1 to 2 Tbsp. Moroccan seasoning (ras el hanout)
- 2 tsp. chili powder
- ½ tsp. garlic powder
- 1 English cucumber, very thinly sliced
- 2 Tbsp. prepared ranch salad dressing
- 16 Bibb or Boston lettuce leaves

1. Combine the lamb, salsa, preserves, 4 Tbsp. wine, Moroccan seasoning, chili powder and garlic powder. Transfer to a 3-qt. slow cooker. Cook, covered, on low 5-6 hours, or until lamb is tender. Remove lamb; shred with 2 forks. Strain cooking juices; skim fat. Return lamb and cooking juices to slow cooker; heat through. Stir in remaining 2 Tbsp. wine; heat through.
2. Combine cucumber and ranch dressing; toss to coat. Serve lamb mixture in lettuce leaves; top with cucumber mixture.

2 FILLED LETTUCE WRAPS 221 cal., 8g fat (2g sat. fat), 74mg chol., 257mg sod., 13g carb. (8g sugars, 1g fiber), 24g pro.
DIABETIC EXCHANGES 3 lean meat, 1 starch.

EASY SLOW-COOKER MAC & CHEESE

"You're the best mom in the world," my sons cheer whenever I make this creamy mac and cheese perfection. You can't beat a response like that!

—Heidi Fleek, Hamburg, PA

PREP: 25 min. • **COOK:** 1 hour • **MAKES:** 8 servings

2 cups uncooked elbow macaroni
1 can (10¾ oz.) condensed cheddar cheese soup, undiluted
1 cup 2% milk
½ cup sour cream
¼ cup butter, cubed
½ tsp. onion powder
¼ tsp. white pepper
⅛ tsp. salt
1 cup shredded cheddar cheese
1 cup shredded fontina cheese
1 cup shredded provolone cheese

1. Cook macaroni according to package directions for al dente. Meanwhile, in a large saucepan, combine soup, milk, sour cream, butter and seasonings; cook and stir over medium-low heat until blended. Stir in the cheeses until melted.

2. Drain macaroni; transfer to a greased 3-qt. slow cooker. Stir in cheese mixture. Cook, covered, on low 1-2 hours or until heated through.

¾ CUP 346 cal., 23g fat (14g sat. fat), 71mg chol., 712mg sod., 20g carb. (4g sugars, 1g fiber), 15g pro.

"My daughter made this when I came to lunch this week. She adds small pieces of ham and some cooked broccoli to make a complete meal. She also said you could freeze the leftovers, and it heats up beautifully just like the first time. I thought it was delicious!"

—NEWGRANDMA, TASTEOFHOME.COM

TOMATO BASIL TORTELLINI SOUP

When my family tried this soup, they all had to have seconds, and my husband is happy anytime I put it on the table. Sometimes I include cooked, crumbled bacon and serve it with mozzarella cheese.

—Christy Addison, Clarksville, OH

PREP: 25 min. • **COOK:** 6¼ hours • **MAKES:** 18 servings (4½ qt.)

2 Tbsp. olive oil
1 medium onion, chopped
3 medium carrots, chopped
5 garlic cloves, minced
3 cans (28 oz. each) crushed tomatoes, undrained
1 carton (32 oz.) vegetable broth
1 Tbsp. sugar
1 tsp. dried basil
1 bay leaf
3 pkg. (9 oz. each) refrigerated cheese tortellini
¾ cup half-and-half cream
shredded Parmesan cheese
minced fresh basil

1. In a large skillet, heat oil over medium-high heat. Add onion and carrots; cook and stir until crisp-tender, 5-6 minutes. Add the garlic; cook 1 minute longer. Transfer to a 6- or 7-qt. slow cooker. Add the tomatoes, broth, sugar, basil and bay leaf. Cook, covered, on low until vegetables are tender, 6-7 hours.
2. Stir in tortellini. Cook, covered, on high for 15 minutes. Reduce heat to low; stir in cream until heated through. Discard bay leaf. Top with the Parmesan cheese and basil before serving.

FREEZE OPTION Discard bay leaf. Before stirring in half-and-half cream, cool soup and freeze in freezer containers. To use, partially thaw in refrigerator overnight. Heat through in a saucepan, stirring occasionally; add cream as directed.
1 CUP 214 cal., 7g fat (3g sat. fat), 23mg chol., 569mg sod., 32g carb. (9g sugars, 4g fiber), 9g pro. **DIABETIC EXCHANGES** 2 starch, 1 fat.

COUNTRY CASSOULET

This bean stew is great with fresh dinner rolls and your favorite green salad.
It's a hearty meal that's perfect after a long day in the garden.

—Suzanne McKinley, Lyons, GA

PREP: 40 min. + soaking • **COOK:** 6 hours • **MAKES:** 10 servings

1 lb. dried great northern beans
2 uncooked garlic-flavored pork sausage links
3 bacon strips, diced
1½ lbs. boneless pork, cut into 1-in. cubes
1 lb. boneless lamb, cut into 1-in. cubes
1½ cups chopped onion
3 garlic cloves, minced
2 tsp. salt
1 tsp. dried thyme
4 whole cloves
2 bay leaves
2½ cups chicken broth
1 can (8 oz.) tomato sauce

1. Rinse and sort beans. Place in a large saucepan; add water to cover by 2 in. Let soak, covered, overnight. Drain and rinse beans, discarding liquid.

2. Return beans to saucepan; add water to cover by 2 in. Bring to a boil. Boil for 15 minutes. Drain and rinse the beans, discarding liquid.

3. In a large skillet over medium-high heat, brown sausage links; transfer to a 5-qt. slow cooker. Add bacon to skillet; cook until crisp. Remove with a slotted spoon to slow cooker.

4. In bacon drippings, cook the pork and lamb until browned on all sides. Place in slow cooker. Stir in beans and remaining ingredients.

5. Cover and cook on low until beans are tender, 6-8 hours. Discard the cloves and bay leaves. Remove sausage and cut into ¼-in. slices; return to slow cooker and stir gently.

1 CUP 375 cal., 12g fat (4g sat. fat), 74mg chol., 950mg sod., 32g carb. (5g sugars, 10g fiber), 35g pro.

CASSOULET ORIGINS

Cassoulet, a classic stew from southern France, combines slow-cooked white beans, sausage and meats such as duck or pork. Modern versions simplify the dish by using chicken, canned beans or vegetarian swaps.

AIR-FRYER CHICKEN
PARMESAN, 249

288

259

291

GO-TO GEAR

TURKEY QUESADILLAS WITH CRANBERRY SALSA

These quesadillas stuffed with turkey and cheese get amped up when you add sweet-tart cranberry salsa. You might want to make extra; the salsa goes great with chicken or pork too!

—Jodi Kristensen, Macomb, MI

TAKES: 30 min. • **MAKES:** 4 servings

¾ cup fresh or frozen cranberries
2 Tbsp. sugar
¼ cup water
1 small pear, chopped
¼ cup chopped red onion
1 jalapeno pepper, seeded and chopped
3 Tbsp. chopped celery
2 tsp. grated lemon zest
1 Tbsp. lemon juice
½ tsp. ground cumin
4 flour tortillas (6 in.)
2 cups cubed cooked turkey breast
1 cup shredded reduced-fat white or yellow cheddar cheese

1. For the salsa, in a small saucepan, combine cranberries, sugar and water; bring to a boil. Reduce heat to medium; cook, uncovered, until berries pop, about 10 minutes, stirring occasionally. Remove from heat; cool slightly. Stir in the pear, onion, jalapeno, celery, lemon zest and juice, and cumin.

2. Preheat griddle over medium heat. Top half of each tortilla with ½ cup turkey; sprinkle with ¼ cup cheese. Fold tortilla to close. Cook on griddle 1-2 minutes per side or until golden brown and cheese is melted. Serve with salsa.

NOTE Wear disposable gloves when cutting hot peppers; the oils can burn skin. Avoid touching your face.

1 QUESADILLA WITH ⅓ CUP SALSA
321 cal., 10g fat (4g sat. fat), 80mg chol., 449mg sod., 27g carb. (12g sugars, 2g fiber), 32g pro. **DIABETIC EXCHANGES** 3 lean meat, 1½ starch, 1 fat, ½ fruit.

"The salsa was surprisingly amazing! I didn't have enough turkey, so I combined chicken and turkey. And I had sour cream on the side mixed with salsa. Yummy!"

—WENDY769, TASTEOFHOME.COM

AMISH CHICKEN & WAFFLES

A down-home diner special gets weeknight-easy with the help of rotisserie chicken. Want 'em even faster? Make the waffles ahead of time and freeze till dinnertime.

—Lauren Reiff, East Earl, PA

TAKES: 30 min. • **MAKES:** 6 servings

3 Tbsp. butter
3 Tbsp. all-purpose flour
½ tsp. salt
¼ tsp. pepper
½ cup chicken broth
1¼ cups 2% milk
2 cups coarsely shredded rotisserie chicken

WAFFLES
2 cups all-purpose flour
2 Tbsp. sugar
4 tsp. baking powder
½ tsp. salt
2 large eggs, room temperature
1½ cups 2% milk
5 Tbsp. butter, melted
Sliced green onions, optional

1. In a large saucepan, melt the butter over medium heat. Stir in flour, salt and pepper until smooth; gradually whisk in broth and milk. Bring to a boil, stirring constantly; cook and stir until thickened, 1-2 minutes. Stir in chicken; heat through. Keep warm.

2. Preheat waffle maker. Whisk together flour, sugar, baking powder and salt. In another bowl, whisk together the eggs, milk and melted butter; add to dry ingredients, stirring just until moistened.

3. Bake the waffles according to manufacturer's directions until golden brown. Top waffles with chicken mixture and, if desired, green onions.

2 WAFFLES WITH ⅔ CUP CHICKEN MIXTURE 488 cal., 23g fat (13g sat. fat), 154mg chol., 981mg sod., 45g carb. (10g sugars, 1g fiber), 24g pro.

CHICKEN & WAFFLES TIPS

Why do people eat chicken and waffles together?

In America, people have been eating chicken and waffles together for generations. It was first seen in the Amish/Pennsylvania Dutch communities. The Dutch brought the waffle over from Holland and early Americans found it was the perfect vessel for stewed chicken and gravy. The sweetness from the waffle balances with the savory chicken, plus all those deep waffle pockets are perfect for pooling up gravy (or syrup!).

What goes with chicken and waffles?

It's pretty much a meal in itself, but there are plenty of recipes that go with chicken and waffles. Try them with mashed potatoes, stuffing or french fries.

Do you put syrup on chicken and waffles?

This recipe is delicious on its own with all that velvety chicken gravy, so you can skip the syrup here. But for the version that uses fried chicken, you'll definitely want to douse it in golden maple syrup.

GRILLED CHICKEN CAESAR SALAD

Whenever we're invited to potlucks, I'm asked to bring a salad because people know it's one of my specialties. This dish is especially good on summer days when it's too hot to cook on the stove. This is a wonderful marinade. The ingredients are easy to remember and can easily be doubled or halved.

—Deb Weisberger, Mullett Lake, MI

PREP: 15 min. + marinating • **GRILL:** 15 min. • **MAKES:** 6 servings

½ cup red wine vinegar
½ cup reduced-sodium soy sauce
½ cup olive oil
1 Tbsp. dried parsley flakes
1 tsp. dried basil
1 tsp. dried oregano
½ tsp. garlic powder
½ tsp. pepper
6 boneless skinless chicken breast halves (4 oz. each)
1 large bunch romaine, torn (12 cups)
1½ cups Caesar salad croutons
1 cup halved cherry tomatoes
⅔ cup creamy Caesar salad dressing
Grated Parmesan cheese, optional

1. In a bowl or shallow dish, combine the first 8 ingredients; add chicken and turn to coat; cover and refrigerate for at least 4 hours.
2. Drain chicken, discarding marinade. Grill chicken, uncovered, over medium-low heat for 6-8 minutes on each side or until a thermometer reads 165°.
3. Meanwhile, in a large bowl, combine the romaine, croutons and tomatoes; add dressing and toss to coat. Divide among 6 salad plates. Slice chicken; arrange on salads. If desired, garnish with grated Parmesan cheese.

1½ CUPS 376 cal., 25g fat (4g sat. fat), 74mg chol., 688mg sod., 12g carb. (3g sugars, 3g fiber), 26g pro.

"Very tasty, restaurant-quality Caesar salad. I've been using this recipe for years. Always a pleaser at my house. Highly recommend."

—MICHAEL151, TASTEOFHOME.COM

GREEK GRILLED CHICKEN PITAS

I switched up my mom's recipe to create this tasty pita pocket variation. It's delicious and perfect for warm days, with a creamy cucumber sauce that goes great with fresh, crunchy veggies.

—Blair Lonergan, Rochelle, VA

PREP: 20 min. + marinating • **GRILL:** 10 min. • **MAKES:** 4 servings

1 lb. boneless skinless chicken breast halves
½ cup balsamic vinaigrette

CUCUMBER SAUCE

1 cup plain Greek yogurt
½ cup finely chopped cucumber
¼ cup finely chopped red onion
1 Tbsp. minced fresh parsley
1 Tbsp. lime juice
1 garlic clove, minced
¼ tsp. salt
⅛ tsp. pepper

PITAS

8 pita pocket halves
½ cup sliced cucumber
½ cup grape tomatoes, chopped
½ cup sliced red onion
½ cup crumbled feta cheese

1. Marinate chicken in vinaigrette, covered, in refrigerator for at least 4 hours or overnight. In a small bowl, combine the sauce ingredients; chill until serving.

2. Drain chicken, discarding marinade. On a lightly oiled grill rack, grill chicken, covered, over medium heat or broil 4 in. from the heat until a thermometer reads 165°, 4-7 minutes on each side.

3. Cut chicken into strips. Fill each pita half with chicken, cucumber, tomatoes, onion and cheese; drizzle with sauce.

2 FILLED PITA HALVES 428 cal., 14g fat (6g sat. fat), 85mg chol., 801mg sod., 41g carb. (7g sugars, 3g fiber), 33g pro.

GRILLED GROUND TURKEY BURGERS

Bite into these juicy, tender patties on whole wheat buns. We especially like to grill them, but you could also pan-fry them.

—Sherry Hulsman, Louisville, KY

TAKES: 30 min. • **MAKES:** 6 servings

- 1 large egg, lightly beaten
- ⅔ cup soft whole wheat bread crumbs
- ½ cup finely chopped celery
- ¼ cup finely chopped onion
- 1 Tbsp. minced fresh parsley
- 1 tsp. Worcestershire sauce
- 1 tsp. dried oregano
- ½ tsp. salt
- ¼ tsp. pepper
- 1¼ lbs. lean ground turkey
- 6 whole wheat hamburger buns, split

1. In a small bowl, combine the egg, bread crumbs, celery, onion, parsley, Worcestershire sauce and seasonings. Crumble turkey into bowl and mix lightly but thoroughly. Shape into 6 patties.
2. On a greased grill, cook, covered, over medium heat or broil 4 in. from the heat for 5-6 minutes on each side or until a thermometer reads 165° and juices run clear. Serve on buns.
1 BURGER 293 cal., 11g fat (3g sat. fat), 110mg chol., 561mg sod., 27g carb. (3g sugars, 4g fiber), 22g pro. **DIABETIC EXCHANGES** 3 lean meat, 2 starch.

ASPARAGUS-STUFFED AIR-FRYER CHICKEN ROLLS

This elegant-looking dish is really simple to make. I serve it to company a lot, but also make it many weeknights—especially when asparagus is in season.

—Louise Ambrose, Kingston, NY

PREP: 20 min. • **COOK:** 15 min. • **MAKES:** 2 servings

8 fresh asparagus spears
2 boneless skinless chicken breast halves (5 oz. each)
1 Tbsp. Dijon mustard
4 fresh sage leaves
2 slices provolone cheese (1 oz. each)
2 slices deli ham (¾ oz. each)
¼ cup all-purpose flour
1 large egg, lightly beaten
½ cup dry bread crumbs
¼ cup grated Parmesan cheese
Cooking spray

1. In a large skillet, bring ½ in. of water to a boil. Add asparagus; cover and boil for 3 minutes. Drain and immediately place asparagus in ice water. Drain and pat dry.

2. Flatten chicken to ¼-in. thickness. Spread mustard over 1 side of each chicken breast. Down the center of each, place 2 sage leaves, 1 cheese slice, 1 ham slice and 4 asparagus spears. Fold chicken over asparagus; secure with toothpicks.

3. Preheat air fryer to 325°. Place flour and egg in separate shallow bowls. In another shallow bowl, combine bread crumbs and Parmesan cheese. Dip chicken into the flour, then egg, and then bread crumb mixture.

4. Place chicken in a single layer on greased tray in air-fryer basket; spritz with cooking spray. Cook until chicken is no longer pink, 15-20 minutes. Discard toothpicks.

1 STUFFED CHICKEN BREAST HALF
382 cal., 15g fat (7g sat. fat), 167mg chol., 849mg sod., 14g carb. (2g sugars, 1g fiber), 46g pro.

HOW TO PREP ASPARAGUS

After rinsing, bend each stalk near the bottom. The stalk will naturally break at the tough part, which is not as tasty and tender as the rest. Discard this tough portion or save it for making soup stock.

If stalks are large, use a vegetable peeler to peel off the tough outer stems.

PRESSURE-COOKER CHICKEN TORTILLA SOUP

Don't be shy about loading up the spices and shredded chicken in your pressure cooker. This soup tastes wonderful as leftovers the next day. Your family will thank you for this one!

—Karen Kelly, Germantown, MD

PREP: 15 min. • **COOK:** 25 min. + releasing • **MAKES:** 10 servings (2½ qt.)

1 Tbsp. canola oil
1 medium onion, chopped
3 garlic cloves, minced
1 lb. boneless skinless chicken breasts
1 carton (32 oz.) reduced-sodium chicken broth
1 can (15 oz.) black beans, rinsed and drained
1 can (14 oz.) fire-roasted diced tomatoes
1½ cups frozen corn
1 Tbsp. chili powder
1 Tbsp. ground cumin
1 tsp. paprika
½ tsp. salt
¼ tsp. pepper
¼ cup minced fresh cilantro
Optional: Crumbled tortilla chips, chopped avocado, jalapeno peppers and lime wedges

1. Select saute setting on a 6-qt. electric pressure cooker and adjust for medium heat; add oil. Add onion; cook and stir 6-8 minutes or until tender. Add garlic; cook 1 minute longer. Press cancel. Add the next 10 ingredients. Stir. Lock lid; close pressure-release valve.

2. Adjust to pressure-cook on high for 8 minutes. Allow pressure to release naturally for 12 minutes, then quick-release any remaining pressure.

3. Remove chicken from the pressure cooker. Shred with 2 forks; return to pressure cooker. Stir in cilantro. Serve with optional toppings as desired.

1 CUP 141 cal., 3g fat (0 sat. fat), 25mg chol., 580mg sod., 15g carb. (3g sugars, 3g fiber), 14g pro. **DIABETIC EXCHANGES** 2 lean meat, 1 starch.

TORTILLA SOUP TIPS

Are there tortillas in this tortilla soup?

This version doesn't use soft tortillas in the recipe like some do. Instead, the soup is topped with crumbled tortilla chips.

What other methods can I use to make this chicken tortilla soup?

You can also make this chicken tortilla soup on the stovetop. In a Dutch oven, cook the onion in oil over medium heat for 6-8 minutes until tender. Add the garlic and cook for 1 minute; stir in the next 10 ingredients. Bring soup to a boil. Cover; reduce heat to low and simmer for 25 minutes. Remove the chicken and shred with 2 forks; return to the pot. Stir in cilantro and top with desired toppings.

AIR-FRYER CHICKEN PARMESAN

Quick, simple and oh, so tasty, this chicken Parmesan recipe is the perfect weeknight dish to have. It's just as crispy as the classic, if not crispier!

—*Taste of Home* Test Kitchen

TAKES: 20 min. • **MAKES:** 4 servings

2 large eggs
½ cup seasoned bread crumbs
⅓ cup grated Parmesan cheese
¼ tsp. pepper
4 boneless skinless chicken breast halves (6 oz. each)
1 cup pasta sauce
1 cup shredded mozzarella cheese
   Optional: Chopped fresh basil and hot cooked pasta

1. Preheat air fryer to 375°. In a shallow bowl, lightly beat the eggs. In another shallow bowl, combine bread crumbs, Parmesan cheese and pepper. Dip chicken into egg, then coat with crumb mixture.

2. Place chicken in a single layer on a greased tray in air-fryer basket. Cook 10-12 minutes or until a thermometer reads 165°, turning halfway through. Top chicken with sauce and mozzarella. Cook until cheese is melted, 3-4 minutes longer. If desired, sprinkle with chopped basil and additional Parmesan cheese and serve with pasta.

1 CHICKEN BREAST HALF 416 cal., 16g fat (7g sat. fat), 215mg chol., 863mg sod., 18g carb. (6g sugars, 2g fiber), 49g pro.

CHICKEN PARMESAN TIPS

How do you keep the breading on your chicken Parmesan?
To keep breading on Air-Fryer Chicken Parmesan, first dunk the chicken in beaten egg to help bread crumbs stick. You can also press bread crumbs gently onto the chicken and refrigerate the coated pieces for 30 minutes to set the breading.

What's the best temperature to cook chicken in an air fryer?
For juicy and evenly cooked chicken, set your air fryer between 350° and 400°, depending on your model and the type of chicken dish. This range ensures thorough cooking without drying out the meat.

What can you serve with Air-Fryer Chicken Parmesan?
Serve Air-Fryer Chicken Parmesan with warm bread and pasta topped with extra marinara sauce. It also pairs well with green salads like Caesar or a simple Italian salad. For a sweet finish, serve gelato or tiramisu.

PESTO CHICKEN CIABATTA SANDWICHES

Cheesy, crispy and fresh sandwiches transport you to your favorite bistro. These pesto chicken sandwiches are the perfect meal with an easy side. You can substitute turkey or pork for the smoked chicken.

—Jen Pahl, West Allis, WI

TAKES: 15 min. • **MAKES:** 2 servings

- 4 Tbsp. prepared pesto
- 2 ciabatta rolls
- 6 oz. thick-sliced deli smoked chicken breast
- 4 slices provolone cheese
- ½ cup roasted sweet red peppers, drained
- ½ cup fresh baby spinach

1. Preheat air fryer to 300°. Spread pesto on cut sides of both tops and bottoms of each roll. On each of the bottom halves, layer 3 oz. chicken and 1 slice cheese. On each of the top halves, layer ¼ cup red pepper and 1 slice cheese.

2. On a greased tray in air-fryer basket, cook until heated through and cheese is melted, 4-6 minutes. Add spinach to bottom halves and replace tops.

1 SANDWICH 468 cal.,26g fat (11g sat. fat), 63mg chol., 1771mg sod., 24g carb. (2g sugars, 2g fiber), 32g pro.

CHUNKY CHICKEN SALAD WITH GRAPES & PECANS

This chicken salad with grapes is ready in a snap when using rotisserie chicken and a few quick chops of pecans, sweet onion and celery.

—Julie Sterchi, Campbellsville, KY

TAKES: 25 min. • **MAKES:** 8 servings

- ½ cup mayonnaise
- 2 Tbsp. sour cream
- 1 Tbsp. lemon juice
- ⅛ tsp. salt
- ⅛ tsp. pepper
- 4 cups shredded rotisserie chicken
- 1¼ cups seedless red grapes, halved
- ½ cup chopped pecans
- ½ cup chopped celery
- ¼ cup chopped sweet onion, optional
    Optional: Lettuce leaves or whole wheat bread slices

In a large bowl, combine the first 5 ingredients. Add the chicken, grapes, pecans, celery and, if desired, onion; mix lightly to coat. If desired, serve with lettuce leaves or whole wheat bread.

¾ CUP CHICKEN SALAD 311 cal., 22g fat (4g sat. fat), 70mg chol., 180mg sod., 6g carb. (5g sugars, 1g fiber), 21g pro.

"A trusty, classic chicken salad recipe. We had ours on croissants! Mmm ..."

—MAMAMEESE, TASTEOFHOME.COM

AIR-FRYER SOUTHWESTERN CHICKEN ENCHILADAS

These air-fryer enchiladas are not only quick and easy but a perfect dinner for Taco Tuesday or any day of the week. Use rotisserie chicken for a quick substitute for cooked chicken. Dinner will be on the table in less than half an hour.

—Joan Hallford, North Richland Hills, TX

PREP: 20 min. • **COOK:** 10 min./batch • **MAKES:** 6 servings

2 cups shredded cooked chicken
1¼ cups shredded Monterey Jack cheese or pepper jack cheese, divided
1¼ cups shredded sharp cheddar cheese, divided
½ cup hominy or whole kernel corn, rinsed and drained
½ cup canned black beans, rinsed and drained
1 can (4 oz.) chopped green chiles
1 Tbsp. chili seasoning mix
¼ tsp. salt
¼ tsp. pepper
12 flour tortillas (6 in.), warmed
1 cup enchilada sauce
Optional toppings: Sour cream, guacamole, salsa and limes

1. Do not preheat air fryer. In a large bowl, combine chicken, ½ cup Monterey Jack cheese, ½ cup cheddar cheese, hominy, beans, chiles and seasonings. Line air-fryer basket with foil letting ends extend up side; grease foil. Place ¼ cup chicken mixture off center on each tortilla; roll up. In batches of 3, place seam side down in air fryer. Top with about 1 Tbsp. each enchilada sauce, Monterey Jack cheese and cheddar cheese.

2. Cook at 350°, until heated through and cheeses are melted, 10-12 minutes. Repeat with remaining ingredients. Serve with toppings as desired.
2 ENCHILADAS 525 cal., 24g fat (12g sat. fat), 86mg chol., 1564mg sod., 43g carb. (3g sugars, 3g fiber), 33g pro.

QUICK APRICOT CHICKEN

This is one of my favorite ways to fix chicken in a hurry. Everybody loves it, and leftovers are just as good the next day. For variation, I've used pork instead of chicken and added ingredients like pineapple, mandarin oranges, snow peas and broccoli.

—Vicki Ruiz, Twin Falls, ID

TAKES: 15 min. • **MAKES:** 4 servings

- ½ cup apricot preserves
- 2 Tbsp. reduced-sodium soy sauce
- 1 Tbsp. chicken broth or sherry
- 1 Tbsp. canola oil
- 1 Tbsp. cornstarch
- 1 tsp. minced garlic
- ¼ tsp. ground ginger
- 1 lb. boneless skinless chicken breasts, cut into strips
- 1 medium green pepper, chopped
- ½ cup salted cashews
  Hot cooked rice
  Crushed red pepper flakes, optional

1. In a shallow microwave-safe dish, combine the first 7 ingredients; stir in chicken. Cover and microwave on high for 3 minutes, stirring once.

2. Add green pepper and cashews. Cover and microwave on high for 2-4 minutes or until chicken is no longer pink, stirring once. Let stand for 3 minutes. Serve with rice and, if desired, sprinkle with red pepper flakes.

1 CUP 391 cal., 16g fat (3g sat. fat), 63mg chol., 673mg sod., 34g carb. (26g sugars, 2g fiber), 28g pro.

AIR-FRYER ARTICHOKE PESTO CHICKEN PIZZA

These super delicious air-fryer pizzas are made with a garlic and herb cream cheese spread, lemon artichoke pesto and rotisserie chicken. If you want to keep the first pizzas warm while air-frying the second batch, place them in the oven at the lowest temperature available.

—Sharyn LaPointe Hill, Las Cruces, NM

TAKES: 15 min. • **MAKES:** 4 servings

1 pkg. (8.8 oz.) naan flatbreads
Cooking spray
½ cup spreadable garlic and herb cream cheese
¼ cup sun-dried lemon artichoke pesto
1½ cups shredded rotisserie chicken
1 cup shredded Italian cheese blend

1. Preheat air fryer to 375°. Spritz both sides of flatbread with cooking spray. Arrange in a greased air fryer. Cook until lightly crisp, 3-4 minutes. Remove to cutting board. Top each with cream cheese, pesto, chicken and cheese.
2. Cook until heated through and cheese has melted, 4-5 minutes. To serve, cut each flatbread in half.

½ FLATBREAD 455 cal., 23g fat (11g sat. fat), 92mg chol., 988mg sod., 32g carb. (5g sugars, 1g fiber), 27g pro.

BLUEBERRY CHICKEN SALAD

On weekday mornings, I whip up this fresh chicken and blueberry combo to take for lunch. It also works as a nice light summer supper, and it's a cinch to double for a shower or potluck.

—Kari Kelley, Plains, MT

TAKES: 15 min. • **MAKES:** 4 servings

2 cups fresh blueberries
2 cups cubed cooked chicken breast
¾ cup chopped celery
½ cup diced sweet red pepper
½ cup thinly sliced green onions
¾ cup lemon yogurt
3 Tbsp. mayonnaise
½ tsp. salt
Bibb lettuce leaves, optional

1. Set aside a few blueberries for topping salad. In a large bowl, combine chicken, celery, red pepper, green onions and remaining blueberries. In a small bowl, mix yogurt, mayonnaise and salt. Add to chicken mixture; gently toss to coat.
2. Refrigerate until serving. If desired, serve over lettuce. Top with reserved blueberries.

1 CUP 277 cal., 11g fat (2g sat. fat), 60mg chol., 441mg sod., 21g carb. (16g sugars, 3g fiber), 23g pro. **DIABETIC EXCHANGES** 3 lean meat, 1 starch, 1 fat, ½ fruit.

CHICKEN YAKITORI

I grew up in Tokyo, and some of my favorite memories include eating street food like this dish with my friends. Although we now live thousands of miles apart, my friends and I still reminisce about our nights sharing secrets and bonding over delicious meals. This one is easy to re-create at home, which makes it perfect for when I'm feeling homesick. I like to serve it with rice.

—Lindsay Howerton-Hastings, Greenville, SC

TAKES: 30 min. • **MAKES:** 6 servings

½ cup mirin (sweet rice wine)
½ cup sake
½ cup soy sauce
1 Tbsp. sugar
2 large sweet red peppers, cut into 2-in. pieces
2 lbs. boneless skinless chicken thighs, cut into 1½-in. pieces
1 bunch green onions

1. In a small saucepan, combine the first 4 ingredients. Bring to a boil over medium-high heat. Remove from heat; set aside half the mixture for serving.

2. Thread the peppers onto 2 metal or soaked wooden skewers. Thread chicken onto 6 metal or soaked wooden skewers. Grill the chicken, covered, over medium heat 10-12 minutes or until meat is cooked through, turning occasionally and basting frequently with soy sauce mixture during the last 3 minutes.

3. Grill peppers, covered, until tender, 4-5 minutes, turning occasionally. Grill onions, covered, until lightly charred, 1-2 minutes, turning occasionally. Serve chicken and vegetables with reserved sauce for dipping.

4 OZ. COOKED CHICKEN 332 cal., 11g fat (3g sat. fat), 101mg chol., 1316mg sod., 14g carb. (11g sugars, 1g fiber), 32g pro.

YAKITORI TIPS

What should I serve with Chicken Yakitori?
Pair Chicken Yakitori with sides like sushi rice, flavored with minced ginger and scallions, or a simple bowl of hot ramen or cold sesame noodles. For appetizers, edamame makes a perfect starter for the yakitori.

How can you make sure Chicken Yakitori is juicy?
To keep yakitori juicy, cook chicken thighs to an internal temperature of 175°. Cut pieces to the same size for even cooking, and brush with basting sauce several times. Keep the grill cover closed between bastings to seal in the heat and promote good browning.

5i

STEAK & POTATO FOIL PACKS

As a park ranger, I've cooked a lot of meals outdoors. I often assemble foil packs and toss them into my backpack with some ice. Then when I set up camp, it's easy to cook them over a campfire. If I'm at home, I use my grill, and the food is just as good.

—Ralph Jones, San Diego, CA

PREP: 20 min. • **GRILL:** 20 min. • **MAKES:** 8 servings

2 beef top sirloin steaks (1½ lbs. each)
3 lbs. red potatoes, cut into ½-in. cubes
1 medium onion, chopped
4 tsp. minced fresh rosemary
1 Tbsp. minced garlic
2 tsp. salt
1 tsp. pepper

1. Prepare grill for medium heat or preheat oven to 450°. Cut each steak into 4 pieces. In a large bowl, combine steak, potatoes, onion, rosemary, garlic, salt and pepper.
2. Divide mixture among eight 18x12-in. pieces of heavy-duty foil, placing food on dull side of foil. Fold foil around potato mixture, sealing tightly.

3. Place packets on grill or in oven; cook until potatoes are tender, 8-10 minutes on each side. Open packets carefully to allow steam to escape. If desired, sprinkle with additional rosemary.
1 PACKET 348 cal., 7g fat (3g sat. fat), 69mg chol., 677mg sod., 29g carb. (2g sugars, 3g fiber), 40g pro. **DIABETIC EXCHANGES** 5 lean meat, 2 starch.

5i

MY JUICY LUCY

Friends in Minnesota introduced me to the Juicy Lucy burger, a local favorite. Instead of putting the cheese on top, it gets stuffed inside, keeping the meat around the cheese nice and juicy. We love the meltiness of American cheese, but it works with any cheese you'd like.

—Brigette Kutschma, Lake Geneva, WI

TAKES: 30 min. • **MAKES:** 4 servings

1 lb. ground beef
8 Tbsp. shredded American or cheddar cheese
½ tsp. salt
½ tsp. pepper
4 hamburger buns, split and toasted
Optional: Tomato slices, onion slices, lettuce

1. Shape beef into 8 thin patties. Divide cheese among 4 patties; top with remaining patties and press edges firmly to seal. Sprinkle with salt and pepper.
2. Grill burgers, covered, over medium heat or broil 4 in. from heat until a thermometer reads 160° and juices run clear, 6-8 minutes on each side. Serve on buns with toppings of your choice.
1 BURGER 376 cal., 19g fat (8g sat. fat), 84mg chol., 756mg sod., 23g carb. (4g sugars, 1g fiber), 27g pro.

DELUXE CHEESEBURGER SALAD

I was planning to grill burgers, and then it dawned on me: How about a cheeseburger salad? Tomato adds a fresh flavor boost.

—Pam Jefferies, Cantrall, IL

TAKES: 30 min. • **MAKES:** 4 servings

- 1 lb. ground beef
- 2 tsp. Montreal steak seasoning
- 6 cups torn iceberg lettuce
- 2 cups shredded cheddar cheese
- 1 cup salad croutons
- 1 medium tomato, chopped
- 1 small onion, halved and thinly sliced
- ½ cup dill pickle slices
  Thousand Island salad dressing

1. In a large bowl, combine beef and steak seasoning, mixing lightly but thoroughly. Shape into twenty ½-in.-thick patties. Grill mini burgers, covered, over medium heat, 3-4 minutes on each side or until a thermometer reads 160°.

2. In a large bowl, combine lettuce, mini burgers, cheese, croutons, tomato, onion and pickles. Serve with salad dressing.

FREEZE OPTION Place patties on a waxed paper-lined baking sheet; cover and freeze until firm. Remove from sheet and transfer to an airtight container; return to freezer. To use, cook frozen patties as directed, increasing time as necessary for a thermometer to read 160°.

1 SERVING 511 cal., 34g fat (17g sat. fat), 128mg chol., 1033mg sod., 14g carb. (4g sugars, 3g fiber), 36g pro.

"We thought this was very good. Dinner was on the table in 30 minutes or less. I didn't make the patties. I cooked and crumbled the meat in the skillet and used shredded Colby-Jack cheese. We will have this again."

—CYNTHIA175, TASTEOFHOME.COM

GRILLED SKIRT STEAK WITH RED PEPPERS & ONIONS

This fun dish is a welcome part of our family cookouts. It makes a quick and delicious steak-and-vegetable combo that's ideal for lunch or dinner.

—Cleo Gonske, Redding, CA

PREP: 30 min. + marinating • **GRILL:** 20 min. • **MAKES:** 6 servings

- ½ cup apple juice
- ½ cup red wine vinegar
- ¼ cup finely chopped onion
- 2 Tbsp. rubbed sage
- 3 tsp. ground coriander
- 3 tsp. ground mustard
- 3 tsp. freshly ground pepper
- 1 tsp. salt
- 1 garlic clove, minced
- 1 cup olive oil
- 1 beef skirt steak (1½ lbs.), cut into 5-in. pieces
- 2 medium red onions, cut into ½-in. slices
- 2 medium sweet red peppers, halved
- 12 green onions, trimmed

1. In a small bowl, whisk the first 9 ingredients until blended; gradually whisk in oil. Cover and refrigerate ½ cup marinade. Pour remaining marinade into a dish or large bowl. Add beef; turn to coat. Cover and refrigerate overnight. .

2. In a large bowl, toss vegetables with ¼ cup of reserved marinade. Grill red onions and peppers, covered, over medium heat, until tender, 4-6 minutes on each side. Grill green onions until tender, 1-2 minutes on each side.

3. Drain beef, discarding marinade. Grill, beef covered, over medium heat until meat reaches desired doneness (for medium-rare, a thermometer should read 135°; medium, 140°; medium-well, 145°), 4-6 minutes on each side. Baste with remaining ¼ cup marinade during last 4 minutes of cooking. Let steak stand 5 minutes.

4. Slice vegetables into smaller pieces; transfer to a large bowl. Cut steak diagonally across the grain into thin slices; add to vegetables and toss to combine with any remaining reserved marinade.

1 SERVING 461 cal., 32g fat (7g sat. fat), 67mg chol., 311mg sod., 12g carb. (5g sugars, 3g fiber), 32g pro.

SKIRT STEAK TACOS Thinly slice the grilled meat, peppers and onions. Serve with tortillas, guacamole and pico de gallo.

EASY SWEDISH MEATBALLS

While the tender homemade meatballs are cooking in the microwave, make your favorite noodles on the stovetop.

—Sheryl Ludeman, Kenosha, WI

TAKES: 30 min. • **MAKES:** 4 servings

- 1 small onion, chopped
- 1 large egg
- ¼ cup seasoned bread crumbs
- 2 Tbsp. 2% milk
- ½ tsp. salt
- ⅛ tsp. pepper
- 1 lb. ground beef

SAUCE

- 1 can (10¾ oz.) condensed cream of mushroom soup, undiluted
- ½ cup sour cream
- ¼ cup 2% milk
- 1 Tbsp. dried parsley flakes
- ¼ tsp. ground nutmeg, optional
  Hot cooked noodles
  Minced fresh parsley, optional

1. In a large bowl, combine onion, egg, bread crumbs, milk, salt and pepper. Crumble beef over mixture; mix lightly but thoroughly. Shape into 24 meatballs. Place in a shallow 1½-qt. microwave-safe dish. Cover and microwave on high for until meat is no longer pink, about 7½ minutes; drain.

2. Combine the soup, sour cream, milk, parsley and, if desired, nutmeg; pour over meatballs. Cover and cook on high until heated through, 5-6 minutes. Serve with noodles and, if desired, top with parsley.

6 MEATBALLS WITH SAUCE 366 cal., 21g fat (10g sat. fat), 135mg chol., 1055mg sod., 15g carb. (4g sugars, 1g fiber), 26g pro.

SOUTHWEST BURGER

We love burgers and have them every Saturday in summer. We also have a favorite burrito recipe. One day, we got the bright idea to combine the two favorites. *Voila!* Our southwestern burgers were born.

—Tammy Fortney, Deer Park, WA

TAKES: 30 min. • **MAKES:** 8 servings

- 1 can (4 oz.) chopped green chiles
- 4 tsp. ground cumin
- 1 tsp. chili powder
- ¾ tsp. garlic powder
- ¾ tsp. salt
- ½ tsp. pepper
- 2 lbs. lean ground beef
- ¾ lb. bulk pork sausage
- 8 slices Monterey Jack cheese
- 8 hamburger buns, split, toasted
- 8 lettuce leaves
- 1 large tomato, sliced
- 1 to 2 ripe avocados, peeled and sliced
  Optional: Mayonnaise or mustard

1. In a large bowl, combine the first 6 ingredients. Crumble the beef and sausage over mixture; mix lightly but thoroughly. Shape into 8 patties.

2. Grill, covered, over medium heat for 5 minutes on each side or until a thermometer reads 160° and juices run clear. Top each burger with a cheese slice.

3. Grill 1-2 minutes longer or until cheese begins to melt. Serve on buns, with the lettuce, tomato, avocado and mayonnaise or mustard if desired.

1 BURGER 516 cal., 29g fat (11g sat. fat), 105mg chol., 888mg sod., 27g carb. (5g sugars, 3g fiber), 34g pro.

PRESSURE-COOKER SHREDDED BEEF BURRITO FILLING

Create a taco or burrito bar! For a variation, I make beef and bean burritos by mixing a can of refried beans into 3 or 4 cups of cooked beef filling.

—Hope Wasylenki, Gahanna, OH

PREP: 20 min. • **COOK:** 40 min. + releasing • **MAKES:** 6 servings

2½ lbs. boneless beef chuck roast, cut into 4 pieces
1 Tbsp. canola oil
1 Tbsp. chili powder
1½ tsp. ground cumin
   Dash salt
1 small onion, finely chopped
1 jalapeno pepper, seeded and finely chopped
1 garlic clove, minced
1 can (14½ oz.) crushed tomatoes in puree
1 cup (8 oz.) salsa verde
¼ cup beef broth
   Optional: Tortillas, shredded cheddar cheese, sour cream, guacamole, salsa and fresh cilantro leaves

1. Season roast with chili powder, cumin and salt. Select saute setting on a 6-qt. electric pressure cooker; adjust for high heat. Add oil; brown roast on all sides. Place onions, peppers and garlic on meat. Top with crushed tomatoes, salsa verde and beef broth. Lock lid; close pressure-release valve. Adjust to pressure-cook on high for 40 minutes.
2. Allow pressure to naturally release for 10 minutes, then quick-release any remaining pressure. Remove roast; shred with 2 forks. Skim fat from cooking juices. Return meat to pressure cooker; heat through. Using tongs, serve on tortillas for burritos or tacos; add toppings as desired.

NOTE Wear disposable gloves when cutting hot peppers; the oils can burn skin. Avoid touching your face.
FREEZE OPTION Freeze cooled meat mixture in freezer containers. To use, thaw in refrigerator overnight. Heat through in a saucepan, stirring occasionally.
1 SERVING 380 cal., 21g fat (7g sat. fat), 123mg chol., 553mg sod., 10g carb. (5g sugars, 2g fiber), 39g pro.

"This was tender and delicious! Will definitely make again. I'm going to try it with a pork roast. Very good flavor."

—QUEENLALISA, TASTEOFHOME.COM

MEXICAN BURGERS

The unique ingredients like breadcrumbs, cilantro and cumin set these delicious burgers apart. With a lovely avocado spread, they will surely be a hit at your next barbecue!

—Francine Lizotte, Langley, BC

PREP: 20 min. + chilling • **GRILL:** 10 min. • **MAKES:** 6 servings

⅓ cup panko bread crumbs
¼ cup finely chopped red onion
1 Tbsp. chopped fresh cilantro
½ tsp. salt
½ tsp. pepper
½ tsp. ground cumin
1½ lbs. ground beef
½ cup shredded aged cheddar cheese

AVOCADO SPREAD
1 medium ripe avocado, peeled
1½ tsp. lime juice
2 Tbsp. sour cream
1 garlic clove, minced
¼ tsp. salt
⅛ tsp. hot pepper sauce
6 hamburger buns, split and toasted

1. In a large bowl, combine bread crumbs, onion, cilantro, salt, pepper and cumin. Add beef and cheese; mix lightly but thoroughly. Shape into six ½-in.-thick patties. Cover and refrigerate for 30 minutes.

2. Grill burgers, covered, over medium heat until a thermometer reads 160°, 3-4 minutes on each side. Meanwhile, in a small bowl, mash avocado and lime juice. Stir in sour cream, garlic, salt and hot sauce. Serve burgers on buns topped with avocado mixture.

1 BURGER 431 cal., 23g fat (8g sat. fat), 83mg chol., 651mg sod., 28g carb. (4g sugars, 3g fiber), 28g pro.

CHEESE OPTIONS

While aged cheddar works well in this recipe, you can use Oaxaca cheese or Manchego for a more authentic Mexican flavor. You can also top the burgers with crumbled queso fresco for a fresh and tangy contrast.

AIR-FRYER STEAK FAJITAS

Zesty salsa and tender strips of steak make these traditional fajitas special.

—Rebecca Baird, Salt Lake City, UT

TAKES: 30 min. • **MAKES:** 6 servings

2 large tomatoes, seeded and chopped
½ cup diced red onion
¼ cup lime juice
1 jalapeno pepper, seeded and minced
3 Tbsp. minced fresh cilantro
2 tsp. ground cumin, divided
¾ tsp. salt, divided
1 beef flank steak (about 1½ lbs.)
1 large onion, halved and sliced
6 whole wheat tortillas (8 in.), warmed
  Optional: Sliced avocado and lime wedges

1. For salsa, place first 5 ingredients in a small bowl; stir in 1 tsp. cumin and ¼ tsp. salt. Let stand until serving.

2. Preheat air fryer to 400°. Sprinkle steak with the remaining 1 tsp. cumin and ½ tsp. salt. Place on a greased tray in air-fryer basket. Cook until meat reaches desired doneness (for medium-rare, a thermometer should read 135°; medium, 140°; medium-well, 145°), 6-8 minutes per side. Remove from basket and let stand 5 minutes.

3. Meanwhile, place onion on tray in air-fryer basket. Cook until crisp-tender, 2-3 minutes, stirring once. Slice steak thinly across the grain; serve in tortillas with onion and salsa. If desired, serve with avocado slices and lime wedges.

NOTE Wear disposable gloves when cutting hot peppers; the oils can burn skin. Avoid touching your face.

1 FAJITA 309 cal., 9g fat (4g sat. fat), 54mg chol., 498mg sod., 29g carb. (3g sugars, 5g fiber), 27g pro. **DIABETIC EXCHANGES** 4 lean meat, 2 starch.

"I love this fajita meal in the air fryer. Getting to use just one cooking appliance to make this dish was so nice and simple. Great flavor with all the spices."

—ANGEL182009, TASTEOFHOME.COM

REUBEN SALAD IN A JAR

We couldn't resist making Reuben salad into an extra-portable version. Get ready to be asked for the recipe.

—*Taste of Home* Test Kitchen

TAKES: 30 min. • **MAKES:** 4 servings

- 2 Tbsp. butter, melted
- ⅛ tsp. pepper
- 2 cups cubed rye bread
- ¾ cup Thousand Island salad dressing
- 2 cups chopped pastrami
- 1 cup sauerkraut, rinsed and well drained
- 1 large tomato, diced
- 8 green onions, thinly sliced
- 1 cup shredded Swiss cheese
- 1 pkg. (6 oz.) ready-to-serve salad greens

1. In a bowl, combine butter and pepper. Add bread cubes and toss to coat. Arrange in a single layer in an ungreased 15x10x1-in. baking pan. Bake at 400° until golden brown, 8-10 minutes, stirring occasionally. Cool.

2. In each of four 1-qt. wide-mouth canning jars, divide and layer ingredients in the following order: dressing, pastrami, sauerkraut, tomato, green onions, cheese and salad greens. Cover and refrigerate until serving. Divide croutons among 4-oz. glass jars or other small containers; cover. To serve, transfer salads and croutons into bowls; toss to combine.

1 SERVING 509 cal., 35g fat (13g sat. fat), 81mg chol., 1454mg sod., 24g carb. (10g sugars, 4g fiber), 24g pro.

GRILLED PORK
BURGERS

GRILLED PORK BURGERS

We live on a working hog farm, and we love this savory burger. Everyone will love these burgers—even if your pork comes from the grocery store, not the farm!

—Dawnita Phillips, Drexel, MO

TAKES: 25 min. • **MAKES:** 6 servings

1 large egg, lightly beaten
¾ cup soft bread crumbs
¾ cup grated Parmesan cheese
1 Tbsp. dried parsley flakes
2 tsp. dried basil
½ tsp. salt
½ tsp. garlic powder
¼ tsp. pepper
2 lbs. ground pork
6 hamburger buns, split
 Optional: Lettuce leaves, sliced tomato and sweet onion

1. In a large bowl, combine the first 8 ingredients. Crumble the pork over mixture and mix lightly but thoroughly. Shape into 6 patties.
2. Grill burgers, covered, over medium heat for 4-5 minutes on each side or until a thermometer reads 160°.
3. Serve on buns; top with lettuce, tomato and onion if desired.

1 BURGER 522 cal., 28g fat (11g sat. fat), 145mg chol., 690mg sod., 28g carb. (4g sugars, 2g fiber), 38g pro.

"Good burger. I used dried bread crumbs instead of soft and couldn't tell a difference. Nice and moist. I use a 5-cheese grated blend instead of Parmesan in all my recipes that call for Parm. It has more flavor. Will make this again."

—GRANDMASCOOKING22, TASTEOFHOME.COM

CURRIED PORK & ORANGE KABOBS

I love the sweet flavor of red, yellow and orange peppers. I always go for these in the summer when they are inexpensive and plentiful. I think they taste a whole lot better than green peppers.

—Liv Vors, Peterborough, ON

TAKES: 30 min. • **MAKES:** 4 servings

½ cup canola oil
2 Tbsp. dried minced onion
1 garlic clove, minced
1 to 2 Tbsp. curry powder
½ tsp. each ground cumin, coriander and cinnamon
1½ lbs. pork tenderloin
1 large sweet red pepper
1 large sweet yellow or orange pepper
1 small onion
1 large unpeeled navel orange

1. In a small bowl, mix oil, minced onion, garlic and spices; reserve half of mixture for basting kabobs while cooking. Cut pork, peppers, onion and unpeeled orange into 1-in. pieces. On 4 metal or soaked wooden skewers, alternately thread pork, vegetables and orange; brush with remaining curry mixture.

2. Grill the kabobs, covered, over medium heat 10-15 minutes or until vegetables and pork are tender, turning occasionally. Baste frequently with the reserved curry mixture during the last 4 minutes of cooking.

1 KABOB 515 cal., 34g fat (4g sat. fat), 95mg chol., 73mg sod., 16g carb. (8g sugars, 4g fiber), 36g pro.

DRY-RUB PORK CHOPS OVER CANNELLINI BEANS & GREENS

My family was not a huge fan of pork until I tried this recipe. Feel free to incorporate your favorite herbs into the dry rub. You can use the rub on boneless skinless chicken breast or other meats too.

—Michael Cirlincione, Stockton, NJ

PREP: 20 min. • **COOK:** 25 min. • **MAKES:** 4 servings

1 Tbsp. olive oil
1 medium onion, chopped
2 garlic cloves, minced
1 can (15 oz.) cannellini beans, rinsed and drained
1 cup water-packed artichoke hearts, drained and chopped
¾ cup pitted Greek olives, chopped
¼ cup dry white wine or chicken broth
¼ cup chicken broth
¼ tsp. salt
¼ tsp. smoked paprika
¼ tsp. pepper
4 bone-in pork loin chops (8 oz. each)
2 tsp. Greek seasoning or seasoning of your choice
5 oz. fresh baby spinach (about 6 cups)

1. In a large skillet, heat oil over medium-high heat. Add onion; cook and stir until tender 4-5 minutes. Add the garlic; cook 1 minute longer. Stir in beans, artichokes, olives, wine, broth, salt, paprika and pepper. Bring to a boil; reduce heat. Simmer until liquid is almost evaporated, 12-15 minutes.
2. Meanwhile, rub chops with the Greek seasoning. Grill pork chops over medium heat until a thermometer reads 145°, 6-8 minutes on each side. Let stand 5 minutes before serving.
3. Stir spinach into bean mixture; cook and stir until wilted, 2-3 minutes. Serve with pork.

1 SERVING 530 cal., 29g fat (8g sat. fat), 111mg chol., 1345mg sod., 22g carb. (1g sugars, 6g fiber), 42g pro.

"I love this recipe! Great for families and very healthy. Recommended for everyone— super fast and convenient. The combination of flavors is amazing."

—AAA892, TASTEOFHOME.COM

PORK SPRING ROLLS

I thought rice paper wrappers would be a quick, fun way to turn salad ingredients into a hand-held meal. I also make these rolls with shrimp and dried cranberries. Go ahead—experiment!

—Marla Strader, Ozark, MO

TAKES: 30 min. • **MAKES:** 4 servings

- 2 cups thinly sliced romaine
- 1½ cups cubed cooked pork
- 1 cup thinly sliced fresh spinach
- ¾ cup julienned carrot
- ⅓ cup thinly sliced celery
- ⅓ cup dried cherries, coarsely chopped
- 1 Tbsp. sesame oil
- 12 round rice paper wrappers (8 in.)
- ¼ cup sliced almonds
- ¼ cup wasabi-coated green peas
  Sesame ginger salad dressing

1. In a large bowl, combine the first 6 ingredients. Drizzle with oil; toss to coat.

2. Fill a large shallow dish partway with water. Dip a rice paper wrapper into water just until pliable, about 45 seconds (do not soften completely); allow excess water to drip off.

3. Place wrapper on a flat surface. Layer salad mixture, almonds and peas across bottom third of wrapper. Fold in both ends of wrapper; fold bottom side over filling, then roll up tightly. Place on a serving plate, seam side down. Repeat with remaining ingredients. Serve with dressing.

3 SPRING ROLLS 356 cal., 12g fat (3g sat. fat), 48mg chol., 100mg sod., 41g carb. (11g sugars, 3g fiber), 20g pro. **DIABETIC EXCHANGES** 3 lean meat, 1 starch, 1 vegetable, 1 fat.

PRESSURE-COOKER SOUTHWESTERN PORK & SQUASH SOUP

I adapted a pork and squash stew recipe, using tomatoes and southwestern-style seasonings. My husband and sons loved it, and the leftovers were even better the next day! Try it with fresh corn muffins.

—Molly Andersen, Portland, OR

PREP: 20 min. • **COOK:** 3 min. • **MAKES:** 6 servings (2¼ qt.)

1   Tbsp. canola oil
1   lb. pork tenderloin, cut into 1-in. cubes
1   medium onion, chopped
3   cups reduced-sodium chicken broth
1   medium butternut squash, peeled and cubed
2   medium carrots, sliced
1   can (14½ oz.) diced tomatoes with mild green chiles, undrained
1   Tbsp. chili powder
1   tsp. ground cumin
1   tsp. dried oregano
½   tsp. pepper
¼   tsp. salt

Select saute setting on a 6-qt. electric pressure cooker and adjust for medium heat; add oil. When oil is hot, cook and stir pork and onion in oil until browned. Press cancel. Stir in the remaining ingredients. Lock lid; close pressure-release valve. Adjust to pressure-cook on high for 3 minutes. Quick-release pressure. (A thermometer inserted into pork should read at least 145°.)

1½ CUPS 228 cal., 5g fat (1g sat. fat), 42mg chol., 637mg sod., 27g carb. (9g sugars, 8g fiber), 19g pro. **DIABETIC EXCHANGES** 2 starch, 1 lean meat, 1 fat.

HOW TO SAFELY VENT A PRESSURE COOKER

Just pick up a pair of tongs for safe, easy venting of your electric pressure cooker.

Use the tongs to carefully turn the release valve—and be sure to keep your hands and face clear of the steam vent.

PRESSURE-COOKER MUSHROOM PORK RAGOUT

Savory, quickly made pork is luscious served in a delightful tomato gravy over noodles. It's a nice change from regular pork roast. I serve it with broccoli or green beans on the side.

—Connie McDowell, Greenwood, DE

PREP: 20 min. • **COOK:** 10 min. • **MAKES:** 2 servings

1 pork tenderloin (¾ lb.)
⅛ tsp. salt
⅛ tsp. pepper
1½ cups sliced fresh mushrooms
¾ cup canned crushed tomatoes
¾ cup reduced-sodium chicken broth, divided
⅓ cup sliced onion
1 Tbsp. chopped sun-dried tomatoes (not packed in oil)
1¼ tsp. dried savory
1 Tbsp. cornstarch
1½ cups hot cooked egg noodles

1. Rub pork with salt and pepper; cut in half. Place in a 6-qt. electric pressure cooker. Top with sliced mushrooms, tomatoes, ½ cup broth, onion, sun-dried tomatoes and the savory.

2. Lock lid and close pressure-release valve. Adjust to pressure-cook on high for 6 minutes. Quick-release pressure. (A thermometer inserted in the pork should read at least 145°.) Remove pork; keep warm.

3. In a small bowl, mix cornstarch and remaining broth until smooth; stir into the pressure cooker. Select the saute setting and adjust for low heat. Simmer, stirring constantly, 1-2 minutes or until thickened. Serve with noodles.

1 SERVING 387 cal., 8g fat (2g sat. fat), 119mg chol., 613mg sod., 37g carb. (8g sugars, 4g fiber), 43g pro. **DIABETIC EXCHANGES** 5 lean meat, 2 vegetable, 1 starch.

AIR-FRYER STUFFED PORK CHOPS

This is one of my favorite dishes to serve to guests because I know they'll love it.

—Lorraine Darocha, Mountain City, TN

PREP: 40 min. • **COOK:** 20 min. • **MAKES:** 4 servings

½ tsp. olive oil
1 celery rib, chopped
¼ cup chopped onion
4 slices white bread, cubed
2 Tbsp. minced fresh parsley
⅛ tsp. salt
⅛ tsp. rubbed sage
⅛ tsp. white pepper
⅛ tsp. dried marjoram
⅛ tsp. dried thyme
⅓ cup reduced-sodium chicken broth

PORK CHOPS
4 pork rib chops (7 oz. each)
¼ tsp. salt
¼ tsp. pepper

1. In a large skillet, heat oil over medium-high heat. Add the celery and onion; cook and stir until tender, 4-5 minutes. Remove from the heat. In a large bowl, combine bread and seasonings. Add celery mixture and broth; toss to coat.
2. Cut a pocket in each pork chop by making a horizontal slice almost to the bone. Fill chops with bread mixture; secure with toothpicks if necessary.
3. Preheat air fryer to 325°. Sprinkle chops with salt and pepper. Arrange in single layer on greased tray in air-fryer basket. Cook 10 minutes. Turn and cook until a thermometer inserted in center of stuffing reads 165° and thermometer inserted in the pork reads at least 145°, 6-8 minutes longer. Let stand 5 minutes; discard toothpicks before serving.

1 PORK CHOP 274 cal., 10g fat (4g sat. fat), 63mg chol., 457mg sod., 16g carb. (2g sugars, 1g fiber), 28g pro. **DIABETIC EXCHANGES** 4 lean meat, 1 starch.

LONG-LASTING HERBS

To keep parsley fresh for up to a month, trim the stems and place the bunch in a tumbler with an inch of water. Be sure no leaves are in the water. Tie a produce bag around the tumbler to trap humidity; store in the refrigerator. Each time you use the parsley, change the water and turn the bag inside out so any moisture built up inside can escape.

MARINATED PORK KABOBS

This recipe was originally for lamb, but I adapted it to pork and adjusted the spices. It's always requested when the grill comes out for the season.

—Bobbie Jo Miller, Fallon, NV

PREP: 15 min. + marinating
GRILL: 15 min. • **MAKES:** 8 servings

- 2 cups plain yogurt
- 2 Tbsp. lemon juice
- 4 garlic cloves, minced
- ½ tsp. ground cumin
- ¼ tsp. ground coriander
- 2 lbs. pork tenderloin, cut into 1½-in. cubes
- 8 small white onions, halved
- 8 cherry tomatoes
- 1 medium sweet red pepper, cut into 1½-in. pieces
- 1 medium green pepper, cut into 1½-in. pieces
  Salt and pepper to taste

1. In a shallow dish, combine yogurt, lemon juice, garlic, cumin and coriander. Add pork and turn to coat; cover and refrigerate 6 hours or overnight.

2. Alternate pork, onions, tomatoes and peppers on 8 metal or soaked wooden skewers. Sprinkle with salt and pepper. Grill, covered, over medium heat until meat juices run clear, 15-20 minutes, turning occasionally.

1 KABOB 190 cal., 5g fat (2g sat. fat), 67mg chol., 63mg sod., 11g carb. (7g sugars, 2g fiber), 25g pro. **DIABETIC EXCHANGES** 3 lean meat, 1 vegetable, ½ fat.

CHAR SIU PORK

I based this juicy pork on Asian influence in Hawaii. It's tasty as is, in a bun or over rice. Use leftovers with fried rice, ramen and salads.

—Karen Naihe, Kamuela, HI

PREP: 25 min. + marinating
COOK: 1¼ hours + releasing
MAKES: 8 servings

- ½ cup honey
- ½ cup hoisin sauce
- ¼ cup soy sauce
- ¼ cup ketchup
- 4 garlic cloves, minced
- 4 tsp. minced fresh gingerroot
- 1 tsp. Chinese five-spice powder
- 1 boneless pork shoulder butt roast (3 to 4 lbs.)
- ½ cup chicken broth
  Fresh cilantro leaves

1. Combine the first 7 ingredients; pour into a large shallow dish. Cut roast in half; add to dish and turn to coat. Cover and refrigerate overnight.
2. Transfer pork and marinade to a 6-qt. electric pressure cooker. Add chicken broth. Lock lid; close pressure-release valve. Adjust to pressure-cook on high for 75 minutes. Allow pressure to naturally release for 10 minutes, then quick-release any remaining pressure.
3. Remove pork; when cool enough to handle, shred meat using 2 forks. Skim fat from cooking juices. Return pork to pressure cooker. Select saute setting and adjust for low heat; heat through. Top pork with fresh cilantro.

1 SERVING 392 cal., 18g fat (6g sat. fat), 102mg chol., 981mg sod., 27g carb. (24g sugars, 1g fiber), 31g pro.

GRILLED HAM BURGERS

My family loves my ham loaf, so I decided to make the ham loaf mixture into patties and grill them—they were an instant hit. Arugula gives these burgers a peppery bite, and honey mustard dressing adds just the right sweet and sour flavor.

—Susan Bickta, Kutztown, PA

PREP: 20 min. + chilling • **GRILL:** 10 min. • **MAKES:** 8 servings

1½ lbs. fully cooked boneless ham
¾ lb. ground pork
2 large eggs, beaten
⅔ cup graham cracker crumbs
⅓ cup packed brown sugar
⅓ cup canned unsweetened crushed pineapple plus 3 Tbsp. juice
1 Tbsp. spicy brown mustard
¼ tsp. ground cloves
8 slices Swiss cheese (1 oz. each)
8 kaiser rolls, split
2 large tomatoes, cut in sixteen ¼-in. slices
½ cup honey mustard salad dressing
1½ cups fresh baby arugula
Additional honey mustard salad dressing, optional

1. Pulse ham in food processor until finely ground. Combine with pork, eggs, cracker crumbs, brown sugar, pineapple and juice, mustard and cloves. Mix lightly but thoroughly. Shape into 8 patties. Using your fingertips, make a shallow indentation in center of each patty so it remains flat while grilling. Refrigerate 1 hour.

2. Grill burgers, covered, on a greased rack over medium-high direct heat for 5-6 minutes; turn and grill another 3-4 minutes. Add a slice of cheese to each burger; grill, covered, until cheese melts, 1-2 minutes more. Remove from heat when a thermometer reads 160°.

3. Place burgers on roll bottoms; top with tomato slices. Drizzle each with 1 Tbsp. honey mustard dressing. Divide arugula among burgers; replace roll tops. If desired, serve with additional dressing.
1 BURGER 632 cal., 28g fat (9g sat. fat), 149mg chol., 1430mg sod., 55g carb. (18g sugars, 2g fiber), 40g pro.

PRESSURE-COOKER PORK TACOS WITH MANGO SALSA

I've made quite a few tacos in my day, but you can't beat the tender filling made in a pressure cooker. These are by far the best pork tacos we've had—and we've tried plenty. Make the mango salsa from scratch if you have time!

—Amber Massey, Argyle, TX

PREP: 25 min. • **COOK:** 5 min. • **MAKES:** 12 servings

2 Tbsp. white vinegar
2 Tbsp. lime juice
3 cups cubed fresh pineapple
1 small red onion, coarsely chopped
3 Tbsp. chili powder
2 chipotle peppers in adobo sauce
2 tsp. ground cumin
1½ tsp. salt
½ tsp. pepper
1 bottle (12 oz.) dark Mexican beer
3 lbs. pork tenderloin, cut into 1-in. cubes
¼ cup chopped fresh cilantro
1 jar (16 oz.) mango salsa
24 corn tortillas (6 in.), warmed
Optional toppings: Cubed fresh pineapple, cubed avocado and queso fresco

1. Puree the first 9 ingredients in a blender; stir in beer. In a 6-qt. electric pressure cooker, combine pork and pineapple mixture. Lock lid; close pressure-release valve. Adjust to pressure-cook on high for 3 minutes. Quick-release pressure. A thermometer inserted into pork should read at least 145°. Stir to break up pork.

2. Stir cilantro into salsa. Using a slotted spoon, place pork mixture in tortillas. Serve with salsa, and toppings as desired.

FREEZE OPTION Freeze cooled meat mixture and cooking juices in freezer containers. To use, partially thaw in refrigerator overnight. Heat through in a saucepan, stirring occasionally.

2 TACOS 284 cal., 6g fat (2g sat. fat), 64mg chol., 678mg sod., 30g carb. (5g sugars, 5g fiber), 26g pro. **DIABETIC EXCHANGES** 3 lean meat, 2 starch.

GRILLED PORK CHOPS WITH SPICY FENNEL RELISH

Pork chops are great for grilling! If you have time, marinate the pork chops for several hours or overnight before grilling for even more flavor. You could also add lemon juice and zest to the marinade to add a bright citrus note to the pork.

—Gilda Lester, Millsboro, DE

PREP: 20 min. • **GRILL:** 15 min. • **MAKES:** 4 servings

½ cup lemon juice, divided
½ cup extra virgin olive oil, divided
2 garlic cloves, minced
1½ tsp. salt, divided
1 tsp. ground cumin
4 bone-in pork loin chops (1 in. thick and 8 oz. each)
1 medium sweet red pepper, halved
½ large onion, cut into ½-in. slices
½ medium fennel bulb, cut into ½-in. slices
¼ cup coarsely chopped pitted green olives
2 Tbsp. chopped fresh basil
⅛ tsp. crushed red pepper flakes

1. In a shallow dish, combine ¼ cup lemon juice, ¼ cup oil, garlic, 1 tsp. salt and cumin. Add pork; turn to coat. Let stand while preparing vegetables.
2. Place red peppers, onion and fennel in grill basket; brush with 2 Tbsp. oil. Grill, covered, over medium-high heat until lightly charred, 4-5 minutes. Remove to a cutting board and finely chop. In a large bowl, combine vegetables, olives, basil, remaining ¼ cup lemon juice, remaining 2 Tbsp. oil, remaining ½ tsp. salt and red pepper flakes.

3. Drain pork, discarding marinade. Grill pork, covered, over medium-high heat until a thermometer reads 145°, 6-8 minutes on each side. Let stand 5 minutes before serving with relish.

1 PORK CHOP WITH ½ CUP RELISH
487 cal., 34g fat (9g sat. fat), 111mg chol., 864mg sod., 8g carb. (4g sugars, 2g fiber), 37g pro.

GRILLED SUMMER SAUSAGE SALAD

It's not often you see sausage in a salad, but I say why not? The grilled meat and garden vegetables make for a garlicky, fresh-tasting, super-filling salad. I'll even grill the romaine on occasion!

—Noelle Myers, Grand Forks, ND

TAKES: 30 min. • **MAKES:** 8 servings

1   lb. garlic summer sausage, casing removed, quartered lengthwise
2   small zucchini, cut in half lengthwise
2   yellow summer squash, cut in half lengthwise
1   medium sweet red pepper, halved and seeded
1   medium sweet orange pepper, halved and seeded
2   Tbsp. olive oil
½   tsp. salt
¼   tsp. pepper
1   pkg. (5 oz.) spring mix salad greens
½   English cucumber, chopped
2   celery ribs with leaves, chopped
½   cup Italian salad dressing

1. Brush summer sausage, zucchini, yellow squash and peppers with olive oil; sprinkle with salt and pepper. Grill sausage and vegetables on an oiled rack, covered, over medium heat for 5-6 minutes on each side or until crisp-tender. Remove to cutting board; coarsely chop vegetables and sausage.

2. Place salad greens in a large bowl; add cucumber, celery, grilled vegetables and sausage. Drizzle with dressing; toss to coat. Divide among 8 bowls. If desired, sprinkle with additional black pepper.

2 CUPS 260 cal., 21g fat (6g sat. fat), 35mg chol., 1048mg sod., 10g carb. (4g sugars, 2g fiber), 10g pro.

"This was very good! I added some onion and cherry tomatoes to the mix, since they needed to be used up. We also added cheese."

—AHMOM, TASTEOFHOME.COM

5i

PRESSURE-COOKER MAC & CHEESE

This gooey, cheesy Velveeta recipe reminds me so much of my grandma's macaroni and cheese. It is easier to make than from a box and has a nice homemade touch from the pepper.

—Jennifer Stowell, Deep River, IA

PREP: 10 min. • **COOK:** 15 min. **MAKES:** 4 servings

1 pkg. (16 oz.) elbow macaroni
2½ cups chicken broth
½ cup butter, cubed
1 pkg. (8 oz.) Velveeta, cubed
1 cup heavy whipping cream
   Pepper to taste

1½ CUPS 1009 cal., 62g fat (38g sat. fat), 184mg chol., 1470mg sod., 90g carb. (9g sugars, 4g fiber), 27g pro.

CUSTOMIZE IT

Velveeta works perfectly in Pressure-Cooker Mac & Cheese, melting smoothly without curdling. For a deeper flavor, try stirring in shredded Gruyere, sharp cheddar, or Parmesan at the end for added creaminess and a nutty finish.

1. In a 6-qt. electric pressure cooker, add the first 4 ingredients in order; do not stir. Lock lid; close pressure-release valve. Adjust to pressure-cook on high for 7 minutes. Let pressure release naturally for 5 minutes; quick-release any remaining pressure.
2. Stir to combine then gradually stir in cream and pepper.

GRILLED SALMON WITH AVOCADO SALSA

I'm not usually a seafood fan, but I ordered a similar salmon dish at a restaurant, and I couldn't stop eating it. My recipe re-creation has become a favorite with family and friends.

—Renee McIlheran, Channahon, IL

TAKES: 25 min. • **MAKES:** 4 servings

- 1 large tomato, seeded and chopped
- 1 medium ripe avocado, peeled and chopped
- 1 small onion, chopped
- ½ cup minced fresh cilantro
- 1½ tsp. olive oil
- 1 garlic clove, minced
- 2 Tbsp. plus 2 tsp. balsamic vinaigrette, divided
- 4 salmon fillets (4 oz. each)
- ¼ tsp. salt
- ¼ tsp. pepper

1. In a small bowl, combine the tomato, avocado, onion, cilantro, oil, garlic and 2 Tbsp. vinaigrette. Chill until serving.

2. Moisten a paper towel with cooking oil; using long-handled tongs, lightly coat the grill rack. Sprinkle salmon with salt and pepper. Place salmon skin side down on grill rack. Grill, covered, over medium heat for 7-9 minutes or until the salmon flakes easily with a fork. Brush with remaining vinaigrette. Serve with salsa.

1 FILLET WITH ½ CUP SALSA 301 cal., 21g fat (3g sat. fat), 57mg chol., 295mg sod., 9g carb. (3g sugars, 4g fiber), 21g pro. **DIABETIC EXCHANGES** 3 lean meat, 2 fat.

CHIMICHANGAS

Though this is still debated, Tucson is generally credited as the original home of the chimichanga (fried burro, as we call them, stuffed with meat, onions and chiles). I've combined several recipes into this one, and it's fairly authentic.

—Laura Towns, Glendale, AZ

TAKES: 30 min. • **MAKES:** 12 servings

¼ cup bacon grease
2 cups chopped or shredded cooked beef, pork or chicken
1 medium onion, diced
2 garlic cloves, minced
2 medium tomatoes, chopped
2 cans (4 oz. each) chopped green chiles
1 large peeled boiled potato, diced
1 tsp. salt
1½ tsp. dried oregano
1 to 2 tsp. chili powder or to taste
2 Tbsp. minced fresh cilantro
12 flour tortillas (12 in.), warmed
Canola oil
Optional toppings: Shredded cheddar cheese, sour cream, guacamole, salsa, shredded lettuce, chopped tomatoes and sliced ripe olives

1. In a large skillet, heat bacon grease over medium heat. Add beef, onion, garlic, tomato, chiles and potato. Stir in salt, oregano, chili powder and cilantro. Simmer until liquid has reduced, 2-3 minutes.

2. To assemble, place ½ cup off-center on each tortilla. Fold up edge nearest filling; fold in both sides and roll up. If needed, secure with a toothpick.

3. In an electric skillet or deep-fat fryer, heat oil to 375°. Cook chimichangas until golden brown, turning to cook all sides. Drain on paper towels. Serve with toppings of your choice.

1 CHIMICHANGA 343 cal., 13g fat (4g sat. fat), 25mg chol., 862mg sod., 41g carb. (2g sugars, 7g fiber), 16g pro.

CHIMICHANGA TIPS

Can you bake chimichangas instead of frying them?
Yes. To make chimichangas lighter, bake them instead of frying. Prepare as usual, but bake at 375° for 20–30 minutes or until golden brown.

How do you store chimichangas?
Refrigerate chimichangas for up to 3 days. For longer storage, wrap cooled chimichangas in foil and place in a freezer-safe bag. They can be frozen for up to 3 months, making them perfect for busy nights!

What's the best way to reheat chimichangas?
Reheat chimichangas in a skillet with hot oil, in the oven, or in an air fryer. The air fryer works particularly well for restoring crispiness.

AIR-FRYER SHRIMP CAKE SLIDERS

My family loves these shrimp sliders. The slaw dressing and shrimp cake patties can be made ahead. When you're ready to serve, toss the cabbage slaw, air-fry the shrimp cakes, assemble and enjoy.

—Kim Banick, Turner, OR

PREP: 30 min. + chilling • **COOK:** 10 min./batch • **MAKES:** 12 sliders

1 lb. uncooked shrimp (41-50 per lb.), peeled and deveined
1 large egg, lightly beaten
½ cup finely chopped sweet red pepper
6 green onions, chopped and divided
1 Tbsp. minced fresh gingerroot
¼ tsp. salt
1 cup panko bread crumbs
¼ cup mayonnaise
1 Tbsp. Sriracha chili sauce
1 Tbsp. sweet chili sauce
5 cups shredded Chinese or napa cabbage
12 mini buns or dinner rolls, toasted
3 Tbsp. canola oil
   Additional Sriracha chili sauce, optional

1. Place shrimp in a food processor; pulse until chopped. In a large bowl, combine the egg, red pepper, 4 green onions, ginger and salt. Add shrimp and bread crumbs; mix gently. Shape into twelve ½-in.-thick patties. Refrigerate 20 minutes.

2. Meanwhile, in a large bowl, combine mayonnaise and the chili sauces; stir in cabbage and remaining green onions.

3. Preheat air fryer to 375°. In batches, place patties in a single layer on greased tray in air-fryer basket. Cook until golden brown, 8-10 minutes. Serve on buns with slaw; secure with toothpicks. If desired, serve with additional chili sauce.

1 SLIDER 210 cal., 10g fat (1g sat. fat), 63mg chol., 321mg sod., 20g carb. (3g sugars, 1g fiber), 11g pro.

"The first time I made them, my husband said these were the stars of the show! They're always a big hit. My go-to recipe for shrimp cakes, hands down."

—BETH5849, TASTEOFHOME.COM

HERBED TUNA SALAD

HERBED TUNA SALAD

Cooking for two is a challenge for us since my husband and I do not care for leftovers. This well-seasoned salad with a distinctive dill flavor is my favorite lunch recipe.

—Rebecca Schweizer, Chesapeake, VA

TAKES: 15 min. • **MAKES:** 2 servings

1 can (6 oz.) light water-packed tuna, drained and flaked
2 Tbsp. finely chopped red onion
1 tsp. minced fresh parsley
1½ tsp. dill weed
⅛ tsp. garlic salt
⅛ tsp. dried thyme
⅛ tsp. pepper
  Pinch cayenne pepper
2 Tbsp. fat-free mayonnaise

1 Tbsp. reduced-fat sour cream
3 cups Boston lettuce leaves
6 grape tomatoes, sliced
  Optional: Sliced cucumber and fresh dill

1. In a small bowl, combine the first 8 ingredients. Combine the mayonnaise and sour cream; stir into the tuna mixture.

2. Divide the salad greens between 2 plates. Top with tuna mixture and tomatoes and, if desired, cucumbers and dill.

1 SERVING 170 cal., 2g fat (1g sat. fat), 30mg chol., 452mg sod., 14g carb. (0 sugars, 4g fiber), 25g pro. **DIABETIC EXCHANGES** 3 lean meat, 2 vegetable.

AIR-FRYER CHICKPEA & RED ONION BURGERS

When chilly days arrive and we retire the grill to the garage, I make a batch of air-fryer chickpea burgers that even die-hard meat eaters can't resist.

—Lily Julow, Lawrenceville, GA

TAKES: 30 min. • **MAKES:** 6 servings

1 large red onion, thinly sliced
¼ cup fat-free red wine vinaigrette
2 cans (15 oz. each) chickpeas or garbanzo beans, rinsed and drained
⅓ cup chopped walnuts
¼ cup toasted wheat germ or dry bread crumbs
¼ cup packed fresh parsley sprigs
2 large eggs
1 tsp. curry powder
½ tsp. pepper
  Cooking spray

⅓ cup fat-free mayonnaise
2 tsp. Dijon mustard
6 sesame seed hamburger buns, split and toasted
6 lettuce leaves
3 Tbsp. thinly sliced fresh basil leaves

1. Preheat air fryer to 375°. In a small bowl, mix onion and vinaigrette; set aside. Place chickpeas, walnuts, wheat germ and parsley in a food processor; pulse until blended. Add the eggs, curry powder and pepper; process until smooth.

2. Shape into 6 patties. In batches, place patties in a single layer on a greased tray in air-fryer basket, spray with cooking spray. Cook until a thermometer reads 160°, 8-10 minutes, flipping halfway through cooking.

3. In a small bowl, mix mayonnaise and mustard; spread over cut sides of buns. Serve patties on buns with lettuce, basil and onion mixture.

1 BURGER 381 cal., 13g fat (2g sat. fat), 62mg chol., 697mg sod., 54g carb. (10g sugars, 9g fiber), 16g pro.

AIR-FRYER FISH & CHIPS

Looking for easy air-fryer recipes? Try these simple fish and chips. The fish fillets have a fuss-free coating that's healthier but just as crunchy and golden as the deep-fried kind. Simply seasoned, the crispy fries are perfect on the side.

—Janice Mitchell, Aurora, CO

PREP: 15 min. • **COOK:** 25 min. • **MAKES:** 4 servings

1 lb. potatoes (about 2 medium)
2 Tbsp. olive oil
¼ tsp. pepper
¼ tsp. salt
FISH
⅓ cup all-purpose flour
¼ tsp. pepper
1 large egg
2 Tbsp. water
⅔ cup crushed cornflakes
1 Tbsp. grated Parmesan cheese
⅛ tsp. cayenne pepper
1 lb. haddock or cod fillets
¼ tsp. salt
  Tartar sauce, optional

1. Preheat air fryer to 400°. Peel and cut potatoes lengthwise into ½-in.-thick slices; cut slices into ½-in.-thick sticks.
2. In a large bowl, toss potatoes with oil, pepper and salt. Working in batches, place potatoes in a single layer on tray in air-fryer basket; cook until just tender, 5-10 minutes Toss potatoes to redistribute; cook until lightly browned and crisp, 5-10 minutes longer.
3. Meanwhile, in a shallow bowl, mix flour and pepper. In another shallow bowl, whisk egg with water. In a third bowl, toss cornflakes with cheese and cayenne. Sprinkle fish with salt. Dip into flour mixture to coat both sides; shake off excess. Dip in egg mixture, then in cornflake mixture, patting to help the coating adhere.

4. Remove fries from basket; keep warm. Place fish in a single layer on tray in air-fryer basket. Cook until fish is lightly browned and just beginning to flake easily with a fork, 8-10 minutes, turning halfway through cooking. Do not overcook. Return fries to basket to heat through. Serve immediately. If desired, serve with tartar sauce.
1 SERVING 312 cal., 9g fat (2g sat. fat), 85mg chol., 503mg sod., 35g carb. (3g sugars, 1g fiber), 23g pro. **DIABETIC EXCHANGES** 3 lean meat, 2 starch, 2 fat.

FISH & CHIPS TIPS

How long do you cook fish in the air fryer?
Cook fish fillets in the air fryer for 8 to 10 minutes, or until the fish flakes easily with a fork. Cooking times may vary depending on the fillet size and air fryer brand.

Can you use frozen fish fillets to make air-fryer fish fillets?
Only use thawed fish fillets. Thawing the fish overnight in the fridge ensures the coating sticks properly and prevents the outside from overcooking before the center is fully done.

How do you make the coating stick to the fish fillets?
Pat the fillets dry with a paper towel to remove excess moisture. Dip the fish in egg, then press the coating mixture (like cornflakes) onto the fillets to ensure it adheres.

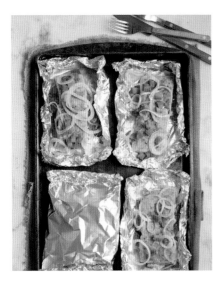

SALMON GRILLED IN FOIL

This tender salmon steams up in foil packets, meaning easy cleanup later.

—Merideth Berkovich, The Dalles, OR

TAKES: 20 min. • **MAKES:** 4 servings

- 4 salmon fillets (4 oz. each)
- 1 tsp. garlic powder
- 1 tsp. lemon-pepper seasoning
- 1 tsp. curry powder
- ½ tsp. salt
- 1 small onion, cut into rings
- 2 medium tomatoes, seeded and chopped

1. Place each salmon fillet, skin side down, on a double thickness of heavy-duty foil (about 18x12 in.). Combine the garlic powder, lemon pepper, curry powder and salt; sprinkle over salmon. Top with onion and tomatoes. Fold foil over fish and seal tightly.

2. Grill, covered, over medium heat for 10-15 minutes or until fish flakes easily with a fork. Open foil carefully to allow steam to escape.

1 PACKET 199 cal., 11g fat (2g sat. fat), 57mg chol., 436mg sod., 5g carb. (2g sugars, 1g fiber), 20g pro. **DIABETIC EXCHANGES** 3 lean meat.

"I have tried this recipe twice, and I love it! The first time, I had fresh salmon and put it on the grill. The next time, I used halibut steaks and cherry tomatoes instead of chopped, and I added asparagus and mushrooms. I cooked it in the oven at 400° for 30 minutes. The steaks came out delicious, the fish was flaky and tender, and the seasoning, perfect!"

—ZERBMEISTER, TASTEOFHOME.COM

HOW TO MAKE PERFECT FOIL PACKS

Following the recipe closely is the best way to ensure everything is done at the same time in your foil packets. This recipe uses small fillets and thinly sliced onions, which will cook more quickly than large pieces.

If you were using a much larger or thicker fillet of salmon, you'd cut the veggies larger or introduce sturdy veggies such as chopped potatoes, broccoli florets and carrot sticks. If you'd like to include these veggies with small fish portions, simply parcook them before adding to the packs.

AIR-FRYER TUNA BURGERS

My family was hesitant to try these, but any skepticism disappeared after one bite.

—Kim Stoller, Smithville, OH

TAKES: 30 min. • **MAKES:** 4 servings

1 large egg, lightly beaten
½ cup dry bread crumbs
½ cup finely chopped celery
⅓ cup mayonnaise
¼ cup finely chopped onion
2 Tbsp. chili sauce
1 pouch (6.4 oz.) light tuna in water
4 hamburger buns, split and toasted
  Optional: Lettuce leaves and sliced
  tomato

1. Preheat air fryer to 350°. In a small bowl, combine first 6 ingredients; fold in tuna. Shape into 4 patties.

2. In batches, place patties in a single layer on greased tray in air-fryer basket. Cook until lightly browned, 5-6 minutes per side. Serve on buns. If desired, top with lettuce and tomato.

1 BURGER 366 cal., 17g fat (3g sat. fat), 64mg chol., 665mg sod., 35g carb. (6g sugars, 2g fiber), 17g pro.

---

⑤ⅰ

BACON-WRAPPED SCALLOPS WITH PINEAPPLE QUINOA

Bacon-wrapped scallops seem so decadent and fancy that oftentimes I forget how easy they are to prepare. This elegant entree can be ready in 30 minutes.

—Laura Greenberg, Lake Balboa, CA

TAKES: 30 min. • **MAKES:** 4 servings

1 can (14½ oz.) vegetable broth
1 cup quinoa, rinsed
¼ tsp. salt
⅛ tsp. plus ¼ tsp. pepper, divided
10 bacon strips
16 sea scallops (about 2 lbs.), side muscles removed
1 cup drained canned pineapple tidbits

1. In a small saucepan, bring broth to a boil. Add quinoa, salt and ⅛ tsp. pepper. Reduce heat; simmer, covered, 12-15 minutes or until liquid is absorbed.

2. Meanwhile, preheat air fryer to 400°. Arrange 8 strips of bacon in a single layer on tray in air-fryer basket. Cook 3 minutes or until partially cooked but not crisp. Remove and set aside. Add remaining 2 bacon strips; cook until crisp, 5-6 minutes. Finely chop crisp bacon strips. Cut remaining partially-cooked bacon strips lengthwise in half.

3. Wrap a halved bacon strip around each scallop; secure with a toothpick. Sprinkle with remaining pepper.

4. Arrange scallops in a single layer on greased tray in air-fryer basket. Cook until scallops are firm and opaque, 8-10 minutes.

5. Remove quinoa from heat; fluff with a fork. Stir in pineapple and chopped bacon. Serve with scallops.

4 SCALLOPS WITH ¾ CUP QUINOA 455 cal., 12g fat (3g sat. fat), 75mg chol., 1717mg sod., 45g carb. (10g sugars, 3g fiber), 41g pro.

FRITTATA GOES TO MEXICO

I love that I can multitask while I'm air-frying. These individual Mexico-inspired mini frittatas are fast, easy and loaded with flavor! Serve with fresh fruit salad and toasted English muffins.

—Sharyn LaPointe Hill, Las Cruces, NM

PREP: 20 min. • **COOK:** 15 min. • **MAKES:** 4 servings

½ lb. Yukon Gold potatoes, cubed (about 2 cups)
1 Tbsp. olive oil
½ tsp. garlic salt
4 large eggs
2 Tbsp. half-and-half cream
¼ cup spreadable spicy jalapeno cream cheese, softened
½ tsp. ground cumin
½ cup shredded Mexican cheese blend
½ cup cherry tomatoes, quartered
2 Tbsp. minced fresh cilantro
1 Tbsp. minced seeded jalapeno pepper
Thinly sliced jalapeno pepper

1. Preheat air fryer to 400°. Place potatoes, oil and garlic salt in a large bowl; toss to coat. Place potatoes on tray in air-fryer basket. Cook until tender and lightly browned, 14-16 minutes, shaking basket occasionally to redistribute.

2. In another bowl, whisk eggs, half-and-half, cream cheese and cumin until blended. Stir in shredded cheese, tomatoes, cilantro and minced jalapeno. Divide potatoes among 4 greased 8-oz. ramekins. Pour egg mixture over top; cover with foil. Place ramekins in air-fryer basket. Cook for 12 minutes. Remove foil and cook until set and a knife inserted in center comes out clean, about 3 minutes longer. Let stand 5 minutes before serving. Top with jalapeno slices.

NOTE Wear disposable gloves when cutting hot peppers; the oils can burn skin. Avoid touching your face.
1 FRITTATA 262 cal., 17g fat (7g sat. fat), 212mg chol., 498mg sod., 14g carb. (2g sugars, 1g fiber), 12g pro.

HERBED LAMB KABOBS

This colorful kabob wouldn't be the same without its delicious herb marinade and tender-crisp vegetables. Together, they add delicious flavor and texture to the lamb pieces.

—Janet Dingler, Cedartown, GA

PREP: 15 min. + marinating • **GRILL:** 20 min. • **MAKES:** 8 servings

- 1 cup canola oil
- 1 medium onion, chopped
- ½ cup lemon juice
- ½ cup minced fresh parsley
- 3 to 4 garlic cloves, minced
- 2 tsp. salt
- 2 tsp. dried marjoram
- 2 tsp. dried thyme
- ½ tsp. pepper
- 2 lbs. boneless lamb, cut into 1-in. cubes
- 1 medium red onion, cut into wedges
- 1 large green pepper, cut into 1-in. pieces
- 1 large sweet red pepper, cut into 1-in. pieces

1. In a small bowl, combine the first 9 ingredients. Pour 1 cup into a shallow dish; add lamb and turn to coat. Cover; refrigerate for 6-8 hours. Cover and refrigerate remaining marinade for basting.

2. Drain and discard marinade. On 8 metal or soaked wooden skewers, alternately thread lamb and vegetables. Grill, uncovered, over medium-hot heat for 8-10 minutes on each side or until meat reaches desired doneness (for medium-rare, a thermometer should read 135°; medium, 140°; medium-well, 145°), basting frequently with reserved marinade.

1 SERVING 366 cal., 28g fat (5g sat. fat), 69mg chol., 591mg sod., 6g carb. (3g sugars, 2g fiber), 22g pro.

"I don't have a grill, so I made these on a large indoor griddle. It still turned out amazing! I used pork instead of lamb because of cost constraints, but I feel the marinade would have been good on anything. I will recommend this to anyone looking for a good marinade!"

—THEHEAT01, TASTEOFHOME.COM

BLACK BEAN CHIMIS FROM THE AIR FRYER

BLACK BEAN CHIMIS FROM THE AIR FRYER

These chimichangas get a little love from the air fryer, so they're healthier than their deep-fried counterparts. Black beans provide protein, and the recipe is a smart way to use up leftover rice.

—Kimberly Hammond, Kingwood, TX

PREP: 20 min. • **COOK:** 5 min./batch • **MAKES:** 6 servings

2 cans (15 oz. each) black beans, rinsed and drained
1 pkg. (8.8 oz.) ready-to-serve brown rice
⅔ cup frozen corn
⅔ cup minced fresh cilantro
⅔ cup chopped green onions
½ tsp. salt
6 whole wheat tortillas (8 in.), warmed
4 tsp. olive oil
Optional: Guacamole and salsa

1. Preheat air fryer to 400°. In a large microwave-safe bowl, mix beans, rice and corn; microwave, covered, until heated through, 4-5 minutes, stirring halfway. Stir in cilantro, green onions and salt.
2. Spoon ¾ cup bean mixture across the center of each tortilla. Fold bottom and sides of tortilla over filling and roll up. Brush with olive oil.

3. In batches, place seam side down on greased tray in air-fryer basket. Cook until golden brown and crispy, 2-3 minutes. If desired, serve with guacamole and salsa.
1 CHIMICHANGA 337 cal., 5g fat (0 sat. fat), 0 chol., 602mg sod., 58g carb. (2g sugars, 10g fiber), 13g pro.

GARDEN CHICKPEA SALAD

Looking for something different on a hot summer's day? This refreshing salad makes a terrific cold entree.

—Sally Sibthorpe, Shelby Township, MI

TAKES: 25 min. • **MAKES:** 2 servings

½ tsp. cumin seeds
¼ cup chopped tomato
¼ cup lemon juice
¼ cup olive oil
1 garlic clove, minced
¼ tsp. salt
¼ tsp. cayenne pepper
SALAD
¾ cup canned garbanzo beans or chickpeas, rinsed and drained
1 medium carrot, julienned
1 small zucchini, julienned

2 green onions, thinly sliced
½ cup coarsely chopped fresh parsley
¼ cup thinly sliced radishes
¼ cup crumbled feta cheese
3 Tbsp. chopped walnuts
3 cups spring mix salad greens

1. For dressing, in a dry small skillet, toast cumin seeds over medium heat until aromatic, stirring frequently. Transfer to a bowl. Stir in tomato, lemon juice, oil, garlic, salt and cayenne pepper.

2. In another bowl, combine chickpeas, carrot, zucchini, green onions, parsley, radishes, cheese and walnuts. Stir in ⅓ cup dressing.
3. To serve, divide greens between 2 plates; top with chickpea mixture. Drizzle with remaining dressing.
1 SERVING 492 cal., 38g fat (6g sat. fat), 8mg chol., 619mg sod., 30g carb. (7g sugars, 9g fiber), 12g pro.

GARLIC-HERB SALMON SLIDERS

I serve these as full-sized burgers on kaiser rolls too. The fresh flavors of the salmon and herbs are just unbeatable.

—Margee Berry, White Salmon, WA

PREP: 25 min. • **GRILL:** 10 min.
MAKES: 4 servings

⅓ cup panko bread crumbs
4 tsp. finely chopped shallot
2 tsp. snipped fresh dill
1 Tbsp. prepared horseradish
1 large egg, beaten
¼ tsp. salt
⅛ tsp. pepper
1 lb. salmon fillet, skin removed, cut into 1-in. cubes
8 whole wheat dinner rolls, split and toasted
¼ cup reduced-fat garlic-herb spreadable cheese
8 small lettuce leaves
8 slices red onion

1. In a large bowl, combine the first 7 ingredients. Place salmon in a food processor; pulse until coarsely chopped, and add to bread crumb mixture. Mix lightly but thoroughly. Shape into eight ½-in.-thick patties.
2. On a lightly greased grill rack, grill burgers, covered, over medium heat or broil 4 in. from heat until a thermometer reads 160°, 3-4 minutes on each side. Serve on rolls with spreadable cheese, lettuce and onion.
2 SLIDERS 446 cal., 17g fat (5g sat. fat), 112mg chol., 719mg sod., 43g carb. (7g sugars, 6g fiber), 30g pro. **DIABETIC EXCHANGES** 3 starch, 3 lean meat, 1 fat.

SHRIMP CAESAR SALAD

My friend Jane and I have a favorite lunch spot that serves a fantastic salad on Wednesdays. I created my own version at home so I can eat it whenever I want. To save prep time, buy peeled, deveined shrimp and prewashed lettuce.

—Marla Clark, Albuquerque, NM

TAKES: 30 min. • **MAKES:** 4 servings

- 2 romaine hearts, coarsely chopped
- 1 cup cherry tomatoes, halved
- ¼ cup shredded Parmesan cheese
- ½ cup all-purpose flour
- ¾ tsp. salt
- ½ tsp. pepper
- 1 lb. uncooked large shrimp, peeled and deveined
  Oil for frying
- ½ cup creamy Caesar salad dressing
  Additional shredded Parmesan cheese and pepper, optional

1. In a large bowl, combine romaine, tomatoes and cheese; refrigerate until serving. In a shallow bowl, mix flour, salt and pepper. Add shrimp, a few pieces at a time, and toss to coat; shake off excess.
2. In a deep skillet, heat ¼ in. oil to 375°. Fry shrimp, a few at a time, 1-2 minutes on each side or until golden brown. Drain on paper towels.
3. Drizzle dressing over romaine mixture and toss to coat. Top with shrimp. If desired, sprinkle with additional cheese and pepper; serve immediately.
1 SERVING 405 cal., 31g fat (5g sat. fat), 153mg chol., 680mg sod., 8g carb. (2g sugars, 2g fiber), 23g pro.

FRIED FISH TACOS

This fried fish taco recipe is easy to make for dinner any night of the week. Use cod, halibut, walleye or any flaky whitefish that can stand up to a good beer batter and hot oil. Serve with crunchy cabbage and warm tortillas.

—*Taste of Home* Test Kitchen

PREP: 25 min. + chilling • **COOK:** 5 min./batch • **MAKES:** 6 servings

- 2 cups shredded cabbage
- 3 Tbsp. mayonnaise
- 2 Tbsp. minced fresh cilantro
- 2 Tbsp. sour cream
- 1 Tbsp. lime juice
- 1 Tbsp. honey
- ¼ tsp. salt
  Oil for deep-fat frying

BATTER
- 1 cup all-purpose flour
- 1½ tsp. baking powder
- ¾ tsp. salt
- ¼ tsp. cayenne pepper
- 1 cup very cold beer or nonalcoholic beer
- 1 lb. cod fillets, cut into 1-in. strips
- 6 corn tortillas (6 in.), warmed
  Optional toppings: Diced tomatoes, sliced avocado and pickled red onion

1. In a small bowl, combine the first 7 ingredients. Refrigerate, covered, at least 30 minutes. Meanwhile, in an electric skillet or deep-fat fryer, heat oil to 375°. In a shallow bowl, combine flour, baking powder, salt and cayenne pepper. Stir in beer until smooth. In batches, dip fillets in batter; allow excess to drip off.

2. Fry fish in batches until golden brown, 2-3 minutes on each side. Drain on paper towels. Serve in tortillas with cabbage mixture. Top with tomato, avocado and onion if desired.

1 TACO 303 cal., 15g fat (2g sat. fat), 35mg chol., 448mg sod., 26g carb. (4g sugars, 2g fiber), 15g pro.

FISH TACO TIPS

What other kinds of fish can I use?
We've used cod here because it holds batter easily and stays succulent at a high frying temperature. You could try other types of white fish, however, including halibut, mahi mahi, tilapia or catfish. Avoid dark oily fish, such as salmon, mackerel or tuna.

What can I serve with fish tacos?
These tacos are light in texture but substantial once you've factored in the tortilla, so they're best served with a bright-tasting salsa or a green salad.

INDEXES | CATEGORY INDEX

GRIDDLE

GRILL

LAMB

MEATLESS

MICROWAVE

NO-COOK

OTHER PROTEINS

PORK | STOVETOP

PORK | OVEN

PORK | SLOW COOKER

PORK | OTHER EQUIPMENT

POULTRY | STOVETOP

POULTRY | OVEN

POULTRY | SLOW COOKER

POULTRY | OTHER EQUIPMENT

PRESSURE COOKER

SEAFOOD

WAFFLE IRON

INDEXES | RECIPE INDEX